C.M. Yonge

The Story Of The Christians And Moors Of Spain

C.M. Yonge

The Story Of The Christians And Moors Of Spain

ISBN/EAN: 9783742849045

Manufactured in Europe, USA, Canada, Australia, Japa

Cover: Foto ©Andreas Hilbeck / pixelio.de

Manufactured and distributed by brebook publishing software (www.brebook.com)

C.M. Yonge

The Story Of The Christians And Moors Of Spain

PREFACE.

IN the earlier times of the awakening of romance in modern days, Spanish chivalry was the fashion. Scott and Southey both did their parts in making it known; and the fantastic honour and dauntless bravery of the Castilian knight were favourite subjects; so that Washington Irving in America, and Herder in Germany, were alike inspired with the same enthusiasm. Modern criticism on the one hand, and modern persiflage on the other, have done their part to discredit these legends. Research has shown the small foundation on which stood some of the favourite stories, and then they have been parodied and laughed at. Perhaps Babieca is more familiar as the horse of Don Fernando Gomezales than of the Cid; and even Don Quixote has been so far forgotten that there has been little inclination to seek out either the facts or the fictions that formed his character.

Thus it has seemed to me that the eight hundred years' struggle between the Moslem and the Christian was little recollected at the present day; nor, indeed, could I find its history, romance, and poetry anywhere brought into combination. Viardot has admirably written the Moorish history, and Dozy has brought microscopic research to bear upon it; but they take history alone, and from the Moorish side. Durden's is a very good English complete history of Spain, full of matter, but many-volumed and almost forgotten; and Lady Callcott's stands nearly alone as a short popular history of great excellence.

Washington Irving has dealt with the romance of the Arab conquest, Southey with the Cid, Lockhart with the ballad lore, Perez de Hyta with the civil wars of Granada; but, as far as I have seen, no one has tried to combine in a general view Spanish and Moorish history, together with tradition, romance, and song. It is a presumptuous effort, only properly to be carried out by one with as much access to original documents and private knowledge as Mr. Ford, to whose handbook I am much indebted; but he is out of sympathy with the spirit of the Spaniards, and more inclined to dwell on their evil qualities than their good ones. This, then, is only a compilation to give a surface idea of that strange warfare, and which may, perhaps, give a hint of unexplored fields of wondrous interest.

Where it has been possible, I have availed myself of existing translations of Spanish poetry.

Having no knowledge of Arabic, I am afraid the names of the Moorish princes may not be always correctly spelt, as authors vary a good deal in their mode of expressing them.

C. M. YONGE.

May 31*st*, 1878.

TABLE OF THE MOORISH, CASTILIAN, AND ARAGONESE SOVEREIGNS,

Arranged Chronologically.

Kings of the Asturias and Leon.	Khalifs of Cordova.
718 Pelayo.	
737 Favila.	
739 Alfonso I.	
	756 Abd el Rhaman I.
768 Aurilio.	
774 Fruela I.	
784 Mauregato.	
788 Bermudo I.	788 Hoschem I.
791 Alfonso II.	
	796 Al Hakhem I.
	822 Abd el Rhaman II.
842 Ramiro I.	
850 Ordono I.	
	852 Mohammed I.
866 Alfonso III.	
	886 Al Mondhyr.
	888 Abd Allah.
909 Garcia.	
	912 Abd el Rhaman III.
914 Ordono II.	
924 Fruela II.	
925 Alfonso IV.	
930 Ramiro II.	
950 Ordono III.	
955 Sancho I.	
	961 Al Hakem II.
967 Ramiro III.	
	976 Haschem II.
982 Bermudo II.	
999 Alfonso V.	

(Ommeyades.)

CHRONOLOGICAL TABLE.

Kings of the Asturias and Leon.	Kings of Aragon.	Khalifs of Cordova.
		1008 Mohammed II.
		1009 Suleiman.
		Period of confusion, during which Emirs governed in their own cities.
1027 Bermudo III.		
1027 Fernando I.		
	1037 Ramiro I.	
	1063 Sancho.	
1067 Sancho II.		
1073 Alfonso VI.		Almoravid Khalifs.
		1091 Yousuf Ebu Taschfyn.
	1094 Pedro I.	
	1104 Alfonso IV.	
		1107 Ali Abu Taschfyn.
1108 Urraca.		
1126 Alfonso VII.		
	1134 Ramiro III.	
	1137 Petronila.	
		1143 Taschfyn.
		Almohad Khalifs.
1157 Sancho III.		1157 Abd el Moumem.
1158 Alfonso VIII.		
	1162 Alfonso I.	
		1163 Yousuf Abou Yakoub.
		1184 Yakoub Ebu Yousuf.
1188 Alfonso IX.		
	1196 Pedro II.	
		1199 Mohammed Ebu Yakoub.
	1213 Jayme I.	1213 Yousuf Ebu Mouhamm.
1216 Fernando III.		
		Confusion.
		Kings of Granada.
		1238 Al Hamar.
1252 Alfonso X.		
		1273 Mohammed II.

CHRONOLOGICAL TABLE.

Kings of the Asturias and Leon.	Kings of Aragon.	Kings of Granada.
1284 Sancho IV.	1276 Pedro III.	
	1285 Alfonso III.	
	1291 Jayme II.	
1295 Fernando IV.		
1312 Alfonso XI.		1305 Al Nassar.
		1312 Ismael.
		1325 Mohammed IV.
	1327 Alfonso IV.	
	1336 Pedro IV.	1333 Yousuf.
		1354 Mohammed V.
1359 Pedro I.		1359 Ismael II.
		1361 Abou Said.
		1362 Mohammed.
1369 Enrique I.		
1379 Juan I.		
	1387 Juan I.	
1390 Enrique II.		
		1391 Yousuf II.
	1395 Martin.	
		1396 Mohammed VI.
1407 Juan II.		
		1408 Yousuf III.
	1412 Fernando I.	
	1416 Alfonso V.	
		1425 Mohammed VII.
		1431 Yousuf IV.
1454 Enrique IV.		
	1458 Juan II.	
		1466 Aboul Hacem.
1474 Isabel.		
	1479 Fernando II.	
		1482 Abou Abdallah (Boabdil).

CONTENTS.

CHAPTER VI.
THE PASS OF RONCESVALLES. 39

CHAPTER VII.
LITTLE CHRISTIAN STATES 49

CHAPTER VIII.
SANTIAGO, THE PATRON OF SPAIN 54

CHAPTER IX.
THE COUNT OF THE LAND OF CASTLES . . . 64

CHAPTER X.
THE AUGUSTAN AGE OF CORDOVA 69

CHAPTER XI.
THE LOSS OF COMPOSTELLA 79

CHAPTER XII.
THE INVINCIBLE AL MANSOUR 89

CHAPTER XIII.
THE FALL OF THE KHALIFATE 115

CONTENTS.

CHAPTER I.
THE GOTH AND THE ARAB . . .

CHAPTER II.
THE BATTLE OF GUADALETE . .

CHAPTER III.
THE CONQUEST . . . . .

CHAPTER IV.
THE LIMIT TO THE MOSLEM . .

CHAPTER V.
THE FIRST SPANISH KHALIF . . .

CHAPTER XIV.
The Union of Castille and Leon 122

CHAPTER XV.
Ruy, mi Cid Campeador 129

CHAPTER XVI.
The Almoravides and their Conquest . . . 143

CHAPTER XVII.
Don Alfonso, the Battle-fighter of Aragon . 157

CHAPTER XVIII.
The broken Chains of Navas de Tolosa . . 166

CHAPTER XIX.
The Conquests of San Fernando and Jayme el Conquistador 179

CHAPTER XX.
The Cream of the West 199

CHAPTER XXI.
The Battle of Salado 210

CHAPTER XXII.
The Age of Tyrants 226

CHAPTER XXIII.
The Last Bright Days of Granada. . . . 241

CHAPTER XXIV.
The Abencerrages and Zegris 255

CHAPTER XXV.
The Siege of Malaga 270

CHAPTER XXVI.
The Last Sigh of the Moor 284

CHAPTER XXVII.
Woe to the Vanquished 295

THE STORY
OF THE
CHRISTIANS AND MOORS
OF SPAIN.

CHAPTER I.

THE GOTH AND THE ARAB.

NATURE has divided the peninsula of Spain into two great partitions—the mountain land of the north and west, and the sunshiny borders of the Mediterranean towards the south-east. The one portion would naturally breed stern, grave, resolute patriots, hard to dislodge from their mountain nests; the other, a bright genial race, prone to enjoy the gifts of the soil and climate so lavishly bestowed on them.

This distribution of the features of the country has been the key to much of Spanish history. The southern portion has always been easy to conquer, the northern, very difficult; and the inhabitants, though not always good soldiers in the field of battle, have ever excelled in that guerilla warfare which is the most baffling and harassing to the invader, and which develops the most constancy, and also the most ferocity, in the invaded.

To go through the various immigrations and conquests that brought in the nations which formed the

Spanish people would be in vain. It will be enough to say that the aboriginal population, the Vascos or Basques, had been driven up into and over the Pyrenees, into districts where their descendants still retain their native language. The Kelts or Kelt-Iberians, with a fringe of Phœnician and Greek settlements on the coast, had, after a long and fierce struggle, been subdued by the Romans, whose civilisation and language they entirely adopted. Spain gave to Rome an epigrammatist in Martial, the best of her emperors in Theodosius, a Christian poet in Prudentius, and a great divine in St. Isidore; and five centuries had made the whole country as completely Latin as Italy itself. In the break-up of the Western empire, Spain was first overrun by the Vandals, who only ravaged and made no settlement, though some say that they left their name to Andalusia. There followed a struggle between the Suevi (Schwaben) and the Western Goths or Visigoths, ending in 621 with the final conquest of the Peninsula by Swintila the Goth.

This people were already half civilised, and held the Arian doctrine. They were so much less ferocious and savage than the Suevi and Vandals as to be almost like deliverers to the Romanised population. They themselves had a strong feeling for Latin culture, and, settling down in the old cities, entirely adopted it. For some time there was a struggle between the Catholic creed which they found prevailing among the inhabitants and the Arianism they had brought with them; but in the end of the sixth century, King Recared, having been brought over to the Catholic faith by his Frankish wife Ingund, proclaimed himself of the same faith as the rest of the Church.

The old diocesan arrangement had never been broken, and the Goths became devoted sons of the Church. Latin was the language of religion and culture, and, as the population of the country likewise used it, it became universally spoken; so that the High German of the Goth can only be traced in the proper names of persons and places and in a few imported terms. Many of the Latin inflections of nouns were dropped, but the accusative was retained as the usual plural termination, giving that peculiarly dignified sound which distinguishes the language. The writing was always in Latin, and all the habits, manners, and methods of warfare were copied from the Romans, who, as usual even when conquered, had leavened and subdued the minds of their victims.

Toledo was the Gothic capital, where the kings led a life little disturbed by the wars and inroads that ravaged the lands north of the Pyrenees, and thus they constantly became more luxurious, and lost more and more of the original vigour of the first conquerors.

Like all the Teutonic races, the Goths had a royal family, deriving its descent from Odin, and from whom the king must be taken. Theirs was called the Baltir, and reigned in Spain for two centuries, falling latterly into a state of much corruption and lawless violence. In 708, Wittich, or Witiza, the reigning king, was deposed for his tyranny, and in his stead was crowned his cousin Roderich,* while his two sons, Ebba and Sisebut, took refuge with their uncle Oppas, Archbishop of Seville. His sister was the wife of Julian,

---

* Gothic, Roderich (famous king); Spanish, Rodrigo; English, Roderick.

count, or commander, of the southern province, which included part of the opposite coast of Africa.

Meantime a terrible power was advancing from the East. The sons of Ishmael had been like the sands of their own desert—wild, scattered, incapable of united action, save in tribes or clans—until the wonderful impulse given by the promulgation of the Koran drew them together under one head, and filled them with indomitable energy. To restore the original patriarchal worship of Abraham and proclaim the One God, overthrowing the gross idolatries of the Arabs, including their fanatical adoration of the Kaaba or Black Stone of Mekka, was at first the object of Mahommed; and to this end were directed all the messages that he declared to be divine, and which finally formed the Koran. Of Christianity he knew nothing save through the distorted medium of the heresies then prevailing in the East; of Judaism he knew much, and borrowed a great deal, and he would have amalgamated with both, if they would have accepted him as the one last and complete Prophet. He would have made Jerusalem the centre of religion to the whole world, but the passion of the Arabs for the Kaaba and for Mekka was too strong for him. The Black Stone, purified from the idols that surrounded it, became the cynosure of every professor of Islam—*i.e.* the Faith; and the city of Mekka, supposed to stand where the Angel revealed the well to the fainting Hagar, is the place to which the Faithful turn in prayer, and whither they make their pilgrimage.

The adoption of the Kaaba won enough of the Arabs to Mahommed to enable him to overcome, assimilate, or destroy the recusant tribes. The faith he taught adapted itself to their national character—alike to their intense pride of birth, their wild poetical imagination, their fierceness, their lavish generosity and scrupulous hospitality, their capacity of bearing hardships, and their licentiousness of spirit. It was, in fact, Judaism without its hopes, with its law cut down to suit the wild Ishmaelite, and its paradise made grossly material. Moreover it was devoid of all elements of growth or adaptation. The Koran, which professed to be dictated by the Angel Gabriel to Mahommed, was the final revelation, binding the Faithful as the Law of Moses bound the Jews. Of course the Divine inspiration was lacking, so that no power of expansiveness was in it; and it was, at the very best, the ideal code of a half-civilised Arab, while great part of it was composed under the impulse of fierce passions excited against his enemies. Thus the Koran has often trained savage nations up to a certain point, and the impulse has carried them beyond it; but there is sure to be then a reaction—a recall to the more rude elements such as the Prophet left them. A kind of Puritanism arises, and the attempts at a higher tone of philosophy or civilisation are extinguished, usually in blood.

The first ardour of new converts to Islam is generally irresistible, and when Mahommed died in 632 he was master of the Arabian peninsula. The head of the Arab faith was then called the Successor, or Khalif (from *khalafa*, to succeed), and was at once the pope and emperor of all the Faithful, absolute and despotic in government; and also chief imaum, or interpreter of the will of God.

The immediate successors of Mahommed were near

family connections, elected by the will of the Faithful; and though bloody dissensions raged at the centre of their rule, their dominions were extended with the utmost rapidity over Palestine, Syria, Persia, and Egypt. Saracens, the name by which these Arabs were known to the terrified world, was derived from their own word *Sarakhein*, from *Sarak*, the East; while those who lived farther westwards were termed Mahgrebhyn, or Western Arabs—or, as we call them, Moors.

When Othman was Khalif in 647, and his brother Abdallah, wali, or governor, of Egypt, the dominion of the Moslem began to extend to the west under the brilliant general Okba Aben Nafr. The Atlas mountains, lying in parallel chains along the north of Africa, had many pleasant slopes and rich valleys, inhabited by the Berbers, a tall, noble-looking race of men, fair-skinned, active, high-spirited, and indomitable, living their free life in their date-groves, through all the changes of dynasty and empire that affected the cities on the coast, fighting, in the armies of Carthaginian or Roman, for love of fighting, but never accepting their civilisation or bending to their yoke. The Arabs believed them to be of their own race; and it is likely that this was true, for they had the same patriarchal habits, were divided into clans, and had the same fine Semitic features, with many of the like tastes—being splendid horsemen, and unrivalled in the use of the *djerid*, or reed-lance. Their name of Berber seems to have been taken from the Greeks, who called all foreigners *Barbaroi*, from *Ba-ba*, in derisive imitation of the language they could not understand.

The Berbers were reckoned as belonging to the

Greek empire; when provoked by the exactions of the governors of Carthage, they asked help from the Arabs in Egypt. Okba led an expedition, and advancing between the ranges of the Atlas and the sea, reached the Atlantic. Riding into the ocean up to the girths of his camel, he cried aloud: "Allah! I call Thee to witness that if these deep waters did not stop me, I would bear yet farther the knowledge of Thy great name!"

He had passed by the great old Roman province of Africa of which Carthage was the capital, now a disorganised feeble state, unable to resist him; but on his way back he insulted a Berber chief, and thus roused all the fierce population to oppose him. He perished in the struggle; but his lieutenant, Zohair, continued it, stormed Carthage, and defeated both Greeks and Berbers. However, a Berber woman, called El Kahina, or the Prophetess, roused her whole people, and persuaded them that it was the rich cities that attracted their enemies. The Berbers needed only their pasture-lands and date-groves; let them destroy the towns where Christian and Jew heaped up riches, and their foes would let them alone. They obeyed her. Every town and village from Tripoli to Tangier was laid waste. And for five years she reigned; but then was defeated and slain in a great battle with the Arabs. Then peace was made, and the Berbers were forgiven on condition of their joining the Arab force. Mousa Aben Nassir, a really great man, succeeded in their incorporation into the Moslem empire, and they became enthusiastic believers, though without hating the Arabs less. They even believed themselves the true descendants of Ishmael, and fought for the spread of the faith of the Koran; but never without bitter jealousy of the Sarakhein of the East.

In 710, Walyd Abou-'l-Abbas was Khalif at Damascus, and Mousa, now an old man, wrote to ask permission to carry the faith of the Prophet into what he called "the isle of Andalusia," saying: "It is Syria for the beauty of sky and soil; Yemen for climate; India for flowers and perfumes; Egypt for fruit; China for precious metals." He sketched out a magnificent plan of conquest, beginning with Spain, and then passing through France, Germany, and Hungary to Constantinople; and the Khalif gave ready consent.

On the one side stood the nations freshly stirred into energy by the attainment of a more systematic faith, and stronger principle of unity than they had ever previously known, ardent to spread their doctrine by the sword, and viewing death in Allah's cause as the passport to paradise. On the other side were the broken remnants of the Roman empire, lying about among the fabric that had been set up on its ruin. The luxury of Rome had eaten into the Teuton vigour, and the Teuton lawlessness had corrupted the Church it had received from the Romans.

The youth of one people was launched against the decay of two; the new-born zeal of one religion against the stability of another grievously betrayed by its professors.

CHAPTER II.

THE BATTLE OF GUADALETE.

THE fall of Gothic Spain was one of the disasters that served to justify the saying that all great catastrophes are caused by women. At least, so says tradition and romance, though it is probable that the tide of Arab conquest would have rushed into Europe without any Spanish treachery. Moreover, as Count Julian was the brother-in-law of the deposed Witiza, there was every reason to expect him to hate the actual king, Roderich. So that some modern critics have doubted whether in truth vengeance for Roderich's guilty love for his daughter, Florinda, were the real cause of Julian's invitation to Mousa.

> Long had the crimes of Spain cried out to Heaven;
> At length the measure of offence was full.
> Count Julian called the invader. . . .
> . . . . Mad to wreak
> His vengeance for his deeply injured child
> On Roderick's head, an evil hour for Spain,
> For that unhappy daughter, and himself.
> Desperate apostate, on the Moors he called,
> And, like a cloud of locusts, whom the wind
> Wafts from the plains of wasted Africa,

> The Mussulman upon Iberia's shores
> Descends.   A countless multitude they came:
> Syrian, Moor, Saracen, Greek renegade,
> Persian, and Copt, and Latin, in one band
> Of erring faith conjoined, strong in the youth
> And heat of zeal, a dreadful brotherhood.

Florinda has ever since been execrated by the Spaniards, who call her "La Cava," or the Wicked.

Julian was count, or commander, of the south and of Ceuta. It would seem as if he had been Roman rather than Gothic, and in his wrath he turned to ask the aid of Mousa, who sent his bravest sheik, Thâryk Aben Zyad, with a strong force.

He crossed the strait between what had always been called the Pillars of Hercules, but which the Arabs now named Bab-el-Zéîkab, or the Gate of Defiles. The great couchant lion of the rock of Calpe afforded them landing, though it was vainly defended by the Goths, under Theodomir, and he there built a fortress, which has ever since borne his name, Jebal Thâryk—Gibraltar, the Rock of Thâryk.

It was to the Moors the key of Spain. The invaders spread along the shore and advanced to the river Anas—Wady Ana, as they termed it, after the Arab ravines, now Guadiana—as far as a city built by the Phœnicians, and called after Sidon. They gave it the name of Medina, after the sacred city where Mahommed lay buried, and its present name of Medina-Sidonia is a history in itself.

Roderich had been awakened from his luxurious life at Toledo, by the messages of Theodomir. A wondrous old Spanish romance, which calls itself his truthful history, relates his preparation. Near Toledo stood an ancient tower, ruinous but splendid, and beneath it was a cave, closed up with a strong iron gate, fastened with many locks, and above it was engraven Greek letters, which wise men expounded to mean: "The king who opens this cave and discovers its wonders will learn both good and evil." Many kings had gone as far as the opening, but had been terrified out of life or senses by the tremendous noise within the cavern. The gate had been therefore closed up with nine locks, concluding that though a king was destined to open it, the fated time was not come. But Roderich, in this time of danger, resolved to try his fortune, and consult the oracle of the cavern. The gate was opened, and by torchlight the king moved on in advance of the rest till he came to a magnificent hall, where stood a bronze statue of fierce aspect, holding a battle-axe and striking the ground with a tremendous noise. The king on this began to conjure the statue to cease and give him time to examine the cave, promising to do no harm to it. The figure accordingly became still, and the king began to examine the place, reading the following inscription on the walls:

> Unhappy king, thou hast entered in an evil hour.
> By strange nations thou shalt be dispossessed,
> and thy people degraded.

And on the shoulders and breast of the statue:

> I do my office.
> I call upon the Arabs.

The unfortunate king left the cavern in haste, and closed up the entrance with earth; but at midnight a fearful sound was heard, and the whole ancient tower was discovered to have crashed down to its foundations. Thus in after times did the Spaniards describe the handwriting on the wall, foredooming their Gothic ancestors, heavily laden with crime; and as the last survivor of an effete dynasty, Roderich collected his forces to meet the terrible nation who had been never yet defeated nor turned back, but who had spread from the East as irresistibly as locusts. The two armies met on the banks of the Lethe, now known by the Arab addition, Wady Lete, Guadalete, not far from Xeres. Roderich's army is said to have numbered eighty thousand men, but only the nobles were well armed. The lower classes had no defensive armour, and only used bows and arrows or slings; while the invaders, though in smaller numbers, were all picked men —the terrible horsemen of the deserts.

The battle took place on the 1st of July, 711, and lasted, the Moors say, three days, the Spaniards, a week. Roderich is described as appearing in a "gown of beaten gold," with a gold crown on his head, and covered with precious stones; seated in a car or waggon drawn by two horses, with a richly-embroidered canopy or tent overshadowing it, supported by a pillar of gold. It was guarded by a thousand men, and seems to have resembled the *caroccio* in which the gonfalon, or sacred banner, of the Italian cities was taken out to battle. Roderich seems only to have appeared on this car the first day. Afterwards he mounted his horse, and wore his helmet adorned with horns of gold (as seen in old Gothic coins), and dashed into the thickest of the fray.

It was fought out, day after day; but on the last the broken remnant of the Goths found the horse, called by romance Orelio, and the horned helmet lying on the banks of the river, and never again did they see Roderich the last of the Goths.

The Arab historians declare that "Allah slew him by the hand of Thâryk;" but Mousa sent to the Khalif Walyd what was supposed to be his head preserved in camphor: but Spanish story gives him another fate. Roderich was one of those princes whom their people could never believe to have perished. Here is his lament in one of the beautiful old national ballads, as translated by J. G. Lockhart:

The hosts of Don Rodrigo were scattered in dismay,
When lost was the eighth battle, nor heart nor hope had they;
He, when he saw the field was lost, and all his hope was flown,
He turned him from his flying host and took his way alone.

His horse was bleeding, blind, and lame, he could no farther go,
Dismounted, without path or aim, the king stepped to and fro.
It was a sight of pity to look on Roderick,
For sore athirst and hungry he staggered faint and sick.

All stained and strewed with dust and blood, like to some smouldering brand
Pluck'd from the flame, Rodrigo shew'd. His sword was in his hand;
But it was hacked into a saw of dark and purple tint;
His jewell'd mail had many a flaw, his helmet many a dint.

He climbed unto a hill-top, the highest he could see,
Thence all about of that wild route his last long look took he.
He saw his royal banners where they lay drenched and torn,
He heard the cry of victory, the Arabs' shout of scorn.

He look'd for the brave captains that had led the hosts of Spain,
But all were fled except the dead, and who could count the slain?
Where'er his eye could wander, all bloody was the plain;
And while thus he said the tears he shed ran down his cheeks like rain:

"Last night I was the King of Spain, to-day no king am I;
Last night fair castles held my train, to-night where shall I lie;
Last night a hundred pages did serve me on the knee,
To-night not one I call my own, not one pertains to me.

"O luckless, luckless was the hour, and cursed was the day
When I was born to have the power of this great seigniory;
Unhappy me that I should live to see the sun go down this night;
O Death, why now so slow art thou, why fearest thou to smite?"

So was Roderich supposed to bewail himself in a ballad quoted by Cervantes, and therefore certainly older than the sixteenth century. A worthless man himself, the fact of being the last of his race led to his being pitifully lamented by his people. Long did they look for him to reappear; and gradually a belief grew up that he had spent the end of his life in penance.

His chronicle gives a beautiful legend of how he wandered to a convent near Merida, where a monk named Romano, taking pity on his anguish of mind, went forth with him, carrying with them a little image of the Blessed Virgin, till they came to the mountain of Alcobaça, where they found a cave, which they enlarged with their own hands, and there dwelt together; the good monk comforting the fallen king through his bitter penance and the many temptations from which he suffered in the earlier part of his retirement. After some time Romano died, and Roderich found another hermitage near Visço, where he died; and Spanish chroniclers declared that they had seen a tomb inscribed

> Hic requiescat Rudericus ultimus Rex Gothorum.

Some even said he had entered the tomb alive with a serpent who devoured him.

Two English poets have been smitten with the wild beauty of these legends of Roderich. Scott made his adventure in the tower of Toledo the occasion of a vision of all Spanish history down to the Peninsular War; and Southey, in a blank-verse poem, beautiful in parts, but too long for the impatience of modern readers, has pictured his penitence, and made him, after Romano's death, return to the defence of his people as an unknown warrior, become known to them in the hour of battle, and then—while the cries—

> Roderick the Goth! Roderick and victory!
> Roderick and vengeance!

are still pealing on his ear, vanish once more to his penance.

> Days, months, and years, and generations past,
> And centuries held their course, before, far off,
> Within a hermitage near Visço's walls,
> A humble tomb was found, which bore inscribed
> In ancient characters King Roderick's name.

CHAPTER III.

THE CONQUEST.

THE battle of Guadalete was decisive. The Goths could make no head without a king. His nearest kinsmen were either traitors or were unwilling to come forward, in case he should be still alive. Count Julian advised Thâryk to press forward and give the stricken foe no time to rally; and he divided his forces into three bodies, one of which seized Cordova, another Malaga, while Thâryk himself, taking Jaen by the way, marched on to Toledo; and, meeting the other two parties, laid siege to the capital.

Plunder had been forbidden, and only the combatants were attacked. These first Saracen conquerors were the most merciful invaders the world had yet seen, and great as was the terror of their name, they were found to be kindly and generous masters. So Toledo made small attempt at resistance, and capitulated on the same conditions as the other cities. The Christians were left unmolested in their houses, convents, and churches, on the payment of a tribute called *tadyl*; they were only forbidden to ring church bells, have religious processions, or raise new churches without special permission. They were allowed their own laws and judges, but were not permitted to punish anyone who should become a Mahommedan, while it was death for a Moslem to become a Christian.

These conditions had been made at Jerusalem, Alexandria, and everywhere else, and were readily accepted. Thâryk had pressed on before he could receive Mousa's orders to wait for him at Guadalete, and that chief landing with fresh forces, pushed forward to Merita (so called the colony of the Roman veterans —*emeriti*), where Egilona, wife to Roderich, had shut herself up. Merida (as it is now termed) was very strong; and was so steadily defended that Mousa sent for reinforcements from Barbary under his son Abd-el-Asis.

On their arrival the Meridans were discouraged, and sent persons to treat with the besiegers. Thâryk found Mousa in his tent, an old, withered, white-bearded man; and he promised to consult the sheiks and answer them the next day. At night he had his beard clipped and dyed, and in the morning the messengers were asked how they could hope to resist men who could make themselves young again. They were granted the same terms as Toledo, except that the property of those who had died while fighting against the invaders was confiscated, and Queen Egilona was kept captive.

Mousa was jealous of Thâryk, who came to meet him at Talavera, and treated him ungenerously. A table had been found at the city, still called, from its name in Arabic, *Al Meida* (the table), measuring three hundred and sixty feet in circumference, and made, it was said, of emerald—which of course meant malachite—and further believed to have belonged to

C

Solomon, and have been brought into Spain at the time of the captivity in Babylon. This marvellous table was nearly the ruin of Thâryk: Mousa claimed it for the Khalif, and, when one of its legs was missing, he had Thâryk thrown into prison and beaten with rods; but the Khalif sent commands that they should be reconciled, and Thâryk was restored.

Theodomir, the nearest kinsman of Roderich, had retreated with the remnant of the army into the mountains and hills of eastern Andalusia, where he harassed the Moors in the narrow defiles, carrying on the *guerilla*, or little war, familiar to the Peninsula in all ages. At last, however, he was shut up in the little city of Orihuela, with so few troops that he stationed women on the walls, with helmets on their heads and their hair crossed on their chins to look like beards. It was not to fight, only to obtain favourable terms from Abd-el-Asis, who had pursued him thither. He came himself to the leader's tent, and through him obtained the province of Murcia, with seven cities, to hold under the Khalif, on condition that each able Goth should yearly pay a dinar of gold, or else four measures of wheat, barley, wine, vinegar, oil, and honey; each Roman serf, half the quantity.

In the course of the next two or three years, Mousa, Abd-el-Asis, and Thâryk, had spread their victories far and wide. That beautiful city of the south, Illiberis, fell into the hands of Abd-el-Asis, and changed its name to Garb Nata, or Karnaltah, the Cream of the West. He married Egilona, the Gothic queen, his prisoner, assuring her that he would still treat her as a queen, and never take another wife; and he kept his word. The lady had so many treasures that the Moors called her "Mother of Necklaces."

Mousa was disposed to keep the lands and the spoils as much to themselves as possible, while their victories extended to the northward; and is even said to have brought back silver images from the churches of Narbonne. Thâryk, whose conquests had followed the course of the Ebro, was a disinterested and resolute Arab, and freely divided all the plunder among his warriors. The rivalry between these two chiefs continued, and they were summoned to Damascus.

Walyd was dead, and the reigning Khalif was his brother Suleiman. Thâryk was the first to appear before him, and pleaded his own cause. "Better than even the Faithful," said he, "can the Christians tell whether I have been cowardly, or cruel, or covetous."

Mousa arrived, bringing four hundred Gothic hostages and piles of treasure. Suleiman asked him about the Christians of Spain.

"They are," said he, "lions in their castles, eagles on their horses, women in the plain, goats in the mountains."

"And those of Afrank?" (*i.e.* Gaul, the Frank).

"They are quick and bold in the attack, fearful and cowardly in the retreat."

"And the Berbers?"

"The Berbers are like the Arabs in face, in courage, in patience, in sobriety, in hospitality, and in ways of fighting; but they are the falsest of men, keeping neither their word nor bond."

Mousa produced Solomon's famous malachite table, and presented it to the Khalif; but therewith stepped forth Thâryk with the lost foot, which he had kept all this time to prove to the Khalif that he had been the winner of it. So entirely did it convince Suleiman that, with the utter contempt for personal dignity common among Eastern princes, he caused Mousa to be beaten as cruelly as he had used Thâryk, and banished him to Mekka. The Khalif was in fact afraid of the house of Mousa becoming independent, and sent off ten envoys, five to put to death the two sons of the old general who had been left in charge of Kairwan and Tangier, and the other five to cut off Abd-el-Asis. They found him ruling at Seville, so beloved by the soldiers that they durst not attack him till they had spread reports that Egilona was making him a Christian, and intended him to assume a crown like a Gothic king. Then they followed him to a small mosque where he was in the habit of praying, cut off his head, and showing it in the market-place, read the Khalif's order for his death. His head was brought to the Khalif and shown to his father, who died of grief for the fate of his sons.

In six years all Spain had been overrun, and had been divided into four provinces. The cities and plains mostly retained their former inhabitants. There was no persecution of them as Christians, and they retained their clergy and the old liturgy compiled by the Spanish bishops Leander and Ildefonso, and commonly called the Mosarabic. Every inducement to follow the faith of their conquerors was held out to them, and they were much depressed, while the Moors dwelt in the palaces of the nobles who had been slain or had fled.

The Arabs looked down on them as wretched slaves,

wanting in the brave patient sobriety of the sons of the desert. These conquerors had the simple patriarchal manners of their forefathers, and were at the same time capable of high cultivation, though at present they only showed their high qualities by their mercifulness to the subdued nation.

CHAPTER IV.

THE LIMIT TO THE MOSLEM.

THE hills that border the extreme west of Europe towards the Atlantic have always been the refuge of the remnants of the conquered races. The old Vasco or Basque nation had preserved their language, and virtually their independence, in the Pyrenean heights, through all the successive conquests of Kelt, Roman, and Goth, and were equally able to hold out against the Moors. The fugitives from many of the cities which Tháryk conquered found shelter there, and often resorted to ask counsel from a hermit who dwelt on the mountain of Uruela, and had there built a little chapel to St. John the Baptist.

When he died, no less than six hundred freemen of high birth attended his funeral, and there they agreed to form themselves into a band for the protection of their mountains from the Moor, and to choose a leader. On the hillside then, beside the hermit's little rude church, they raised on their shields, and proclaimed as chief, Garcia Ximenes—that is, Garcia the son of Ximen. He was not of the royal race, though his name was Gothic (*Gar*—meaning war), but he was probably half Basque. He became thus chief of the *Nava*—the clearing of forest, in the Basque language; and this chief of the clearing became the progenitor of the kings of Navarre.

About the same time, farther to the west, where the Sierra Penamerella juts out into the Atlantic, another band of Gothic Christians met round the great cavern of Covadonga, which opened on the long winding ravine of Cangas, or the Shell. The ravine is five miles long, and ends in a beautiful green meadow, where, from mountain torrents, collects the pure bright Deva, and in the mountain that closes it in opens the huge cave, capable of holding three hundred men. This cave was the refuge of several of the Baltir, the royal line of Goths; in especial of Pelagius—or in the Spanish tongue Pelayo—whose father, Favila, son of King Chindaswinth, had been murdered by Witiza. He is said to have been driven to revolt by the loss of his sister, who had become the prey of a Moorish chief; and he had here made his home with his wife, his two children, and Alfonso (*Adelfuns*, noble impetuosity), another young son of the Baltic line. Other Goths, who had fled but never submitted, came and shared his refuge in this meadow; and they raised Pelayo on their shields, and proclaimed him as their king. Thus in 718 began the monarchy which was destined to include for a time, not only the whole Peninsula, but the richest lands beyond the Atlantic.

> Covadonga's conquering site
> Cradle was of Spanish might.

The Arabs sent a troop under a chief called Al Kama against Belay-el-Room—or the Roman, as they called Pelayo—and Archbishop Oppas with it, to offer such terms as his cousin Theodomir had accepted. These were, however, disdainfully rejected, and the Moors, by this time too confident of victory, allowed themselves to be drawn on to attempt to storm the cave of Covadonga. When their van was in the meadow that lay beneath the cave, Pelayo and his few brave comrades on horseback charged them in front; and while their rear was still entangled in the long winding ravines flanked by precipices, the cry broke out from the peasants and women hitherto hidden behind the rocks:

>   "In the name
> Of God! For Spain or vengeance!" And forthwith
> On either side along the whole defile,
> The Asturians shouting: "In the name of God!"
> Set the whole ruin loose; huge trunks, and stones,
> And loosened crags, down, down they rolled with rush,
> And bound, and thundering force.

The destruction was terrible; the torrent Deva swept away the fugitives, Al Kama was taken, and Oppas made prisoner, and put to death as a traitor. Nay, the Asturian peasants believe that the devil carried him away bodily. They still show carvings commemorating the fact, as well as the granite boulders rolled from the tops of the hills, and the streams that ran red with blood. Arab chroniclers do not mention this defeat, but only say that the Christians lived in dens and caves in the mountains; and that when these wild beasts came out they were chastised.

The passes of the Pyrenees were not in the power of either of the little knots of Christians, and across them El Haur ben Abd-el-Rhaman, the emir, led his hordes, hoping to carry on Mousa's scheme and win

"Frandjas." He took Narbonne and besieged Bordeaux; but Eudes, the duke of Aquitaine, hurried to the rescue, with all the men whom he could muster from the Pyrenees to the Loire. He had lately received from Rome three sponges, which had been used to clean the high altar after the Pope had said mass; and these he cut up into small pieces, and distributed to his troops as precious relics. The Moorish leader, on his side, exhorted the Arabs in Eastern phrase like Scripture itself. "Fear not the multitude," he said. "If Allah be for us, who can be against us?"

But the Franks were decreed to be the boundary which the Mussulman power should not pass, and the army was defeated with such slaughter that the Arab writers called the way where they were pursued, between Toulouse and Carcassonne, the Road of the Martyrs. Still, in spite of Eudes, an Arab garrison remained in Narbonne; and on a Pyrenean mountain, which the invaders called *Al Bab*, or the Gate, was a fastness held by a renowned Berber chief, Othman ben Abi Nessa. In some foray on Aquitaine, Abi Nessa captured Lampegia, the beautiful daughter of Eudes himself; he married her, and for her love made alliance with her father. Eudes was glad enough thus to secure himself on the south, for on the north the great mayor of the palace and Duke of the Franks, Karl of the Hammer, or Charles Martel, who ruled for the helpless *fainéant* Meerwing king, Hlotar II., was attacking his northern border on the Loire, and he had to hasten to the defence.

But in Spain Abi Nessa's friendship with him was held as treason. Abd-el-Rhaman brought all his forces against him. He shut himself up in his fortress, but was so closely pursued that he was forced to fly into the Pyrenean gorge with his wife and a few faithful followers. They gained a little valley where they hoped to be safe, and he laid the exhausted Lampegia on the grass beside a waterfall, and was giving her drink when the cry of their enemies was heard. The servants fled, but Abi Nessa, with his wife in his arms, was overtaken. He perished, either being slain or leaping down a precipice, and Lampegia was deemed too lovely for any fate but the wretched one of being sent to the Khalif's harem at Damascus.

Abd-el-Rhaman then traversed the Pass of Roncesvalles, and, as Eudes hurried back to meet him, routed the forces of Aquitaine and plundered Bordeaux, which was full of riches. He promised his men the spoil of Tours, where the great abbey of St. Martin was one of the richest shrines of the West. Meantime, Eudes had hurried to inform his late enemy, Karl of the Hammer, of the danger. It was no time for disputes among Christians. The question was to be decided whether the Gospel or the Koran should be the rule of the West. Karl saw the need. He was beyond the Rhine when the call reached him, but he sent out the ban or summons to all the dominions of the Meerwings to join him at Tours, and hurried on, his host gathering as he went Austrasian Franks from the eastern forests, Burgundians from the Jura, Neustrian Franks from the farms of the Seine, with their Gaulish vassals, Romanised Gauls from the cities; all feeling the peril of the much-loved shrine of the warrior saint and bishop, if they did not understand the mightier issues of the strife.

Abd-el-Rhaman had reached the very gates of Tours

when he learnt that Karl was approaching. Too prudent to let his men gorge themselves with plunder before the battle was fought, he marched towards Poitiers, and encamped between the rivers Vienne and Clain. He thought of causing his men to destroy all their plunder and keep only their arms and horses; but he feared to offend them, and abstained.

There Karl came up with him and likewise encamped, with the valley between. The two armies lay face to face for a week—Karl probably to give time for his troops to join him, Abd-el-Rhaman probably for a lucky day, for it was he who began the attack with his swarms of light horsemen. The Franks stood in their close serried ranks "like solid walls or banks of ice," said the Spanish historian, and the rush of the Arab and Moorish horse was all in vain. These men were true Franks—tall, blue-eyed, strong and massive, not like the mixed people of the south—and their wall of strength remained unbroken. A few of their reserves made their way into the rear, the Arabs turned to defend their camp, and there was a general confusion; night came on, and the Franks returned to their camp. They would have renewed the battle on the ensuing day, but they found the Arab camp deserted, with all the treasure and hosts of corpses, among which that of Abd-el-Rhaman was found. This battle, one of the fifteen most decisive battles in the world, was fought in the October of 732. The Moors retreated to Narbonne, and it was not for seven years more that Karl succeeded in chasing them beyond the Pyrenees.

Pelayo died in 737, and his rude sepulchre still remains in the little church of St. Eulalia, which he himself built not far from the cave. Even to this day no corpse is allowed to be placed where lay that of the Father of Kings before its final removal to its resting-place.

He was succeeded by his son Favila, who was soon killed by a bear when hunting in the mountains, and the kingdom went to Alfonso, the husband of his sister. The little kingdom included Gijon and Oviedo, wonderful old cities, where may still be seen the low-browed, round-arched, heavily-vaulted churches, built up out of Roman remains, and looking as stern, enduring, and resolute as the men who built them.

CHAPTER V.

THE FIRST SPANISH KHALIF.

THERE was a time of decay and feebleness in the khalifate in the middle of the eighth century. From the first the old clannish feuds of the Arabs had raged fiercely round the seat of empire. A tribe, called the Ommeyads, had always been at war with the Hashimites, from whom Mahommed had sprung, and they had been his fiercest opponents till, after their defeat, they had been driven to accept him as their Prophet. Othman, the fourth Khalif from Mahommed, was of this tribe, and under him the animosities of the race had broken out. Ali, the son-in-law of the Prophet, had rebelled and had died in battle, and his two sons Hasan and Hosein had been murdered. This had led to the great schism of the Moslemah, since all the Persians have adhered to the cause of Ali.

The Ommeyads had, however, the advantage, and reigned at Damascus until rivals arose to them in the family of Abbas, the uncle of Mahommed. In 740, on the banks of the Zab, the Ommeyads were defeated by Abou-'l-Abbas, who earned the title of *Al Ssefah*, or the Bloodshedder, by exterminating the whole family with horrible cruelty. For instance, ninety young men were beaten till they fell down exhausted, and then a carpet was spread over them as they lay, while their executioners seated themselves on it and held a feast, amusing themselves with their heavings and contortions. One youth of twenty, named Abd-el-Rhaman (servant of mercy) escaped the massacre, in which his wife and child perished, and fleeing into Mahgreb, found shelter and a refuge in the valleys of the Atlas, where the great pastoral tribe of Berbers, called Zenetes, received and sheltered him, though he durst not make himself known to any save the aged chief of the tribe.

Meantime the dissensions of the East had been acting on the West. The Emir-al-Bahr, or chief of the sea, as the viceroy of Spain was called, was appointed by the Khalif, and no sooner did one of these emirs arrive than the monarch at Damascus was dethroned and a new one sent by the Successor. Some walis held with the first, some with the second; and by the time the struggle had been settled, either by open war or secret assassination, a third emir would arrive on the scene. Sometimes the walis were chosen by election in the cities, sometimes appointed by the emir; and everything was in confusion. At last ninety sheiks and walis met at Cordova, and agreed to break from their dependence upon the new Abbassid khalifate, but—as they heard it reported that the last of the Ommeyads was in Mahgreb—to offer him the throne, and make him, as they said, "the sun among the stars."

Two of their number were sent in quest of him to the Zenetes, and found him in their tents. He accepted the charge as the message of Allah, and the aged sheik gave his solemn blessing: "My son, since Allah calls thee, fear not. Trust to us to help thee, for the honour of thy house cannot be maintained without the horsemen and the spear." Moreover he sent seven hundred of the choicest of the young men of the Zenetes to fight for him; and with these and five thousand more Berbers did Abd-el-Rhaman land at Almunecar, in 755, and was hailed with delight in Andalusia. He was one of the noblest types of that fine race, the Saracen Arabs—blue-eyed, fair, and ruddy-complexioned, and of a tall active form; and he had received that high culture which the Ommeyads had adopted from Syria and Persia before the ruin of his family had driven him forth to be trained by hardships in strength and endurance, and by misfortunes in forbearance, gentleness, and courtesy. He bore the white standard as an Ommeyad, instead of the black Abbassid colours. It was a long white silk streamer, in the centre of which was a scarlet hand holding an azure key, as a symbol of the book which opens the gates of the world. This had been adopted by the companions of Thâryk, when, at Gibraltar, their swords opened to the Koran the gates of the East.

The Emir Yusuf, appointed by the Abbassid Khalif, opposed him, but was overcome, as was the Successor sent out from Baghdad to put down what was there considered as a rebellion and usurpation. After both these had been reduced, and treated with much clemency, Toledo revolted and held out for two years; and the Moors in Africa, who had likewise set up a separate kingdom, began to harass the coasts of Andalusia, so that it was necessary to maintain a small fleet to protect the harbours.

Abd-el-Rhaman I. seems to have called himself *malek*, or king, but he was prayed for in public instead of the Khalif of Baghdad, and coined money, as only the head of the Faithful could do. Indeed, in his eyes,

Spain was the fragment rescued from the Abbassid usurpers. He was a despot, like all Moslem sovereigns, but he was one of the most merciful of men, and never shed blood save on the battle-field.

In time of peace the only soldiers who retained their arms were a bodyguard, consisting of a few hundred Zenetes, who remained an institution almost as long as the khalifate lasted. There were also a corps of *kaschefs*, a sort of mounted police, who wore mere breastplates over their linen garments, and carried short reed-lances and basket-work shields, with white turbans wound round a steel headpiece with a spike at the top, and the ends of the scarf floating over their long hair behind. Indeed, all Moorish arms were light, and their warfare was matter of skill and dexterity. Their horses were slender and light, but of marvellous swiftness and endurance, and their breed was as carefully attended to as that of any racer in modern times. The warrior, lightly clad, and armed richly, but not heavily, could wheel about with the readiness and grace almost of a bird, on his perfectly trained steed, and use his slender lance of reed with bewildering effect. His other weapons were a sword of the finest steel, generally inlaid in gold with sentences from the Koran, and a dagger in his sash. Every able-bodied man was bound to train himself to arms, and, when called upon, to present himself to the wali, who chose out the numbers that he needed. War, according to Mahommed, was sacred, and the man who died in battle with the unbeliever was sure of paradise; so the call to arms was made in the mosques, and the term for all campaigns against Christians or schismatic Mussulmans, was *al djihed*, or holy war.

There was pay for the soldiers and a regular allotment of the booty, the Khalif having the fifth part, and the rest being equally divided, except that the horseman's share was double that of the foot-soldier.

From the time of Abd-el-Rhaman, the Arab dominion in Spain assumed a regular form, and progressed in all forms of learning and culture. The narrow bounds of the Koran were extended by mystical interpretations, and the Ommeyad dynasty, who had gathered up much of the Greek learning and thought in the East, became further imbued with the remnants of Roman civilisation. These, after surviving the Gothic invasion, again conquered the conquerors, and were improved on by them, even though overthrown again and again by Berber invasions, under the inevitable reactions towards the rude simplicity and materialism of the original Book.

The Khalif was the head of all religion as well as of the state. A minor could not therefore reign, and fifteen years was the lowest age at which a man could be elected. Silk, gold, and silver were forbidden by the Prophet, except when used in binding the sacred books; and the strict observers of the Law carried out the rule, and wore nothing but woollen and linen fabrics; but in Spain, few attended to these regulations. The Khalif's robe was a very ample one, generally of green silk intermingled with threads of gold, with deep borders of embroidery, on which his own name was always repeated a thousand times. A purple baldric sustained his two-edged sword, inlaid with the words, "Aid is from Allah; victory is near." He wore no crown, but a turban of white muslin, with one end over the brow, the other twisted round his neck and hanging over one shoulder; an arrangement that Mahommed was said to have learned from the angels.

Everybody was really equal under the Khalif, but he was assisted in state matters by a *dyouân*, or divan, and the provinces and cities were under walis, or governors, whose rule was as absolute as their master's. The laws were equitable, and were carried out by the *kadi*, or judge, in each place, and apparently very fairly, since no one could transgress the law with impunity but the Khalif; and for more than a century there was an extraordinarily able and merciful family on the throne. The prime minister was called the *al hajib*.

The Khalif was chief imaum, or interpreter, and thus commenced all religious rites. The place of worship was called, in Arabic, *mesgad*, in Spanish, *mesquita*; whence our word mosque. Though often beautiful in form, richly paved and inlaid, they were bare within of everything save a pulpit for the preacher; and there was always an empty niche to show the direction to Mekka.

Abd-el-Rhaman was a great builder. He went through his dominions repairing the ravages of war and neglect: Roman roads and Gothic fortresses were put into order again, mosques and palaces built; and new towns arose at a little distance from the old ones, which were left to the Jews and Mosarabic Christians. These paid a fixed tribute, but were allowed to be governed by their own laws, and suffered no persecution.

The taste for beautiful gardens, which had always prevailed in Syria and on the Mediterranean, was strong in Abd-el-Rhaman, and the grounds around the

Andalusian palaces were lovely beyond imagination, with trees, grass, and artificial marble fountains. Many valuable plants were introduced, especially the date-palm, the banana, the sugar-cane, the cotton-plant; and Abd-el-Rhaman himself planted the first palm brought from his Syrian home in his gardens at Cordova, addressing to it a ballad long popular among the Arabs, of which the following is a distant imitation :—

> Thou, too, art here, my noble palm,
>   In stranger singleness;
> The kisses of the Western world
>   Thy Eastern pride caress.
>
> Thy root is in a fruitful soil,
>   Thy head thou rear'st to heaven;
> But bitter tears like me thou'd'st weep
>   Were feeling to thee given.
>
> But no, thou canst not feel as I
>   The adverse fate's control.
> Ah me! unceasing floods of grief
>   O'erwhelm my troubled soul.
>
> I watered with my tears the palm
>   That by Euphrates rose:
> The palms and restless streams are now
>   Forgetful of my woes.
>
> When driven by unrelenting fate,
>   And El Abbas, I left
> All this torn bosom held most dear,
>   Of my soul's treasures reft.
>
> To *thee*, of my lov'd native land,
>   No fond remembrance clings;
> *I* cannot cease to think, and still
>   The tear unbidden springs.
>
>   From Lady Callcott's "History."

There is something very touching in finding that the lovely groves of Cordova were but banishment to the home-sick Ommeyad, in whose song one hears a distant echo of those of the exiles who once hung their harps on the willows of his own beloved Euphrates. Another reminiscence of his old life and the plains around the great river was the practice of hawking, which Abderraman (as Christian chroniclers contract his name) introduced into Europe. There is an Arabic song of the captive falcon :

> In rocky desert was I born,
> Thence by spoilers was I torn,
> My eyes the hood close muffles round,
> My talons are in fetters bound ;
> But let my glance discern my prey,
> On soaring wing I speed away.
> With my victorious talons cling,
> And in their grip my quarry bring ;
> Malek or Emir is my slave,
> Sheik or warrior so brave.
> For what's the use of each strong hand
> Save for a perch where I can stand?

Abd-el-Rhaman's great work was the mosque called the Aljama, at Cordova. He was himself the architect, and actually worked at it with his own hands for an hour every day. Outside it was a huge unshapely mass, for the Arabs never displayed beauty in the exterior lest it should attract the evil eye: but within, came, first, courts and cloisters leading to the various schools; then, within a wall six feet thick, came a great court, paved with mosaic marble, in compartments. In the centre of each design of the pattern was an orange-tree, overshadowing a marble basin, with jets of water rising from it ready for the ablutions of the faithful, as types of the fount of paradise which washed away all hatred and jealousy.

The mosque itself had nineteen doors, with beautiful Moorish latticework over them. From each of these doors extended an avenue of pillars in the direction of Mekka, so that there were nineteen large aisles or avenues, and thirty-eight smaller ones between them. Each column was of one single stone, and there were one thousand and ninety-three of them, some brought from Nismes and Narbonne, others from Carthage, and different Roman ruins in Spain, of all kinds of marble and styles of ancient architecture. Some were sunk into the earth, some sawn off if too long; others had to be lengthened by fresh capitals. But even now, when so many have been destroyed that only a five-aisled cathedral is left, the effect of the maze of columns, supporting low-arched vaults, is as beautiful as it is grand and strange. Above these was a wonderful edifice of carpentry in odoriferous woods, supporting a dome crowned by a gold pomegranate outside. Within hung four thousand six hundred silver chains supporting lamps of the same metal, and under the dome was the Khalif's pulpit, a kind of platform on four marble columns. The walls were lined with white marble, inlaid with gold letters with verses of the Koran, the Arabic lettering so encrusted with crystal that the characters looked like letters of light.

The work was not finished in Abd-el-Rhaman's

lifetime. It was called *Al Kobbat*, or the Dome, and pilgrims came to it as if to another Mekka. They walked round each column, chanting a verse of the Koran, and the operation lasted full ten days.

CHAPTER VI.

THE PASS OF RONCESVALLES.

IN 778 an event happened which has made a noise in the world quite disproportionate to its actual importance.

The grandson of Karl of the Hammer, Karl the Great, King of the Franks, though not yet Roman emperor, was gathering to himself the greater part of the lands which had once owned the dominion of the Cæsars, and looked on Spain as one of its provinces. Three invitations took him thither: Itusain-el-Abdari, who had been wali of Zaragoza, but had been deprived by Abd-el-Rhaman, and Kasim, a son of Yusuf, both came to him at his great diet of Paderborn, to entreat his aid against the Ommeyad, whom they viewed as an usurper; and, more honourably, the Gothic King Silo, who reigned in right of his wife Adosinda, Alfonso's daughter, promised to submit the little Gothic kingdom of Oviedo to the great Frank if he would aid it against the common enemy.

Karl accepted the invitation, and marched southwards. He divided his forces into two bodies. One entered Spain by the Pass of Roncesvalles, to the west, under his own command; the other, led by his nephew, Duke Bernard, was to surmount the barrier to the east, receiving the submission of Girona and Barcelona; and the two armies were to join at Zaragoza, which its former wali had promised to deliver up to him.

On the way Karl had to pass the lands of the Basques, which, north of the mountains, belonged to Duke Lupus II., of the Meerwing family, and thus an enemy to Karl. However, he came to the camp and swore fidelity to the king, who then pushed on across the mountains, received the surrender of Pampeluna, and marched on to Zaragoza. But there is a remarkable fatality attending invasions of Spain from the north. The advance of the great Christian put an end to Arab dissensions. The city held out resolutely, and offered treasure and hostages if he would draw off. He heard that the whole force of Spain was rising against him, and that on the Elbe the Saxons were revolting; and wiser than his imitators of later years, instead of ruining himself by a peninsular war, he accepted the proposals of the Zaragozans, and marched back, only stopping to dismantle the fortifications of Pampeluna, that it might not revolt again.

He had met with neither loss nor disaster, and himself with his vanguard safely crossed the Pyrenees; but while his rear was slowly threading the mazes of the defile of Roncesvalles, struggling through the narrow pass in almost single file, the sight was too much for the Basques, who were watching in the forests upon the heights, and they burst upon the troops who were guarding the baggage. A battle began, in which the heavily-armed Franks had no chance against the light-footed mountaineers, who overwhelmed them with darts and stones, so that every man perished; among them Ruotland, the warden of the marches of Brittany, Equihard, the king's steward, and Anselm, the pfalzgraf. The Basques dispersed again immediately, and could not be pursued; but Karl seized their Duke Lupus, and had him put to death for his treachery.

So much for history. The place is a sublime one, between high mountains, clothed with forests of oak and chestnut, with a steep winding road between them, opening on a sweet soft green valley, and every here and there stones or marks connected with the name of Roland—a stone which he threw down in his rage when his horse stumbled; a gigantic footmark, called the Tread of Roland; and even a gap in the mountain-top, known as the Breach of Roland, and said to have been cleft by his sword when he threw it away. Above all, and probably with some foundation, there was a story that Karl, far in advance in the valley of Fuente Arabia, heard pealing down the hill the bugle-blast of Roland, which he wound in vain to call for aid.

> Oh for a blast of that dread horn,
> On Fontarabian echoes borne,
>   That to King Charles did come;
> When Roland brave, and Olivier,
> And every paladin and peer,
>   On Roncesvalles died!

Why Roland became the favourite national hero it is hard to tell. Nevertheless, it was of him that Taillefer sang when the Normans marched to victory at Hastings; and he was the prime champion in the chronicle ascribed to Turpin, archbishop of Rheims, and written probably in the time of the Crusades. There one Ganelon is the traitor; and Roland, after doing wonders in the Pass with his sword Durindana, dies, not of wounds, but of exhaustion, using almost his last breath to blow the terrible blast of his horn. Story and song, more than there is space to mention, clustered round the name of Roland, alike in Brittany, Germany, France, and Italy, all that had made common cause under Karl the Great—Carlomagno, or Charlemagne.

Spain must needs have its share. The traditions only remembered that *el Rey Carlos* had crossed the mountains as a victor, and been attacked on his retreat. So the treachery of the Basques of Aquitaine was magnified into a national resistance of the Spaniards to the invasion of the French. The little kingdom was made to include Leon, as no doubt it did when the ballad was composed; and the king, instead of the obscure Silo, who really was Karl's ally, became Alfonso, the son of Froila, whom Adosinda had adopted, he being true heir and future king. A national hero was likewise found in Bernardo del Carpio, the offspring of a stolen marriage between Sancho Diaz, Count of Saldanha, and Ximena, the king's sister. Alfonso placed his sister in a convent, and kept the count in a dungeon in the castle of Luna, but bred up their son Bernardo at Oviedo. According to ballad lore, Alfonso invited *el Rey Carlos*, promising to make him his heir; but Bernardo raised the spirit of the nation, and attacked the Frankish host at Roncesvalles. He even was said to have found Roldan invulnerable to lance or dart, and therefore to have actually squeezed him to death within his brawny

CHAP. VI.] THE PASS OF RONCESVALLES. 43

arms; a feat for which he is regarded as the Spanish Hercules.

There is a spirited ballad, translated by Lockhart, giving his call to arms, and describing the muster.

The peasant hears upon his field the trumpet of the knight—
He quits his team for spear and shield and garniture of might.
The shepherd hears it 'mid the mist—he flingeth down his crook,
And rushes from the mountain like a tempest-troubled brook.

The youth who shows a maiden's chin, whose brows have ne'er been bound
The helmet's heavy ring within, gains manhood from the sound.
The hoary sire beside the fire forgets his feebleness,
Once more to feel the cap of steel a warrior's ringlets press.

As through the glen his spears did gleam, these soldiers from the hills
They swelled his host, as mountain stream receives the roaring rills.
They round his banner flock'd, in scorn of haughty Charlemagne,
And thus upon their swords are sworn the faithful sons of Spain:

"Free were we born!"—'tis thus they cry—"though to our old king we owe
The homage and the fealty behind his crest to go.
By God's behest our aid he shares, but God did ne'er command
That we should leave our children heirs of an enslaved land.

"Our breasts are not so timorous, nor are our arms so weak,
Nor are our veins so bloodless that we our vow should break,
To sell our freedom for the fear of prince or paladin:
At least we'll sell our birthright free, no bloodless prize they'll win."

This song was actually sung by the Spanish peasants when the English, in 1814, passed through Roncesvalles, driving the French before them.

Another ballad tells how the poor Count of Saldanha pined in his prison, and bemoaned himself at the neglect of his son.

> They tell me my Bernardo is the doughtiest lance in Spain,
> But if he were my loyal heir, there's blood in every vein
> Whereof the voice his heart would hear, his hand would not gainsay—
> Though the blood of kings be mixed with mine, it would not have all the sway.
> I hear of many a battle in which thy spear is red,
> But help from thee comes none to me where I am ill bestead.

Bernardo was not, however, so indifferent as his father supposed. Alfonso II. became sole king on Silo's death in 783, and Bernardo, after many vain entreaties to him to release his father, as the reward of his own services, actually made alliance with the Moors, forayed the country round, and made himself so terrible from his castle of Carpio that Alfonso at last bought him over by the promise that his father should be restored on his delivering up all the castles he had gained, even Carpio itself. Bernardo gave up his last castle, and his father, cased in complete armour, was seen on horseback in the midst of a troop of horsemen coming to meet him. He sprang forward and threw his arms round the father he had never seen. A senseless weight was in his arms. The old man was dead—strangled in prison it is said.

Here is Lockhart's version of the grand ballad of his funeral.

> All in the centre of the choir Bernardo's knees are bent;
> Before him for his murder'd sire yawns the old monument.

His kinsmen of the Carpio blood are kneeling at his back,
With knightly friends and vassals good, all garb'd in weeds of black.

He comes to make the obsequies of a basely slaughtered man,
And tears are running down from eyes whence ne'er before they ran.

His head is bow'd upon the stone, his heart, although full sore,
Is strong as when in days bygone he rode o'er Frank and Moor.

And now between his teeth he mutters, that none his words can hear,
And now the voice of wrath he utters, in curses loud and clear.

He stoops him o'er his father's shroud, his lips salute the bier,
He communes with the corse aloud, as if none else were near.

His right hand doth his sword unsheath, his left doth pluck his beard,
And while his liegemen hold their breath, these were the words they heard:

"Go up, go up, thou blessed ghost, into the arms of God,
And fear not lest revenge be lost, when Carpio's blood hath flowed.

"The steel that drank the blood of France, the arm thy foe that shielded,
Still, father, thirsts that burning lance, and still thy son can wield it!"

Then followed a defiance to the king, when not a man would step forward at Alfonso's bidding to seize Bernardo; and then, alas! he made his promise of vengeance good, went over to the ranks of the Moors, and is heard of no more.

We have ended Bernardo's story; but we must return to Roncesvalles to say that there is also a whole garland of Spanish ballads about Roldan, Rinaldos, and all the rest of the twelve peers of France, and among them are recorded two peculiar to Spanish lore, namely, Montesinos and Durandarte.

Montesinos and Oliveros had had, it appears, a desperate single combat about a lady called Aliarda, and had both been picked up nearly dead near St. Denys. On their recovery Charlemagne settled their disputes in the following summary manner, which, though peculiar, seems to have been efficacious. He

> Married each to a sweet damsel
>   Of his palace the most fair,
> On them laid the heaviest penance
>   If one word they e'er should dare
> But to speak to Aliarda,
>   In secret or before the court;
> And if they should disobey him,
>   Then each life should be cut short.
> Thus should they remain in friendship
>   And the empire at rest.
> Soon was Aliarda wedded
>   With of cavaliers the best.
> Everyone remained contented
>   And in his condition blest!

Nevertheless, this delightful state of things was broken by the march to Roncesvalles, and the assailants, instead of, as in the Carpio ballads, being patriotic Spaniards, were Moors, to whom Carlos's traitorous kinsman had betrayed them. Montesinos did wonders, till, having slain various terrible Moors, he found himself with only the stump of his lance in his hand, and set forth to seek among the slain for his cousin Durandarte, whom he tracked by his blood and found at dawn of day lying at the point of death. And thus he spake:

> "Oh my cousin Montesinos,
>   Ill with us this battle went;
> Since the life of Alda's husband,
>   The great Roldan, there was spent.
>
> "Captive have they made Guarinos—
>   Captain of our squadron he—
> And my life is fast departing;
>   Mortal is my misery.
>
> "The first kindness that I ask thee—
>   Breathing it with parting sighs—
> Is, that when I have departed,
>   And my body soulless lies,
>
> "That thou would'st extract my heart
>   With the little dagger here,
> And would'st take it to Belerma—
>   To my lady-love so dear.
>
> "And wouldst tell her as my message,
>   In this battle that I died;
> And a dead man, I have sent her
>   What, living, never her denied.
>
> "Thou wilt give her all the lordships
>   Over which I have held sway."
> And, as these words he uttered,
>   His brave spirit passed away.

Montesinos faithfully performed his commission, and the ballad leaves Belerma—

> Vencida de un gran desmayo

(vanquished by her great dismay, or swoon). Montesinos is said to have had a castle in La Mancha, where he lived with his lady, Florida or Frida; and he certainly left his name to a cave, apparently to the opening of a mine, down which the wondrous fancy of Cervantes caused his hero to be lowered. There Don Quixote fell into a vision, in which Montesinos himself, a venerable old man, in a sad-coloured robe and green satin tippet, introduced him to the wonders of the enchanted cavern. There, having particularly inquired after the "little dagger" of the ballad, the knight was conducted into a crystal palace, where he beheld the unfortunate Durandarte, in flesh and blood, stretched like an effigy on a marble monument, whence, in a feeble voice, he inquired after the execution of his commission; on which Montesinos, kneeling by the tomb with tears in his eyes, gave a circumstantial relation of the extraction of the heart (which weighed two pounds—a sure mark of courage); adding that he wiped it with a laced handkerchief, and at the first halting-place salted it, and then hastened to deliver it to Belerma. They had, however, all been enchanted underground, together with Durandarte's squire, Guadiana, Belerma's duenna, Ruydera, seven daughters, two nieces, and their servant, all waiting till the great and unrivalled knight, Don Quixote de le Mancha, should deliver them from their thraldom. "And if it should not be so," replied the long-suffering Durandarte with a sigh, "patience, cousin, and shuffle the cards!"

CHAPTER VII.

LITTLE CHRISTIAN STATES.

IT is strange that such fiendish cruelty should be ascribed by the Carpio ballads to Alfonso II., for he is in general treated as a saint of the class of Edward the Confessor. The records of his reign are very scanty and much confused, and it appears that on the death of Silo, an illegitimate son of Alfonso I. by a Moorish woman, known as Mauregato (probably a nickname), seized the crown and kept it to his death, paying the Arabs a tribute—which some say had begun under Aurelio—of wheat, wine, olives, and fifty horses, and according to romance, even fifty maidens, every year. He died in 788, and then his uncle Bermudo was chosen as king, though he was a deacon; but he soon retired into a convent, leaving the throne and his two sons to Alfonso II., called *El Casto*, from the monastic vow he had taken.

It was that same year, 788, that Abd-el-Rhaman died, having chosen as his successor his youngest and favourite son Haschem, the son of a wife he had taken among the noble Zenetes of Mount Atlas, and the only one of his children who had been born in Spain. He had been most carefully educated, and was a brave and merciful prince; but he had to fight for his throne, for his two brothers, Abd-Allah and Suleiman, raised Merida and Toledo against him. He overcame and forgave them both, and during his brief reign continued to build mosques and palaces, and imported many choice plants from the East and from Africa, which spread into all the gardens of Europe. He still retained the dignified simplicity of the Ommeyad, and used to work in his garden with his own hands; and he was also a poet, writing Arabic verses which were highly esteemed.

He founded schools, and forbade the use of any language but Arabic, so that his Christian subjects used Arabic gospels. He died in 796, and his son El Hakem had another war with his uncles, Suleiman and Abd-Allah. The former was killed in battle; but the latter, when subdued, was treated with the usual clemency of the Ommeyads.

Al Hakem was, however, beginning to be tainted with the vices engendered by despotism. The title of Khalif was given to him, and he had parted with the simplicity of his forefathers, and began to live luxuriously, and listen to flattery. But conscience was still awake in him. Of him is told a pretty story—that a poor widow's ground having been forcibly taken from her for the site of a pavilion, she went to the kadi, who promised to obtain justice for her. He went to the place, filled a sack with earth, and then begged the Khalif, who was sitting before the pavilion, to help him to place it on the back of his ass. Al Hakem said it was too heavy. "Oh Khalif," then said the kadi, "if thou canst not bear this load of earth, how wilt thou endure the weight of the whole field when the widow comes to demand it of thee at the day of judgment?" Al Hakem was struck by conscience, and at once gave the woman, not only the field, but the whole splendid pavilion. Again, he forgave his cousin Estah, son of Abd-Allah, at the entreaty of his sister. Soon after, there was some disaffection at Toledo, and the governor, Amrou, taking the opportunity of one of the young princes passing through the city, invited four hundred of the chiefs to a feast, and throwing them into a dungeon, had them all beheaded, and their heads placed on stakes outside the palace gates, to the horror of the people, who of course accused the Khalif.

There was further discontent at a treaty made with the King of the Asturias, which offended the more zealous Saracens; and there was a conspiracy for murdering him in the mosque. The plot was revealed, and was revenged by terrible executions. Three hundred heads in the forum of Cordova, with the inscription, "Traitors to the Khalif," horrified the people. Their wrath was increased by a new tax, intended to maintain a guard, consisting of Berbers and of Slavonic slaves brought from the borders of the Adriatic—men who might be the instruments of any tyranny. There was resistance; ten ringleaders were taken, and condemned to be impaled; and when the Cordovans rose and rescued them, the enraged Khalif, in spite of the entreaties of his sons and all his wisest counsellors, charged them with his troops, made a terrible slaughter, impaled his prisoners, pulled down the quarter of the city where the resistance had begun, and banished the survivors. After some wanderings, they established themselves in the island of Crete, and their fortress—*Al Khandak*, or the entrenchment—finally gave the island its modern name of Candia. Remorse for this ferocious action from that time preyed on Al Hakem; he ceased to take pleasure in anything, continually beheld visions of fighting men, and called to his attendants to stop the slaughter, and died, full of grief and horror, in 821.

Meantime the Christians had prospered. Alfonso II. was gaining ground in Galicia, and had even made a foray as far south as Lisbon, whence he brought home a quantity of spoil. He sent Karl the Great a splendid tent, eight richly-caparisoned mules, and eight slaves to lead them, all captured at Lisbon; and he gave to the cathedral at Oviedo a great gold cross, which was its pride for nearly one thousand years.

The son of Karl—called by the French Louis le Débonnaire—made an expedition into Spain, which resulted in the foundation of the little county of Barcelona, under one Bernardo, among the wild eastern Pyrenees. While in the stony hills of Sobrarle, the inhabitants drew together as those of Navarre had done, and formed a league for mutual defence. They met in the assembly called the *cortes*, and had laws, named *fueros*, which gave them rights that made their rule almost independent of the king whom they elected—namely, Iñigo Sanches, Count of Bigorro. Thus commenced the kingdom of Aragon. A county among the hills south of the Asturian chain, under Don Rodrigo Fruelas, and was called Castilla, from the castles which formed its line of defence; so that there were four independent Christian realms in the hills.

Alfonso II. lived to be eighty-five, and during his later years, Ramiro, who had been marked out for his successor, ruled for him. It is this Ramiro who figures in the spirited ballad which sings the cessation of the maiden tribute, which is unmentioned by Arab authors, and therefore supposed to be a fiction. A damsel thus calls upon the king :

"I know not if I'm bounden to call thee by the name
 Of Christian, Don Ramiro, for though thou dost not claim
 A heathen realm's allegiance, a heathen sure thou art—
 Beneath a Spaniard's mantle thou hid'st a Moorish heart.

"For he who gives the Moslem king a hundred maids of Spain,
 Each year when in its season the day comes round again,
 If he be not a heathen, he swells the heathen's train :
 'Twere better burn a kingdom than suffer such disdain.

"And if 'tis fear of battle that makes ye bow so low,
 And suffer such dishonour from God our Saviour's foe,
 I pray you, sirs, take warning ye'll have as good a fright
 If e'er the Spanish damsels arise themselves to right !"

It need not be said that this was the last of the tribute. Another ballad (Portuguese) tells how six damsels were delivered by one knight, armed only with a bough of a fig-tree, and how this put an end to the tribute.

CHAPTER VIII.

SANTIAGO, THE PATRON OF SPAIN.

THE great St. James, son of Zebedee and brother of St. John, was, according to holy Scripture, the first Apostle who met a martyr's death, being slain by the sword of Herod Agrippa, about ten years after the Ascension.

But in the sixth and seventh centuries, when the Teuton conquerors had been converted, a strong desire had arisen for connecting the churches with Apostles. St. Isidore, Bishop of Seville, a considerable author, who died in 636, was the first to record that there was a tradition that St. James had taught in Spain, but showing some confusion as to which St. James it was. Very possibly the notion arose from the similar name of some early teacher in Spain.

But just as Joseph of Arimathea was appropriated by England, and Mary and Martha by Provence, the Spanish Goths clung to the notion of St. Jacobo, or Santiago, as they called him, having been their apostle or patron saint; and early in the ninth century, when the search for relics had become a passion, Pelayo, a hermit who lived near the ruined port of Iria Flava in Galicia, came to his Bishop, Theodomiro, to tell him that he saw lights hovering about a certain desolate place overgrown with grass and bushes. To a Galician Bishop whose learning was in his breviary and legendary, and who viewed as unholy the science of his Arabic neighbours, the presence of the remains of a saint seemed a much more likely explanation than any possibility of luminous vapours in the marshes round a ruin. Search was made, and a great marble sarcophagus containing a skeleton was brought to light, which it was decided could belong to nobody but Santiago, or else why should the lamps of heaven itself have come to point it out?

Immense was the rejoicing. The old king, Alfonso II., at once granted the spot and all the land for three miles round to the Bishop; and a church was built, and came to be called Padron instead of Iria Flava, from the patron saint.

Moreover, to account for a saint so clearly killed in Judea being buried in Galicia, it was declared that the other disciples, not daring to bury the body, took it to Joppa, and put it on board-ship, when the angels guided it to Iria Flava. Nay, the sarcophagus was the ship itself, made of marble, which moulded itself like wax to the body of the saint, and made its way, without sail or rudder, along the Mediterranean to the place of its destination.

Probably all this was not so much conscious falsehood as superstition enhancing the marvellous, and likewise the endeavour to account for two real facts—*i.e.* the lights, the form of the sarcophagus within and without, and for the one monstrous supposition, taken for granted, that this skeleton was that of St. James at all!

It was not easy to go on pilgrimage to Rome, and still harder to go to Jerusalem, so all the Spaniards and all their Provençal and Gascon neighbours were glad to make Padron the shrine of their devotion; and the place became so rich that it was likely to become a dangerous attraction to the heathen Northmen and Danes, whose ships were infesting the coast of Spain. So in 829, Don Ramiro removed the relics to Campus Stellarum, or Compostella, a little hollow valley in the mountains, where the enemy were less likely to penetrate; and when pilgrims wondered how the heavy marble ship, or coffin, was brought up the rugged ascent, it was answered that wild bulls came and offered themselves to the yoke, and drew it up the ascent! The cross and lizard were the badges of Compostella, which thenceforth enjoyed a yearly revenue of a bushel of wheat from every acre of it in Spain, and a share of the spoil of every battle-field; while the Spaniards, his enthusiastic devotees, believed that Santiago, their glorious patron, fought for them in all their battles, and had been absolutely seen on a white horse in the thickest of the fray. Next, the battle must have a local habitation. Now the valley of Clavijo, on the banks of the Lera, a tributary of the Ebro near Calahorra, is full of small fossil cockles or scallops, such as were brought home by pilgrims—at first, of course—from Palestine; but of late they had also become the badge of pilgrimage to Compostella, and thus were connected in the popular mind with Santiago. They were then supposed to mark his presence at Clavijo, and thus arose the belief that King Ramiro (who succeeded Alfonso in 842) had there fought a tremendous battle with the Moors, and that there it was that Santiago had appeared to succour him at the decisive moment. Of course the yearly tribute had been granted in honour of the aid then given; and when, in after times, people grew critical, and asked for evidence of the grant, a charter of Ramiro was produced, dated from Calahorra, which it was said fell into his hands in consequence of the victory. Unfortunately Calahorra was in the hands of the Moors for two centuries longer, and there is no authentic record of there having been any such battle.

Both kings seem to have been chiefly occupied by keeping off the Northmen, who, however, soon found that there was little but hard blows to be had in the Asturian hills, and chiefly made their descents on the far richer and more inviting Moorish territories, which they frequently plundered. At one time a strong body of them were encamped on the Tablada hills above Cordova. The strength of the kingdom was mustered against them, but they evaded a battle and re-embarked safely.

Abd-el-Rhaman followed the policy of his contemporary, Alfred, and set on foot a fleet, whose constant watchfulness abated their ravages. Otherwise he had few wars. He was of that type of Eastern monarch that seems moulded on the character of Solomon—large-hearted, wise, magnificent, tolerant, and peaceful. He was as great a contrast to the stern, ascetic, narrow-minded, but earnest Alfonso and Ramiro, as were his exquisite horseshoe arches, graceful filigree stonework lattices, inlaid jewellery of marble pavements, and slender minarets, to their dark, vault-like, low-browed churches, and solid castles, built out of hard, unmanageable granite. He repaired the old Roman roads and aqueducts, and fostered handicrafts, so that Damascus silks and sword-blades were rivalled at Cordova. A kind of stamped and ornamented leather, for hangings, was also prepared there; and it is from Cordovan leather that shoemakers are called *cordonniers* in French, and cordwainers in English. Arab and Barbary horses—*barbs* as they were called—had of course been brought in with the conquerors, and their pedigrees were carefully recorded in the palace archives. They were used not only in war, but kept in relays along the road to speed intelligence to the court—the germ of postal communication.

He founded schools, and his alms were liberal—three hundred orphans being bred up at his cost at the school attached to the Aljama mosque. So good-natured was he that when one of his female slaves had insolently refused to obey his summons, and declared she would rather die than come, and the chief eunuch wanted to punish her by walling her up, he replied: "Let it be with loose bricks of silver, so that when she changes her mind she may knock them down and come to me."

Yet Abd-el-Rhaman II. is the first Khalif with whom any stories of persecution are connected. And the decree which led to the translation of the Gothic and Latin Christian writings into Arabic had acted in favour rather of the Gospel than the Koran. Hitherto the Christians had been unmolested, marriages between them and the Moors were not unfrequent, and the women of each nation lived much the same outward life; not indeed as free as that of their Northern sisters, but much less secluded than that of the modern Eastern lady. Gothic or Latin Christians were in places of trust, and their churches and monasteries were inviolate.

Near Cordova was one of the great double monasteries of the early Middle Ages, called Tabanos; and it is from a scholar named Eulogio, who was bred there and who became a priest at Cordova, that we have the history—one so simple and veracious as to be a great contrast to the wild and impossible legends of the Galician mountaineers.

It would seem that some Mahommedans had been converted, and that this roused the anger of the "true believers." The Metropolitan Bishop, Recafredo, sided with the authorities, being one of those who thought zeal a dangerous thing; and thus the trial of the Christians was doubly great.

Perfecto, a priest, was beset by Arabs in the streets of Cordova, and challenged to explain why he held out against Islam. He argued the matter out, ending by saying that he durst not speak his opinion of the Prophet. They insisted, declaring that no harm should ensue; but when they thus had forced a denunciation from him, they could not restrain their rage, and dragged him before the kadi. For a little while he yielded and recalled his hot words; but then repenting, he cursed Mahommed and all his followers, and, while still uttering the words, was beheaded for blaspheming the Prophet. His example was followed by one Isaac, a monk of Tabanos, who had forsaken a post under government for the cloister, and was moved to come before the kadi and denounce the Prophet. He too was beheaded; but the prospect of martyrdom had become so precious in the eyes of the Christians that the Abbot Walabouso of Tabanas and four more monks followed in the same path. The Khalif never persecuted Christians, as such, if they refrained either from attempting conversion or from openly denouncing the Prophet. But there were two poor young girls, named Muñila and Alodia, who were the children of a Moslem father and a Christian mother, who had reared them in her own faith, and they grew up so good and lovely that they were called (like the English Eadgyth) "roses springing from thorns." Their father died, and their mother married a less tolerant Moslem, who, finding their faith proof against his threats, brought them before the kadi. Splendid marriages were offered them if they would quit the Christian faith; but they answered that they knew of no spouse equal to their Lord, no bliss comparable to what He could bestow; and persuasion and torture alike failed with them, until they sealed their confession with their lives.

A nun of Tabanos next dreamt that the martyred abbot had appeared to her, telling her that he had a message for his sister Maria, a nun in the same convent. Maria viewed this as a call to follow him, and went into the city, intending to denounce herself; but turning aside into church first to strengthen herself by prayer, she there met another maiden named Flora. This girl had had a Christian mother, and held her faith, though she had been much persecuted by her brother, who had brought her to the judge and had her cruelly beaten and imprisoned. She had escaped; but the meeting with Maria decided her on going again to the tribunal to offer herself. Hand-in-hand the two maidens stood before the kadi, and declared Mahommed a deceiver and a false prophet. They were thrown into the lowest dungeon; but there they met Eulogio, who had been imprisoned, not by the Arabs, but by the time-serving Archbishop Recafredo, as a dangerous person. He comforted and exhorted them, and they were soon visited by two unexpected persons, Aurelio and his wife Sabigote, both Moslems outwardly, but Christians at heart. Shown by the examples before them how unworthily they were acting, they consulted Eulogio, telling him that they were chiefly held back by the thought of their two little children. He replied by assuring them that their little ones would be safe in the mercy of the Father of the fatherless. Flora and Maria were beheaded; and the next night Sabigote dreamt of them like the martyrs of old, in white robes, with palms in their hands, singing among the saints in paradise, and exhorting her to continue in their steps and witness a good confession. Six days later Eulogio was released, and he wrote a poem recounting their history, which is still preserved.

Aurelio and Sabigote began to live as Christians, and so did another married pair, Felix and Liliosa, having first set their affairs in order. Indeed Felix had long been a Christian at heart, but had in fear professed himself a Moslem, until he was roused by the brave constancy of these martyrs to dare the consequences of confessing his faith. Still the pair doubted whether it was right to follow the fashion of going voluntarily to provoke vengeance by cursing Mahommed, and they therefore waited till the accusation was made, when they were brought, not before the kadi, but before the divan, or royal counsel. There persuasions and promises were used against them in vain, and they too were beheaded, together with a deacon of Tabanos, who insisted on sharing their fate.

Abd-el-Rhaman, a most unwilling person too, commanded Recafredo to summon a synod to forbid the Christians to give open provocation and to denounce themselves. The decree was made; but the zealous took it as a token of lukewarmness and time-serving in the higher clergy, and paid no attention to it, so that fresh executions followed. In the midst, Abd-el-Rhaman II. died of paralysis, in 852, leaving forty-five sons and forty-one daughters. His son Mahommed was of a more severe disposition, and martyrdoms became much more frequent; the most notable being that of a beautiful and wealthy maiden named Columba, who had, in spite of all persuasions of her relations, taken the veil at Tabanos. The other nuns were moved by the authorities and shut up at Cordova, to prevent their rushing on destruction; but Columba escaped, reviled Mahommed before the kadi, and perished. It is probable that these voluntary self-sacrifices were the reaction from the indifference which had set in under the toleration of the Khalifs, and they certainly greatly quickened the life of the Mosarabic Church, and won instead of deterring the doubtful.

Eulogio went about encouraging and strengthening waverers, and the clergy of Toledo elected him as their Bishop; but he was viewed as too zealous and uncompromising for promotion, and was immediately after brought before the divan for having hidden a converted Mahommedan girl in the house of his sister. He was beheaded, and his corpse thrown into the river, where a white dove flew over it as it floated down the stream. The Moslem girl was also put to death; but the Arabs seem then to have perceived that the persecution only strengthened the zeal of the

Church, and it was discontinued. Eulogio's history was written by his fellow scholar Alvaro, and is still extant, together with his own acts of the martyrs, and an apology, *i. e.* defence of them as real martyrs, which was denied by the wonder-craving Spaniards in the north because they worked no miracles; because they were simply beheaded, not tortured; because they offered themselves; and because their slayers were not worshippers of many gods, but of *one*.

The feeling is curious which disregarded the veritable contemporary martyrs, and went into the wildest raptures of enthusiasm over such utter impossibilities as the relics of Santiago and the absurd miracles imputed to them.

CHAPTER IX.

THE COUNT OF THE LAND OF CASTLES.

No very marked progress was made by either Moors or Christians during the remainder of the ninth century. The Asturian kingdom extended over Leon and Galicia; and Alfonso III., called the Great, made inroads as far as Lisbon and Coimbra. There were family divisions among the Ommeyads, and though they did not lose much ground, they did not gain. The Christians, however, had a brave champion in Fernando Gonçales, Count of Castille. An Eastern prince, named Abu Alaxi, had written to the Khalif, entreating permission to make his holy campaign, or *al giheb*, in Spain, since all good Moslems understood that fighting under the commander of the Faithful secured an entrance into paradise. Abd-el-Rhaman III. received him most royally. The Moors were then at peace with Leon; indeed, the king, Don Sancho the Fat, had actually come to Cordova to consult the Moorish physicians, whose skill far exceeded those of any Gothic mediciner, since, at Seleucia, the Arabs had obtained and made good use of the writings and traditions of the Greek men of science. Abd-el-Rhaman was no covenant breaker, so he did not assist the zealous Abu Alaxi, and probably refused to let him attack Sancho's kingdom, for it was on the independent county of Castille that the incursion was made. Fernan Gonçales signally defeated him at Pedrahita, and thus raised Castille to such reputation as to excite the jealousy of King Sancho of Leon. The mother of this king was Doña Teresa, the daughter of the king of Navarre, and, by her advice, a strange plot was arranged, which has furnished subjects for another whole cycle of ballads. The count was invited to Oviedo to confer on matters of the Christian defence. Thither he came with a beautiful hawk and hound, which Don Sancho desired to purchase from him, and a bargain was struck that if the price were not paid by a certain time it should be doubled on each succeeding day. Meantime the count, having lately lost his wife, the queen-mother discoursed to him on the charms of her niece, Doña Sancha, and undertook to arrange a marriage with her, at the same time sending word to her brother, King Garcia of Navarre, to have him seized and imprisoned as soon as he set foot in those territories.

Doña Sancha learnt how she had been made the bait to bring about the shameful imprisonment of the best warrior in Spain. The ballad, remarkably enough, makes her informant one of the knights from Normandy, who came to fight with the Moslem exactly from the same belief in holy wars as had brought the Arab champion. It is a testimony how high stood Norman sense of honour.

> The Norman feasts among the guests, but at the evening tide
> He speaks to Garci's daughter within her bower aside :
> " Now God forgive us, lady, and God His Mother dear,
> For on a day of sorrow we have been blithe of cheer.

"The Moors may well be joyful, but great should be our grief,
For Spain has lost her guardian, Castile hath lost her chief;
The Moorish host is pouring like a river o'er the land;
Curse on the Christian fetters that bind Gonçales's hand.

"Gonçales loves thee, lady, he lov'd thee long ago,
But little is the kindness that for his love you show;
The curse that lies on Cava's head, it may be shared by thee.
Arise! let love with love be paid, and set Gonçales free."

The lady answered little, but at the midst of night,
When all her maids were sleeping, she hath risen and ta'en her flight;
She hath tempted the alcayde with her jewels and her gold,
And unto her his prisoner that jailer false hath sold.

She took Gonçales by the hand at the dawning of the day.
She said: "Upon the heath you stand, before you lies the way,
But if I to my father go—alas, what must I do!
My father will be angry—I fain would go with you." *

And so she did, and at the old city of Burgos, his capital, was married to him with great state. He then made war on the perfidious Navarrese king, took him prisoner, and kept him at Burgos till his sister's intercession prevailed for his release. But Fernan had not suspected the further treachery of the Leonese, and again allowed himself to be entrapped into attending the cortes, when he was at once made prisoner and thrown into a dungeon. Doña Sancha on this set out on pilgrimage to Santiago, and, arriving at Leon, begged permission to visit her husband. It was granted. She changed clothes with him, and in the garb of a female prisoner he again escaped. King Sancho, after his first anger, allowed the faithful lady to rejoin her husband; but Fernan now demanded the long-accumulating debt for hawk and hound, and as all the

* Lockhart's "Spanish Ballads."

treasures of Leon and the Asturias would have failed to pay it, the independence of his country was granted him in lieu—at least so saith Castilian ballad and tradition, which assuredly have such a grace that, if not true, they ought to be. He was a real personage, who actually gained several great successes. Pope John XI. sent him a cross which was held to be a preservative from hailstorms. Fierce rivalry, however, continued to exist between Leon and Castille, and at one time Ordoño III. of Leon actually compelled Gonçales and all his family to take refuge at Cordova, where the Moors were always ready to exercise hospitality towards their gallant foes; but he afterwards returned to Castille, and his daughter Urraca was married in succession to two kings of Leon, both named Ordoño—the first of whom divorced her on a quarrel with her father; and the second, son of Alfonso the Monk, was known as Ordoño the Wicked, and was dethroned. In fact, nothing could be more stormy and confused than the state of the little Christian kingdoms and counties. They were always at war or in a state of internal commotion, while, though the Moors were little disposed to trouble them, northern invasions harassed them from time to time. One of these was effectually repulsed by Don Garcia, son to the great Fernan Gonçales, and thus the claim of the family to the allegiance of the county was much strengthened. But altogether everything good was at a low ebb with the Spaniards in this century, just as it was with the Christians elsewhere in France, Germany, and in England. The Moors despised them for their ignorance, rudeness, and, above all, for their want of cleanliness. An ascetic reaction from the excessive Roman luxury of the baths, the great place for voluptuous enjoyment and gossip in the ancient world, had led a certain stamp of religious persons to despise and neglect the body, and to forget that purity without ought to go with purity within; and opposition to the regular ablutions of the Mahommedans led the Spaniards into viewing cleanliness as very far from next to godliness, but rather as opposed to it.

Thus it must be confessed that their clergy became the leaders in that mischievous veneration for dirt and vermin which was a morbid feature of mediæval asceticism.

CHAPTER X.

THE AUGUSTAN AGE OF CORDOVA.

The Cordovan Khalifs were warmly affectionate people. Abd-Allah, who began to reign in 888, had indeed a rebellious son, Mohamed, who died of the wounds received in a battle with his brother; but the Khalif's grief was great, and he adopted the only child of this eldest son, Abd-el-Rhaman, a boy of four years old, whose mother was a Christian slave named Maria. Blue-eyed, fair-haired, gentle, and graceful, the boy was loved by all, even by his victorious uncle, surnamed *Al Modhaffer*, or the Conqueror, who might have aspired to the throne. He was carefully educated. Arabic writers say that he was taught first the Koran; then at eight years old the *Sunnah*, or traditional comment; next *Hadyz*, or historical tradition; also grammar, poetry, the Arabic proverbs, the lives of princes, the science of government, and other sciences, such as mathematics; also to groom a horse, to draw the bow, to wield the lance and sword—to manage all weapons, and understand all strategy. His grace, brilliancy, affability, and ability won all hearts, and when, in 913, Abd-Allah died, as it was said, of grief for the death of his old mother, there was but one voice in favour of the young Abd-el-Rhaman then twenty-two years of age, and his uncle, Al Modhaffer, was the first to take the oath of fealty to him as commander of the Faithful.

There had been, however, a revolt of long standing, conducted by a family called *Ben-Hafsann*, or the sons of Hafsann, who had a retreat in the mountains between the Moorish and Christian lands, and though often defeated by Al Modhaffer, had never been entirely reduced. The war broke out again on the accession of the new Khalif, and was rigorously carried on by Abd-el-Rhaman and his uncle; but the law of Ali (son-in-law to Mahommed) required that in a war between Moslems, the enemy should never be driven to extremities, so that pursuit might not go beyond one province, nor a siege last more than a week. Finding that the observance of this custom perpetuated the civil war, Abd-el-Rhaman convoked the imaums of the Aljama and his divan, and decided that it must be broken. It is said to have been the only instance among the Arabs of the violation of the rule of mercy and forbearance. The last of the Ben-Hafsann was besieged in Toledo, until he made a desperate sally with three thousand horse, and escaped to the Christians in the Asturias. The city, which had for sixty years been the headquarters of the rebellion, was treated with the usual clemency of the Khalifs.

In general, however, the reign was peaceful, and noted for great and beautiful works; in especial was noted the palace of Medina-al-Zohra, in a beautiful valley on the banks of the Guadalquivir, five miles from Cordova. The Greek emperors sent him marbles and workmen, and there were still Roman remains to use. Four thousand three hundred columns of precious marble adorned it. The pavements were of marble, and in the principal rooms were fountains, in basins of porphyry. In the Khalif's hall the central fountain was of jasper, and the water spouted from the bill of a golden swan, beneath a canopy in the centre of which was a wonderful pearl, presented to Abd-el-Rhaman by the Emperor of Constantinople. The woodwork was of costly cedar, and in one pavilion was a fountain of quicksilver, the reflections of which were wonderful. It was in the midst of an exquisite garden, where beautiful shrubs, flowers, and water were arranged so as to be the delight of all beholders. The name *Medina-al-Zohra* (town of the flower) was taken from a fair slave, Zohra, whose statue, in white marble, adorned the gateway. It was contrary to the laws of Islam, which strictly interpreted the second commandment, and forbade all imitations of created things, declaring that the likenesses would become bodies, and at the day of judgment demand their souls from the artists. Greeks were employed by Abd-el-Rhaman for this statue, and the swan came from Constantinople; but the Spanish Arabs were extremely liberal in their interpretation of the Koran.

Music had been absolutely forbidden by the Prophet. "To hear music," he said, "is to sin against the law; to perform music is to sin against religion; to enjoy music is to be guilty of infidelity!" So there were stories of strict believers—when within the sound of instruments that they could not silence—stopping their ears till they were informed that it was over by some boy under fifteen, and therefore exempt from the strict obligation of the law. The only songs tolerated were the muezzin's chanted call to prayer, and a hymn of the pilgrims at Mekka round Hagar's supposed well. But nature had been too strong for Mahommed. The Arabs still sang, and in Spain music was greatly cultivated. There was a chief of the royal musicians, and in the Escorial library are still preserved some remnants of the very extensive musical literature, in especial the works of Al Faraby, on the elements of music, on composition, singing, instruments, and accompaniments, with the Arabic musical writing and notes, and drawings of at least thirty instruments. The first volume of one of the great books of songs is also extant, containing one hundred and fifty airs, and the biographies of fourteen musicians. The whole collection had been the work of fifty years.

Poetry flourished with music. Everyone was a poet. The extraordinary richness of the language, which is so full that the dictionary is in sixty volumes, and the natural cadences lend themselves to verse; and the tone of mind of the nation was poetical, and delighted in figurative imagery and in descriptive or romantic pieces. Professed poets were sure of renown and wealth, and even princes sent letters and challenges in poetry to one another. Story-tellers were also in high honour, and there were an immense number of romances, of which we may guess the style by their Eastern kindred, "The Arabian Nights;" but these were further enlivened by the chivalrous fancies caught from the Goths, and there was also a book of fables showing plainly their common descent with those of Æsop. History, genealogy, grammar, rhetoric, and philosophy were greatly cultivated, and many treatises on them were written, and carried the Arabs to conclusions never dreamt of by Mahommed.

Mathematics were studied earnestly, and the substitution of the nine Arabic figures for the cumbrous Roman method, enabled the operations to be carried much farther than before. *Gebr*, the Arab term for arithmetic, is the source of our term algebra. The sages of Cordova carried their calculations into astronomy, and improved on the systems of Ptolemy. Al Batany, who was born in 877, was the first to measure the obliquity of the ecliptic, and made other great discoveries of practical value. The names of most of the individual stars remain as monuments of our debts to these Arabs; from whom we learnt to talk of the zenith and nadir. Geography was also studied. The Arab descriptions of Spain are still valuable; and travellers were sent out to bring home accounts of the scenery, inhabitants, productions, and natural history of different countries. Treatises on all the branches of natural history abounded, and a few of them still remain, including one on all the methods of the chase with dogs, horses, falcons, &c.

Agriculture was especially studied. Great treatises on irrigation and crops, cattle, grafting, and gardening still exist; for the motto of the Arab landowner was: "He who planteth and soweth, and maketh the earth bring forth fruit for man and beast, hath done alms that shall be reckoned to him in heaven." Even the Khalifs worked in their gardens with their own hands; and Andalusia was like one vast highly-cultivated farm. Many plants were introduced by the Khalifs, which Spain lost and neglected after the discovery of America—such as rice and sugar-cane (*soukhar*, as they called it), saffron and mulberry-trees, ginger, myrrh, bananas, and dates. The Spanish names of many plants show their origin, and some have travelled even to us, such as the apricot, from *albaric aque*; the artichoke, from *alca chofa*; cotton, from *al godon*. Medicinal plants were greatly studied, and the Arab physicians, working on from the discoveries of Celsus and Galen, divided with the Jews all there was of healing skill or knowledge; and though anatomical studies were impossible to a devout believer, their surgeons made some progress in discovery. Chemistry and alchemy alike are derived from their words *al kymia*, altered from the Greek. The terms alembic, alcohol, and alkali mark their progress in discovery; and the signs of apothecaries' weight, only now falling into disuse, are a remnant of the days when the leech was either a Moor or a Jew.

Nor were women excluded from all these studies. They studied enough to be companions to their husbands; and a lady named Maryam had a school for young maidens at Seville, where they could acquire science, mathematics, and history, as well as lighter arts. They went about veiled up to the eyes, and never ate with men; but they were allowed to associate with them in the courts and gardens of their beautiful houses, and join in their conversations, music, and poetry.

Their dress was much the same as that of the ladies of North Africa. Full white muslin trousers were tied at the ankle, and a long, full, white *gilalah*, a mantle of transparent muslin, covered the tighter vest and jacket, both of brilliant colours, over which they wore gold chains, necklaces, and bracelets, with strings of coral, pearl, and amber; while their hair was in little curls, adorned with jewels and flowers. But all this was concealed by the thick muffling outer veil; and they also had horsehair vizards, through which they could see without being seen. They had a gallery fenced in with latticework in the mosque, and were treated as more on an equality with men than their sisters in most of the Mahommedan world.

Cordova was, in fact, the seat of a great literary society, where the descendants of Arab sheiks by turns opened their gorgeous palaces in the evenings to poets, philosophers, and men of science, who debated and recited as in the golden days of Pericles or Mæcenas. Jew and Christian could be freely admitted, and travellers and discoverers related their adventures, showed the curiosities they had brought home, and described the places they had seen. Or anecdotes were related, when story-tellers vied with each other in relating instances of courage, generosity, adroitness, or the like; poems were recited, or arguments held on abstract subjects or mystic explanations of the Koran, stretching its meaning as Mahommed never intended. The impulse he had given had carried these Arabs to the highest point, and their progress was shown in the exquisite taste of all their productions, from their buildings down to the lovely illuminations which enriched the beautiful Arabic writing of their manuscripts.

The Khalif had a splendid library, containing copies of books made by scribes whom he sent through Egypt, Syria, Greece, and Persia to transcribe all that was left of ancient learning; and to this library learned men had free access. They used it not only for study, but for imparting their information and discoveries, or, as we should now call it, giving lectures. The extent of it may be guessed from the fact that the catalogue, compiled by the Khalif and his secretary, was in forty-four volumes of fifty folios each, containing the biography and genealogy of each author. Paper was here used, having been introduced by the Arabs, who had learnt the art of making it from the Chinese.

The habits of the Moorish noble seem to have been to rise early, go through the prayers and ablutions of a true believer, take some light repast of fruit and bread; then attend to business, study, or the exercise of arms till noon, when the chief meal was taken. After this a siesta in the garden pavilions, cooled by the sparkling fountains. This prepared the luxurious for music, the studious for reading, the young for active sports; and it was the Khalif's time for seeing ambassadors, hearing petitions, or giving audiences. Sunset brought the muezzin's summons to evening prayer, preceding supper—the social meal—after which the literary gatherings followed, or songs and music, games at chess and backgammon, and sometimes—among the dissipated—drinking bouts and exhibitions of dances.

In the winter months, the assembly was in a hall, where, instead of a fountain, there was a great vase of charcoal, round which were spread carpets and cushions where the guests reclined, and were sprinkled with rose-water and other perfumes. Their mental fare was the recitation of new poems; their bodily, preparations of lamb or kid, milk boiled or frothed, sweetmeats, fruit, red wine for the unscrupulous, white wine for those who wished to keep the letter without the spirit of the law, and lemonade for the strict observers.

Abd-el-Rhaman was, for the most part, a peaceful sovereign; but he had one great war with Ramiro II., who, being at peace with Navarre and Castille, made an inroad into the Moorish dominions, burning and ravaging to the south of the Douro. The Khalif retaliated by a like foray to the north of the same river, and besieged Simancas, a fortress on the little river Pisuerga, a tributary of the Douro. The invasion was so serious that all the Christian forces of Navarre, Leon, and Castille united under Ramiro, and they gained a splendid victory, being assisted, as they believed, by two angels on white horses. However, the loss on their own side was very severe, and they could not hinder the Khalif and his uncle from taking Zamora, and were soon obliged to make peace, retaining the city, and leaving the Douro as the barrier between the Christian and the Moor.

Abd-el-Rhaman underwent the usual lot of many-wived monarchs. His nomination of his favourite son, Al Hakem, as his successor, led to a conspiracy on the part of another son, Abd-Allah. This plot was discovered in time; he and his adviser were seized and brought to Al Zohra.

"What," said his father, "wert thou offended that thou shalt not reign?"

The prince made no answer but by tears. His Ahithophel went and hanged himself. The divan met and condemned the prince; but Al Hakem and all the other brothers implored their father to pardon him. It was in vain. "I shall go mourning for my son all my days," said the Khalif; "but I must needs think of what is to come, and give an example of justice to my people."

Abd-Allah was put to death in prison, and his father did indeed grieve all the rest of his life. He left the government to Al Hakem, and spent his time in his gardens, trying to find comfort in long conversations with Abu Ayub, a learned and devout man, who, after having been a brave soldier, had dedicated himself to good works, and went about in a coarse woollen garment, bestowing alms.

The Khalif sent many gifts to the poor by his hands, and it was he who recorded the words of Abd-el-Rhaman, in these days of depression, at the end of a prosperous and splendid reign of fifty years. Almost in the words of the Preacher of Israel did he sum up the joys and grandeur of his reign, and then added that he had counted up the days when he had been really and truly happy, and found them to amount to just fourteen!

He grew weaker, and his pleasure was to listen to the songs of Moyna, a lady who acted as his secretary, and of Ayesha, another lady, both highly educated, and modest as any of their Christian sisters.

Abd-el-Rhaman III. died in 961. He had an extensive dominion in Africa, including Ceuta and Tangier; and one of his titles was *Emir-al-Moumenyn*, or Chief of the Faithful, which became on European lips the Miramamolin, when inherited by his successors.

Al Hakem's reign was more peaceful and equally prosperous, being in fact a continuation of that of his father in all essential points; but after his death, in 976, more stormy times began, and the brilliant flower of Moslemism began to pass away.

CHAPTER XI.

THE LOSS OF COMPOSTELLA.

AL HAKEM II. left only one son, Heschem II., who was only ten years old, and was therefore named by the Arabs, *Al Mowayed Bi'llah*, the protected by God; and was proclaimed Khalif, though the law required that the commander of the Faithful should be above fifteen years of age. His mother, Sobeyah, had already exercised much power during his father's latter years, and she made a wise choice of his *hajib*, or grand vizier, namely Mahommed-ben-Abd-Allah, better known by the glorious title he won for himself of *Al Mansour*, or the Invincible.

He had been left an orphan while studying at the Aljama College at Cordova, and had been received among the Khalif's pages. Sobeyah perceived his ability, and made him her secretary, in which capacity she became so sensible of his abilities that she placed the whole power of the state in his hands on her husband's death.

Leon was in an unsettled state, for there had been a dispute as to the succession, and Bermudo II. was scarcely secure on his throne, besides which he was making reforms in the Church which were unpopular among the lazy lower clergy. Castille had a young count, Garcia Fernandes, and Al Mansour deemed that the best way to prevent the sheiks from, as usual, rebelling against a new Khalif, would be to lead them against the Christians. So he made an attack on Castille, and Garcia in vain intreated aid from the kings of Leon, Navarre, and Aragon. With shortsighted policy they left the border county to its fate, and year after year Al Mansour entered the country, generally taking some important town each time, and leading away long trains of captives to be sold at Cordova; for he was a much more stern and cruel conqueror than the Khalifs had been, though he had a grand Arab chivalry about him.

Once, when he had shut in a considerable body of Christians in a narrow defile, and, on his summons to surrender, they had refused, he took the worthier course recommended in the case of the Caudine Forks by Pontius Herennius. He bade his men withdraw, and let them escape. The gallant Arab could not bear to massacre so many brave men who lay at his mercy.

The Spaniards meantime fought on, not only against the Moors but among themselves. Like the Scots, they had a ferocious history of terrible deeds of violence and treachery; and like them, too, they made these the occasion of numerous ballads, casting a halo of romance round what would otherwise have been merely savage and barbarous. None of the actual versions of these songs are traceable beyond the thirteenth century, but they are probably derived from contemporary ones, the Spaniards having learnt the habit of chanting wild verses about the tales that caught their fancy from their Moorish neighbours.

One of these incidents, horrible in itself if true, and at any rate fertile in ballad-lore, was the death of the Infants of Lara. Just as we find *Childe* the term for a young knight, the sons of counts and kings in Spain were termed *Infantes*, and their sisters *Infantas*; and it was not till much later that the title was restricted to youthful royalty.

Don Gonzalo, Count of Lara, in the Asturias, had married Sancha, sister of Don Rodrigo, or Ruy Velasquez, and had seven gallant sons, who were all knighted on one day by Garcia Fernandes, Count of Castille.

They all went to Burgos, with their parents, to the grand wedding of Ruy Velasquez with a lady of high rank, Doña Lambra, a kinswoman of the Count of Castille, who was present at the festival. The entertainments lasted five weeks. In the last week a *tablado* was set up beyond the river as a mark for the knights. This is supposed to mean a wooden castle, fastened together so loosely that a strong blow would make it break to pieces. Canes or reeds—which the Spaniards had learnt from the Moorish sport of the *djerid*, to throw—were launched at it without success, till Alvaro Sanchez, a favourite kinsman of the bride, struck it full. Lambra was delighted, and cried out that no one could mend that cast.

Six of the Infants of Lara were playing at tables— backgammon—and did not heed; but the youngest brother, Gonzalo Gonzales, was nettled, and taking only one squire with a hawk on his wrist, he rode up, cast his djerid, and struck the tablado so sharply as to break it.

The elder brothers were afraid that harm would

come of this exploit, for the bride was angered, and Alvaro gave the victor such abusive language, that young Gonzalo in return gave him a blow which knocked out his teeth. Lambra screamed out that never was damsel so dishonoured at her wedding, and her husband was thus invited to strike his nephew violently. A fray broke out, and blood would have been shed had not the Counts of Castille and Lara interfered, and, as they hoped, made peace.

Afterwards they set forth on a progress through Castille, taking the bridegroom with them, probably in hopes of thus keeping the peace, while the seven Infants were, in the midst of a larger company, to escort Lambra to her new home at Bavardiello. When they arrived the brothers went into a garden, where, under the shade of the trees, Gonzalo bathed his hawk. Doña Lambra, in whose heart malice was still rankling, took this opportunity of offering him the most deadly insult, by sending a slave to fill a gourd with blood and fling it at him. The brothers rushed after him with their swords. He fled to his mistress, and she tried to protect him, but in vain. He was slain at her feet, so that she was sprinkled with his blood; after which they took their mother, and rode home to Salas.

Doña Lambra set up a bed covered with a pall in the courtyard, and she and her women wailed over it eastern fashion. She worked on her husband to exact terrible and treacherous vengeance. He asked the Count of Lara to go to Cordova to obtain from Al Mansour gifts towards defraying the expenses of his wedding. This seems very strange, but it occurs as a matter of course in the chronicle and all the ballads, and it is probable that the Moors were in the habit of bribing, under various specious names, the people of one Christian state not to interfere with them when they made war with another. Moreover, Arabian wealth and profuseness in gifts made a visit from a poor mountaineer seem like going to a perfect mine of riches. Ruy Velasquez, however, gave the poor old count the "letters of Bellerophon," which, says the chronicle, were written for him in Arabic by "a Moor who spoke the Roman tongue," and who was immediately put to death lest he should betray the secret, namely, that the father should be at once put to death, and that the Moors should make an inroad, when Velasquez would betray the seven brothers into their hands, and desired that all should be beheaded, telling Al Mansour that they were the strength of Castille.

This was not the Al Hajib's fashion of making war, and he merely detained the count as a captive. Ruy Velasquez, however, mustered his forces for an attack on the Moors, and the Infants of Lara joined him, though not without warnings from their wise old tutor Nuño Salido, who suspected treachery.

At Almenaz, Velasquez and his troops deserted them in the midst of a battle, leaving them and two hundred horse alone among the whole Moorish army, and refusing to succour them, or let anyone else go to their aid. After desperate fighting, six were made prisoners, Fernando, the eldest, having fallen. The Moors at first treated them honourably; but Ruy Velasquez went to the two chiefs and declared that Al Mansour intended these youths to be slain, and would punish those who spared their lives. Therefore they were all massacred, and Nuño Salido with them: their heads were cut off and sent to Cordova.

Al Mansour, according to both chronicle and ballad, had the barbarity knowingly to invite the count to come with him and tell whose were the seven young heads and the one old one which had been brought home by his warriors. We quote from Lockhart's translation:

He took their heads up one by one, he kiss'd them o'er and o'er;
And aye ye saw the tears down run, I wot that grief was sore.
He closed the lids on their dead eyes, all with his fingers frail,
And handled all their bloody curls, and kissed their lips so pale.

"Oh had ye died all by my side upon some famous day,
My fair young men, no weak tears then had wash'd your blood away;
The trumpet of Castille had drowned the misbelievers' horn,
And the last of all the Lara's line a Gothic spear had borne."

With that it chanced a man drew near to lead him from the place,
Old Lara stoop'd him down once more and kiss'd Gonzalo's face;
But 'ere the man observ'd him, or could his gesture bar,
Sudden he from his side had grasp'd that Moslem's scymetar.

With it the old man slew thirteen Moors in his frenzy before he could be mastered. He besought Al Mansour to put him to death; but the Khalif, shocked at the treachery, released him and sent him home. A Moorish woman, who had been his solace in captivity, became the mother of a son, whom she named Mudarra, and bred up with a full knowledge of his father's wrongs. He was trained to arms and knighted by Al Mansour; and when he was fourteen was sent with the token of half a ring, which his father and mother had broken between them, to Salas, where he was warmly welcomed by the Count, and likewise by the Countess Sancha, who loved him for his likeness to that youngest and choicest of all her sons, Gonzalo.

He did amply avenge the deaths of his brethren when he met Rodrigo.

> "Now the mercy you dealt to my brothers of old,
> Be the hope of that mercy the comfort you hold.
> Die, foeman to Sancha! die, traitor to Lara!"
> As he spake, there was blood on the spear of Mudarra.
> *Lockhart.*

Mudarra was baptised, and on the day of his christening Doña Sancha adopted him by putting on an immensely wide smock, then taking him by the hand, drawing him through it, and kissing him. His illegitimacy was thus taken away, and he became heir to Salas, his progeny bearing the surname of Manriquez. It is also said that after the death of the Count of Castille, he caused Lambra to be burnt as the author of all the mischief.

There is no knowing the truth or falsehood of this wild and terrible story. Ballads are many, and there is extant a series of prints with the history of the Infants. Two chests used to be shown at Cordova where it was said their heads had been placed, also a building called the prison; and there were also discoveries of their headless skeletons in the church of St. Millan in 1602, and of their seven skulls at Salas in 1587.

The Moors only made summer campaigns; in the autumn they returned home with their slaves and booty, rarely leaving garrisons in the conquered cities, and this gave the Spaniards time to rally each year.

Too late Bermudo of Leon and Garcia of Navarre saw their error in leaving the border county to its fate. The Bishop of Compostella, Pelayo, offended by the king's endeavour to restrain the corruptions of the clergy, went over to the Moors; and, except that Bermudo was a good and pious man, and his comrades stanch warriors, the story of the first conquest seemed about to repeat itself.

Simancas and Zamora fell in succession, though the saying was:

> Zamora si prende in un hora.

Al Mansour threatened Leon; but Bermudo, to save his capital, gave battle on the banks of the Ezla, and at first gained some advantage, until Al Mansour, to stop the flight of his people, threw himself from his horse, and lying down on the ground, swore that if they chose to fly, they must leave him behind. A fresh charge secured the victory, but with such loss that he was forced to retreat, vowing, however, to punish Leon next year. This gave time to many families to escape; and Bermudo even carried away the bodies of his predecessors to the old refuge in the Asturian hills.

Al Mansour kept his word and utterly demolished Leon, but was repulsed by the strong Asturian castle of Luna, though he took Astorga and Salamanca. On his way to his next campaign he visited the city of Murcia, where he had to wait for some troops from Algarve.

Ahmed, the governor of the place, feasted him and all his troops for twenty-three days. All the officers slept in beds of silk and gold tissue, and daily bathed in rose-water; and the soldiers were located with proportionate sumptuousness. When Al Mansour took leave he said: "I shall take care to send none of my warriors here. They whose rest should be in battle ought not to lie on soft cushions. But as so great a lord ought not to pay tribute like a mere vassal, in the name of my lord the Khalif, I exempt thee from taxes."

The attack this year was against Barcelona, whose count was defeated and fled by sea, leaving his capital to fall into the all-conquering hands. In 994 came the turn of Coimbra, Braga, and all the northern cities of Portugal, and, greatest blow of all to the Christians, he made his way to Compostella—as the Spaniards say—by the contrivance of the wicked Bishop Pelayo. The Arabs considered it an *al djihed*, or holy war, to attack and destroy the shrine of the Christians' prophet, whose influence they had begun to dread. So they were bent on taking and destroying what they called *Sham Yakoub*, where they considered a great figure of St. James, over the sarcophagus, to be the Christian *Kaaba*. They found the place empty and deserted; only one old monk sitting sad and desolate by the tomb. He was led to Al Mansour, and, being asked who he was, replied: "I am a servant of Santiago." The general bade that the old man should go free, but stripped the place, and fed his horse out of the great porphyry font; and purified the place, as he thought, by a destruction of all the images and crosses; but he could not find the body of Santiago, which no doubt had been removed. Still he carried off the two great bells, marked with the cross and lizard, and hung them up as lamps, reversed, in the Aljama at Cordova. The Christians had no comfort but in the belief that the horse died of his sacrilegious meal.

After the fifth part of the spoil of this campaign had been taken for the Khalif—or rather for the hospitals, the schools, and the poor—each foot-soldier had received five *miscáls* of gold, each horseman double that sum. Al Mansour had chosen to share alike with his soldiers.

CHAPTER XII.

THE INVINCIBLE AL MANSOUR.

The loss of Compostella roused the Christians to band together under Garcia Fernandez, Count of Castille, to make a more resolute resistance. The campaign that ensued is so brilliantly and yet so accurately described by M. Viardot, that the following pages are, with a few omissions, translated from his "Histoires des Arabes." Every incident is fact, and for each bit of description there is authority, chiefly from the Moorish historian Conde.

The cry of *al djihed* was chanted by the Khalif of the great mosque of Cordova, and repeated by the imaums of all the mosques. It rang out even in the most distant corners of the empire. The holy war was proclaimed. Thus enjoined in the name of Allah by the Prophet's successor, warfare became a religious service. Every Moslem—except women, children, sick men, and slaves—was as much bound to fulfil it as he was to pray five times a day, to attend the mosque once a week, keep the *Rhamadan* once a year, and go on pilgrimage to Mekka once in his life.

Religion, law, authority, property, duty, and all besides were among the Arabs subject to the one grand principle of unity. Like the world, the state was governed by a single intelligence, ruled by a single power. The Khalif reigned over the empire as God does over the universe. He was chief of the nation because he was pontiff of the Faith. He was supreme judge in every matter, because he was the only interpreter of the only law; he commanded actions because he commanded consciences, and obedience was as much one as was command. Every professor of Islam was subject to the priest as much as to the prince; subject alike in body and soul. Every political duty was a religious duty. The tax was due to the Khalif as a tithe was due in alms to the poor; and it was as needful to obey the wali's summons and muster for the *gasweh* (sacred war), as to attend to the call of the imaum and march round the fields in procession to pray against drought.

This year (998) the Faithful came in multitudes. All the tribes vied with one another in furnishing their contingent. The only difficulty of the Khalif's officers was in the choice. Men of all ranks, trades, and even of all ages, hurried forward with equal eagerness. Beside a scholar of the colleges, still wearing his student's robe, was a gray-bearded merchant, enriched by three voyages to India, and who hoped to gain salvation after gaining his fortune; next to a driver of *al zemyls* (namely, the long strings of beasts of burden —asses, mules, and camels—which transported merchandise from one province to another) stood a shepherd, who had left his huge flocks of sheep on the mountain-chains, where they wandered, according to the season, from the northern to the southern slopes. Citizens were mingled with peasants, artisans with labourers; the paper-maker from Xativa presented himself with the hemp and flax grower from the plains of Valencia; the tanner from Merida with the rice-farmer from Estremadura; the cutler of Jaen with the sugar and cotton planter of Malaga; the silk-weaver of Murcia with the mulberry-owner of the Vega of Granada.

Among all these eager volunteers, the officers first chose the veteran soldiers who had served in the last campaign, filling up their numbers with the strongest youths, and always taking single rather than married men, and never enlisting them for more than a single campaign. At the end of the season the army broke up upon the frontier, and each soldier returned to his family till a new army was called out. The only permanent troops were the Khalif's guard, chiefly African mercenaries; and the *kaschefs*, or police, who kept order at home.

The muster-place was a vast tableland in the district of Toledo, beyond that strong city, but on the south of the mountains separating the two Castilles, and close to a town almost entirely inhabited by Mozarabians. This town, nearly the central point of the Peninsula, afterwards became the capital of the Spanish monarchy, though more from the caprice of an absolute prince than from the advantages of its position.

A few squadrons of Abd-el-Malek's army, who had returned from Africa with their general, had not been disbanded between their winter campaign against the rebels of the south and their summer one against the Giaours of the north. They were already encamped in the meadows bordering the torrent of the *Manzanarés* (apple-trees), whose tortuous sandy channel discharges into the Tagus the water of the snows melted by the spring sunshine on the heights of the Guadarrama. Every day fresh troops from all parts of the empire—from the banks of the Douro to the port of New Carthage, and from the point of Al Gharb (Cape St. Vincent) to the mouths of the Ebro—came to swell this nucleus of the imperial army. In came, in due order, the sons of the Arab tribes of Yemen and Hedjaz, neighbour and sister tribes, but ever rivals from days beyond the ken of history; the sons of Syria, the earliest convert to Islam; the sons of Egypt, who received it almost at the same time, men of noble race, whom the pure Arabs treated as brethren, and who, the first conquered, had shared all the subsequent victories; and lastly the sons of the Mahgreb, the innumerable vanquished race who only adopted the Prophet's faith when overcome by the swords of his disciples, and who inundated Spain with successive immigrations.

These nations, so different in origin, number, and character, but all united by a common faith beneath the sceptre of the pontiff king, formed the Moslem force, of which the Africans were the body and the Arabs the head. The volunteers of their tribes composed the cavalry, that is to say the army—for among the Arabs the horse was a part of the warrior. The soldier, like the ancient centaur, was made up of a man's head and hands upon a horse's strong back and swift legs. In his eyes, to fight on foot was but like the slave using his fists, or the beast his teeth.

Still there were a few bodies of infantry; but these were almost entirely Jewish or Mozarabic Christian. Few Moslems, except the officers who commanded these forces consented to such a servile office. These despised troops seldom had any share in the honours of the combat. It was not to extend in long lines or mass themselves in impenetrable squares that they were called out. With half the rations of the horsemen, they were the servants of the real warriors. Their duty was to spread the tents, plant the palisades, fill up the bed of a river, clear the way on a mountain, dig trenches, drive cattle, prepare victuals for man and horse. A few of them were archers and slingers, carrying the *zembourek*, or foot-bow—a cross-bow which could only be bent with the aid of the foot, and which casts, from a groove, short arrows, balls, or stones. The infantry were a sort of medium between the horsemen and the beasts of burthen. These were always very numerous in the train of a Saracen army, and carried tents and hammocks, stores of arrows, lances, and all kinds of weapons, wheat and rice for men, and barley for horses—all most needful in those border-lands yearly wasted by the forays of both parties. They also drew balistæ, battering-rams, catapults, moving towers—all the siege-machines which raised rampart against rampart, broke gates, and battered walls.

Each fresh troop formed a fresh camp. The tents were arranged in a circle as in the nomadic villages of the Bedouins, touching one another and leaving no opening except towards the *Kebla*, the direction of Mekka, so that for each of his daily prayers, the warrior had only to turn towards the gate of the camp.

While the Arab army was assembling in the camp of Madrid, the *hajib* was fulfilling a ceremony partly religious, partly political, which preceded every campaign or declaration of war. The Koran says: "Fight with your enemies in the warfare of the Faith, but be not the first to attack. Allah hates the aggressor. If they attack you, bathe in their blood. That is the reward due to the unbelievers. If they forsake their errors, Allah is gracious and merciful." Thus, even in the case of an invasion of pure aggression for conquest's sake, the power of council had to be tried before that of the sword. Therefore two heralds were sent to carry to the King of Leon two distinct summonses—one entirely religious, exhorting him and his people to lay aside the worship of idols and adore the true God; the other was entirely political, and called on them to become subjects and tributaries of the Khalif of Cordova. Such summonses were only warnings to the enemy who was threatened by the Moslem armies, and in this case they were the vainest forms. The heralds who bore them, and whose mission had been so often repeated that it was known before they uttered it, were not even admitted to the presence of the king, but were turned back by the *frontero*, or warden of the marches.

Five days after the return of the heralds to Cordova the joyous *Helelis* of the Arab horsemen, in long lines in front of the camp, announced the arrival of the *kaid-al-kowad*, or generalissimo. Without giving himself any time for rest, Al Mansour began the review of his army. Each man, each horse, each mule passed before him. He ascertained that each horseman had lance, bow, sword, and a mace fastened below his knee; that each had an iron cap under his turban, a coat of mail over his long vest, and a light basketwork shield; and that every horse carried his master's quiver of partridge-feathered arrows on one side, and on the other a leathern bag for provisions and a copper vessel for cooking them.

The army was in five divisions, the large tent of the general in the centre, and over it the Mussulman standard—white, with the hand and the book on one side, and, on the other, five verses from the Koran entitled "Victory." Beneath this sacred banner, and, as it were, sheltered by its folds, was a precious relic—a manuscript of the Koran, copied by the very hand of Othman, the fourth of the Khalifs, and which had been brought to Cordova by the Ommeyad who founded the Spanish empire. It was bound in gold plates thickly set with diamonds, and was inclosed in a casket of aromatic wood adorned with rubies and emeralds, and carried on a litter between two richly-caparisoned camels. It was always thus carried in the centre of the army.

The *adalides*, or scouts, were Mozarabic Christians of Toledo, who in many a former expedition had learnt every forest-path, every mountain-path, every river-ford, and had a wonderful power of finding their way in the dark, and recognising the trail of every person and animal; but their fidelity was not so trustworthy that the fate of the army could be allowed entirely to depend upon them, and they were closely watched by Moslem *adalides*, while at their head was an old Arab knight, who had been among the troops sent by Abd-el-Rhaman III. to Sancho the Fat. He had married the daughter of a Leonese baron, and had lived many years at the Christian court; but he considered it an expiation to devote the last years of his life to the service of Islam.

The army encamped every night, and halted by day for meals and prayers. The five prayer-times were reduced to two, and only half the number of prayers were to be said; while, if water were lacking for ablutions, sand, dust, or ashes might be used instead. Signals to march and to halt were given by beating a huge drum at headquarters. It was fifteen cubits in diameter, and was made of ass's skin and sonorous wood. It could be heard in calm weather at half-a-day's march distance, and, the sound being repeated by the timbals and kettle-drums of each division, the order rapidly went through the whole army.

After some days' march the Arab army reached the river Tormès, whose waters so often ran red with the blood of warriors of either faith. They were coasting the left bank upwards to find a fordable place fit for the baggage and engines, when suddenly, like a flash of lightning, a bright little flame appeared on the horizon; then other flames broke out one after another, coming nearer and nearer, and extended themselves almost instantaneously in a line of beacons, as if the first fire had leapt along its course with the rapidity of light itself in gigantic bounds. Immediately the great drum beat to halt, and the word of command was heard from end to end of the army. The scouts in advance had announced an obstacle. Fire was their mode of correspondence, and to render it more visible, and enable it to convey information, chemistry had discovered substances which they could mix with their powdered charcoal and sulphur, especially the saltpetre, which was soon to be put to a more deadly use.

Al Mansour, with a small escort, rapidly rode forward, and, reaching the top of the steep hill whence the first signal had come, he gave a cry of amazement, and sharply reined in his horse. The whole Christian army lay before him encamped on the other side of the Tormès!

Accustomed as Al Mansour was, by twenty years' experience, to the unshaken constancy of the Spaniards and the patient indomitable energy which brought them back to the struggle after twenty defeats, the sight before him was like an incredible dream. It was but a few months since he had beaten these Christians in two bloody encounters, and driven away the remnant of their troops, marched through their provinces, and ransacked their sacred city. Yet already these obstinate men, swifter than himself in preparing for war, were ready to meet him, not hidden in the inaccessible dens of the mountains whither he had chased them, but in the midst of the plain, ready to dispute the passage of the river!

There were their huts, half hollowed out in the ground and half covered with branches, which sheltered the soldiers, and at intervals among them arose the tents of the barons who had collected their vassals beneath their banners. By the assistance of one of the optical instruments by which the Arabic astronomers studied the motions of the heavenly bodies, Al Mansour could count the tents of the nobles in the Christian camp. With an amphitheatre of hills behind it, this camp was in four divisions. The most distant was alone more numerous than the three others put together, and consisted of Leonese, Galicians, and Asturians, the immediate subjects of the King of Leon. Above a tall tent, placed, like the cathedral of a city, in the centre of the dwellings, floated a large standard, where was visible on a red ground the yellow cross and the lizard of Compostella. There must be the old Bermudo II., who had for sixteen years occupied the throne of Pelayo, for no other person could set up the royal banner. The post nearest to the river, forming the advanced guard, was occupied by the warriors of Castille. A square banner, adorned at the four corners by two towers and two lions, announced that their brave count, Garcia Fernandes, was in the midst of his vassals. The third and fourth divisions, placed at a distance from one another a little in the rear of the Castilians, protected the Leonese flanks. In one, there was no princely banner, for it was an auxiliary corps sent by the King of Navarre, Sancho el Mayor, who was more occupied with his own family interests than with his claims as a Christian or his renown as a warrior. In the other, three red hands painted on the banner, with the legend *Irurakbat* (three make one), showed that the three little republics of Alava, Guipuscoa, and Biscay had sent to the Gotho-Iberian army the sons of their people, still as free in the mountains, still as pure from foreign intermixture, and as untouched by foreign conquest as when, a thousand years before, Horace called the natives *Cantaber Indomitus*.

These were the only true volunteers—for they had neither king, lord, nor master of any kind. They were not even Spaniards—only Christians, and joined the war only for conscience' sake. Among the Christians no one fought on horseback but the chiefs and nobles. This was no such disadvantage, as it seemed at first sight, in defensive warfare, or for an escape among rocks and precipices. It had been a mistake on the part of the Arabs to retain in mountainous Celt-Iberia the manner of fighting suited to the sandy steppes of Arabia.

The Spanish camp showed no trace of the splendours and comforts that the Arabs took with them on all their expeditions. Poor, isolated, without arts or commerce, the Spaniards had nothing but their courage to oppose to their rich and industrious enemies. They had not even come to the point of imitation. The sheik of a tribe on pilgrimage to Mekka carried with him a whole caravan of dependants and slaves. He had silver ovens in which to bake fresh bread every day, and his camels bore leathern bags filled with snow, that he might drink iced sherbet in the midst of the desert. A general carried about his court of women, musicians, and poets; and feasts, dances, and *jeux d'esprit* prevailed in his pavilion as much as in his palace at Cordova.

The Christians, on the contrary, slept in hovels of earth and boughs of trees; they lived on barley bread and goats' flesh; the best armour of their barons was a heavy breastplate and headpiece, and their soldiers were clad merely in leathern garments leaving the arms bare, and often had no better weapon than an iron-pointed stake. Instead of the troop of women and musicians, the Spanish host took with them a brotherhood of monks who sung psalms and canticles; and every morning mass was said at a wooden cross planted on a turf altar.

Al Mansour chose the place for his camp; and in a few hours the infantry had dug a deep trench, forming a huge circle, within which the quarters of each division were traced out. It was so near the Christian camp that the outposts could have reached the foremost Spanish sentinels with their arrows. These sentinels were guarding a narrow stone bridge, formed of a single arch, so tall and so pointed that from the water it looked like the doorway of some lonely chapel. It was an important pass, for bridges were scarce; and it was this that the Christians sought to secure. Between the two camps—whose watch-fires were reflected in the stream, like the lights of a city on either side of a river—the warriors of the two religions watered their horses quietly half a bow-shot from one another.

All that night and day passed quietly. Early the next morning the scouts announced a herald. Carrying in his hand a lance, surmounted by a little shield with the royal arms, and at intervals blowing a bull's-horn trumpet, he demanded audience for an envoy of the King of Leon. Shortly after a Spanish bishop, in his robes, rode over the bridge with two horsemen, and was conducted by a guard of honour to Al Mansour's tent, where the hajib and some of his officers were assembled.

Slowly and gravely he spoke: "The Sovereign Lord of three kingdoms, the defender of his people and extender of his dominions, the glorious King Bermudo, the son of Ramiro, my lord, sends me to Mahommed, the son of Amer, and general of Haschem, the son of Al Hakem, calling himself Khalif of Cordova and Commander of the Faithful. Thine army, and that of the king, my lord, are still within their entrenchments. It is too late to fight to-day. To-morrow is Friday, the sacred day of the Moslems; and it is right that thou and thy people should cele-

brate it in peace. Saturday is the Sabbath of the
Jews, who are numerous in each army, and should
have the same privilege. Sunday is the Christian
holyday. I therefore propose a truce for three
days."

Al Mansour replied: "Thus saith the Koran: 'Jews
and Christians, who believe in God and live good
lives, shall receive their reward from the Most High.
They shall be free from danger and punishment.'
Allah forbid that Al Mansour should be accused of
disturbing the prayer of any man. Return to thy
master and tell him that I respect his scruples, and that
the truce for three days is granted. The wrath of
Allah fall on him who breaks it!"

The prelate retired, but Al Mansour, not trusting
the Spanish faith, caused careful watch to be kept, and
his vigilance was unhappily justified, for a troop of
Spaniards crossed the bridge in the night, but they
were at once discovered, and those who could not
swim the river were forced to yield. Whether this
were deliberate treachery of the leaders, or, as is more
likely, the individual attempt of some adventurous and
insubordinate baron, Al Mansour resolved to chastise
it by giving battle immediately; and Bermudo expected
the same consequence, and prepared for a desperate
resistance.

In expectation of an attack from the front, the
Spaniards had filled the whole space between their
camp and the river with their dense masses of infantry;
but they were mistaken. Al Mansour had too much
experience to entangle his cavalry on a narrow fortified
bridge. So, instead of taking the same road as the
Spaniards in their night attack, the Arab army had

left the camp on the opposite side and, forming an immense line on the banks of the Tormès, extended far beyond the crossing guarded by their enemies. With the earliest dawn the scouts, who had reconnoitred and sounded the whole course of the river, dashed into the water to mark the safest landing-place on the other side. Immediately all the squadrons, preceded by their officers, set their horses swimming, most of the horsemen taking up each a cross-bow man behind him, and for a few moments the river vanished under the armed multitude which crowded its waters; and, before the astonished Spaniards could move forwards, the Arab army was drawn up in order of battle.

The Spaniards wheeled swiftly round, so as to present their whole front to the enemy; with the Leonese, Galicians, and Asturians, under the command of King Bermudo, forming a huge square phalanx in the centre. The right wing, towards the river, was composed of Castilians, while the Navarrese and Basques flanked the main body towards the left. Thus arrayed, the Christian army ceased to move, and stood silent and motionless like a wall bristling with iron points. In advance stood men covered with iron or steel breastplates, or coats padded with wool and guarded with steel, and carrying pikes, darts, axes, iron maces, scythes, sickles, bidents and tridents with sharp points; and behind them were the archers and slingers.

Al Mansour resolved to make his principal effort against this main body, sure that its defeat would lead to that of the rest. He sent his son Abd-el-Malek and Suleiman—the Berber general of the African horse—to occupy the Navarrese on the one side, and the

Castilians on the other, while he reserved himself and the Arabs for the chief struggle.

First—as supreme imaum of the army—Al Mansour dismounted from his horse, and, kneeling down, prostrated himself with his beard in the dust; and each captain of a troop in his turn played the part of an imaum, while every horseman repeated after him the brief battle prayer: "Allah, grant us steadfastness and courage, strengthen our feet, and aid us against an unbelieving people." Here and there were warriors with wreaths of flowers on their heads. They were men, who, either in expiation of some crime or out of austere piety, had sworn to die as *schèhyd*, or martyrs, and marched to the battle adorned as victims for sacrifice.

Just as Al Mansour had remounted his war-horse and ridden to the top of a hill to give the word, a Christian baron came forth from the ranks and advanced alone into the field. He was of tall stature, and broad-shouldered, and wore a double cuirass and a large steel cap, whence escaped his long red hair. He was mounted on a heavy powerful horse covered with a bearskin, with the claws crossed over his chest. Halting between the two armies, he flourished his lance three times, as a challenge, and then leant upon it. Single combats often preceded a general engagement. Al Mansour signed to one of his best officers, Mushafa-al-Gamry, to approach.

"How many brave captains have I, dost thou suppose, capable of making head against that infidel?" said he. "Have I a thousand?"

"Not so many," replied Mushafa.

"Have I five hundred?"

"Still less."

"A hundred? or fifty at least?"

"I do not know," replied Gamry, "if there be more than three."

A *nahib*, or captain of the Berber guards, had advanced to break a lance with him; but the Christian scarcely moved in his saddle, drove his weapon right through the body of the Berber, and, withdrawing it drove the horse with the bloody lance to the Christian army, while loud shouts welcomed the victor. Another officer rode from the Arab ranks, and, warned by this fatal experience, avoided the Castilian's deadly lance, and came close enough to grapple with him, hoping to pull him from his horse; but the Christian, grasping a great mace, studded with iron spikes, which hung at his saddle-bow, dashed out the Arab's brains, and sent his body rolling on that of the Berber, while triumphant cries broke out from the Spaniards and while the Moslem army kept a mournful silence.

Al Mansour again called Mushafa. "Canst thou be right," he said; "are there not three men in my army who can meet that infidel? Go and kill him, Mushafa, or I must either send my son or go myself, for I cannot suffer this shame nor this ill-omen."

Mushafa waited no longer. The Christian had changed his horse, and was in front of the Arab ranks. "Who art thou?" he cried. "How art thou distinguished among the noble Moors?"

Mushafa flourished his lance, saying: "Here is my parentage; this is my nobility!"

Wheeling round the heavy Castilian with his rapid Arab steed, baiting him like a mastiff besetting a wild boar, Mushafa at length pierced him at the joint of his armour with his slender scimitar, and the champion fell, expiring. With a second blow, Mushafa cut off his head, and, carrying it by the hair, with the bearskin saddle-cloth thrown over his horse, he returned to the Arab ranks.

At that moment a lad hurried from the camp and bent his knee before Al Mansour, presenting to him a deer in chains, and a letter from the Syrian poet, Saydoben Hassan-al-Robay, who had lately arrived from the East, and had followed the hajib to the camp. Al Mansour, wonderful man that he was, it is said, actually paused to read and admire the poem, which may be thus translated :

>Shelter from every ill,
>   Refuge from every wrong,
>O let thy gracious ear
>   List to thy servant's song.
>
>Thy bounteous hand hath blest,
>   Like the refreshing rain,
>The meadow's verdant grass
>   And the up-springing grain.
>
>May Allah be thy stay,
>   Bless thee and keep from ill,
>From the wrong course preserve,
>   And with all joyaunce fill.
>
>Did not I see thy power,
>   Thy courage, and thy might,
>So timorous am I,
>   I soon should die with fright.
>
>I see the dust arise
>   'Mid yonder tamarisks tall :
>Two leopards seek, with savage eye,
>   Upon their prey to fall.

That victim should I be
　But for thy mighty arm;
Thine humble servant see
　Within that potent charm.

A stag he offers thee,
　And Garcia is its name—
A token how the coming fight
　Shall swell thy mighty fame.

Even as chained it comes,
　If Allah grant my prayer,
Garcia ben Sancho may I see
　His chains and fetters wear.

Oh, happy dawn appear,
　Bring on the welcome hour!
If thou accept my lay,
　Full my reward and dower!
And may thine arrows like a cloud
　Upon the foeman shower.

As soon as the Moslems came within a bow-shot of the Christians, their clarions sounded, and the mounted archers began the combat by riding up almost close to the Christian ranks and discharging their arrows, then galloping back to avoid the arrows shot in return. Many of these were poisoned—those of the Arabs with aconite, those of the Christians with black hellebore. The Arabs shouted, whenever they came on, *Allah akbar!* the Christians, after one first invocation of "*Sant Iago mata moros!*" kept silence, except that from the midst of their ranks the voices of a body of clergy arose, singing the psalm *In exitu Israel de Egypto.*

The number of the Arab archers dashing in small parties against the Spaniards increased. There was a perpetual hurricane of horsemen—going, coming, whirling, dashing about in every direction, clouds of dust rising under their feet, their arms flashing through it, and a perpetual hail of arrows constantly thickening and increasing. The Spaniards, fixed in their place, did not give back a step. The dead and wounded were replaced by fresh combatants, and the ranks still presented a dense mass; but in front lay a line of dead and dying men and horses, like a rampart, making the approach to this living citadel even more dangerous.

Al Mansour put a stop to this useless carnage by commanding the flying troops of archers to disperse and leave the field free. His choicest troops advanced and rushed upon the motionless mass of Christian infantry. Twice they came on, with lance in rest, galloping headlong; twice the floods of Arab fury were broken against the rock of Christian steadiness. Without stirring, the Christians presented the points of their lances and forks at the heads of the horses, and horse and rider rolled in the dust.

After the second attack, the Arab ranks were broken—horses were straying without riders and men without steeds. Many lay dead on the rampart of slain in front of the Christians; the others fell back disordered and discouraged on the banks of the river.

Al Mansour threw himself before them. He tore off his turban, threw down his sword, leapt off his horse, and, flinging himself on the ground, showed that if they meant to fly, it must be over his body. They began to feel shame; the voice of their officers was heard; they rallied; and the hajib, taking in his own hands the Khalif's standard, led them forward again, formed into a deep terrible column, which dashed forward at full speed against the centre of the Christian phalanx. The foremost were forced on by those behind. Their horses were pierced in the breast, but were pushed on upon the weapon, and, as they fell, crushed the enemy and opened a way. Man upon man crowded on—to perish, but to enlarge the breach in the wall, till, like a river carrying away a bank, the Arab cavalry had made a hundred entrances into the shattered Spanish infantry. Then all was over; resistance and flight were equally impossible. Divided, trampled down, unable to use their weapons or to ward off the blows from above, the foot-soldiers had no choice but surrender or death.

The second line, in which were King Bermudo and his principal barons, also began to retreat. Collecting the remnants of the broken battalions, and presenting a formidable front to the pursuing archers, they retreated in good order to the camp, collected the sacred and the valuable articles it contained, and vanished in the mountains which enclosed the battle-field. As Al Mansour had foreseen, the defeat of the King of Leon was that of the whole army. The wings were likewise beaten, but by no means in the same manner. Abd-el-Malek, to whom his paternal affection had allotted the least dangerous task, after keeping back the Navarrese by his mere presence, had seen them take flight as soon as the action became severe; and the Basques, who had been steadier at first, had given way on seeing the centre broken. The youth brought back fifty captives chained together.

The Castilians had bravely maintained their name for valour and fidelity. On seeing the first line or Leonese giving way, the brave Count Garcia had tried to bring aid to his suzerain by breaking through the chain of Berbers, who were skirmishing round the ranks, and keeping him from the decisive struggle. On his side, taking advantage of the count's bold move, Suleiman had also given the word to charge, and there was as terrible and bloody a *mêlée* as in the centre. Riding at the head of his warriors, and serving as a mark for all the hostile archers, the too-daring Garcia almost immediately fell beneath their arrows. The Castillians were left without a leader, and falling back on the bank of the Tormès, guarded their dying count in the midst of their ranks; but they were in a position where their retreat was cut off. They were shut in on all sides. Whilst Suleiman's Berbers occupied the ground where the battle had been fought, Al Mansour's Arabs returned from the pursuit of the Leonese and shut them in from above; so that the Castilians were enclosed in a half-circle of enemies, with the river behind them; nor could they even try to cross it, for the Moslem infantry, who had been left to guard the camp, had no sooner seen the result of the battle than they had hurried to line the opposite bank of the stream.

Al Mansour made a sign to restrain his troops, who, flushed with slaughter, were about to overwhelm the last remains of the Christian army. He wished to spare so many men's lives; and instead of watering the earth with so much generous blood, to supply strong hands for his various works, his fields, his ships, his mines, and monuments. A herald was sent to summon the Castilians to yield on the promise that their lives should be spared. Al Mansour stood on a rising ground, and watched his messenger approach with a green bough in his hand, and the Castilian ranks opening to admit him so as to disclose in their centre their count, lying on a litter formed by crossed lances, while a brotherhood of monks in dark robes prayed around him. As the herald's voice reached his ears, he raised his pale face, tried to speak, but after uttering a word or two fell back and expired; while the monks, raising their arms, chanted aloud, *Requiem æternam dona nobis, Domine*; and all the Castilian warriors, falling on their knees and folding their hands, joined with one voice in the mournful psalmody of the office for the dead.

Al Mansour stood watching with the tears in his eyes when Suleiman came up. "Son of Amer," said he, "why doth not the signal of thy hand command the destruction of those accursed dogs, whose howls defy us and insult heaven."

"Son of Al Hakem," replied Al Mansour, "knowest thou not that it is written: 'He who slayeth one man without having met with violence will be punished like the murderer of all mankind, and he who saveth the life of one man shall be rewarded like the rescuer of all mankind.' Make room, sons of Ishmael, make way. Let these Christians live, and let them bless the name of the clement and merciful God."

At the same time his outstretched arm commanded the Arabs to quit the bank of the Tormès, and his obedient legions flowing back, gradually left the Christians a way to life and liberty. When they saw a passage left open before them, the Castilians accepted it as a miracle granted to the blessed soul of their martyred prince, and rose from their knees in the grave joy and trust of a great deliverance. The monks took up the body of the good count upon their shoulders like a sacred relic, and all the warriors, without interrupting their chanted prayers, marched away bareheaded, with lowered weapons, and in unbroken order.

The Arabs reined in their horses, and kept their ranks without moving; but as the Christian troops moved away, they broke into the song of victory enjoined by the Koran: "Victory cometh from Allah;" and at the same time a carrier-pigeon, let loose from the camp, soared on high to bear to the Khalif at Cordova the tidings that his hajib had deserved more than ever his title of "The Invincible."

The Arab army had suffered enough to be obliged to return immediately, and this gave Bermudo time to prepare for his next invasion by carrying off the remains of the kings and all that was most precious from Leon to their old home at Oviedo. That city was sacked, and so were Toro, Zamora, Braganza, and Tuy; Barcelona followed the next year; and the Christians had lost all the gains of the last two hundred years, and were driven back into the very cradle of their realm, with the Pyrenees and the Sierra Penamerella once more for their boundary.

Had Al Mansour been Khalif, instead of merely al hajib, probably a final blow would have been struck; but at this period of the greatest danger the Spaniards were relieved by a revolt of the Moors in Africa, which called off the forces of the mighty victor. As usual, he subdued everything before him there. His thanksgiving was a noble one. It was an abundant almsgiving, the payment of the debts of many distressed persons, and the freedom of three hundred

Christian slaves and fifteen hundred Christian captives. He was a man of magnificent generosity. When his son Abd-el-Malek was married to his cousin, dowries were given to a great number of orphan girls, gifts were distributed to the schools and hospitals, all his guards were newly clothed, and the poets who composed verses in honour of the occasion were richly rewarded. The wedding-feast was celebrated in the gardens of a beautiful country-house called Almeria, which were illuminated with lamps on every tree and shrub; while on the lakes were boats, whence gentle music was heard. Still, as a remnant of the customs of the desert tribes, who used to carry off their wives by force, the bride was placed in a pavilion, round which her fellow-maidens kept guard with rods of ivory and gold, and fought a mimic struggle with the bridegroom and his attendants, who came with gilt maces to win an entrance.

From these scenes of delight, Al Mansour, in 1001, set forth on his fifty-second warlike expedition, hoping to complete the conquest of Spain. The Christians had had three years in which to rally; they had repented of their fatal divisions, and all their chiefs united: Bermudo II., though so lame with gout that he had to be carried in a chair; Garcia, King of Navarre; and Sancho Garcias, the son and successor of the late Count of Castille. Every man who could wield a lance or a bow was summoned to their tandards.

Al Mansour knew of the league, but was too much accustomed to victory to fear it, or take any steps to enlarge his force, which as usual was partly Arab and partly Berber. His object was to attack the lands of the King of Navarre, who had not yet been pillaged; and his troops were advancing thither beyond the Sierra de Aylon, near Numantia, the city which held out for sixty years against Rome. Near this spot the Christians were encamped at a place called, in Arabic, *Kala't al Nassour*, the Eagle's Rock; by the Spaniards, Calatanazor.

There the battle took place. The tactics on each side were the same as at Tormès; but though the rampart of dead rose higher and higher, the Christian ranks remained unshaken.

> The stubborn spearmen still made good
> The stout impenetrable wood—

And after the fight had raged the whole day, Al Mansour's last desperate charge had ended in his being wounded and carried to the rear. After twelve hours' incessant fighting, night came on, and separated the combatants.

The battle was still undecided. Each army had betaken itself to its camp. The Christians dug long trenches, where their slain were placed with a blessing from the priests; while the Arabs burnt their dead on funeral piles lighted with naphtha. Al Mansour had been carried to his tent, and there waited for his captains to give them orders to renew the attack. His son, Abd-el-Malek, came in with bandaged wounds, and, as each brave warrior was mentioned, answered "slain" or "captive."

The great unconquerable knew he was conquered. For the first time he had to give the word for retreat. Even the great drum was forgotten. As the proverb said:

> A Calatanazor,
> Perdio Almanzor,
> El atambor.

The hajib was carried in a litter over the Douro, and having seen the remnant of his army safely across, and heard that the bridges were destroyed, he refused all nourishment, tore off the bandages of his wounds, and died, in his sixty-third year, his proud heart broken by his first defeat.

Then was opened a small cedar case which he always carried about with him. It held the dust he had shaken from his garments after each of his fifty victories, together with his winding-sheet of hemp grown in his father's little field, and spun and woven by his daughters to form his winding-sheet. In it he was laid in his coffin, and buried in a splendid tomb with an inscription recording his victories.

When morning dawned on the Spaniards, their enemy was gone, and they knew they were saved.

As Al Mansour's first defeat had been his last battle, so Bermudo's first victory was likewise his last. A few weeks later he died, in 1001, leaving his crown to his young son Alfonso V., under the care of his mother Elvira.

CHAPTER XIII.

THE FALL OF THE KHALIFATE.

THE mistake of Al Mansour's life had been a jealousy of power, which made him keep the Khalif back from affairs, and living entirely among the ladies of his harem. Indeed, it is probable that Haschem II. was deficient in the high qualities of mind and body which had lasted unimpaired for so many generations, for, though he was a man of mature age when he lost his great hajib, his mother, Sobeyah, still took the direction of affairs. At first, the family of Al Mansour seemed to be becoming a sort of mayors of the palace, for the eldest son was made hajib; and on his sudden death in 1008, at the same time as that of Sobeyah, his younger brother, Abd-el-Rhaman, was appointed to the same office.

He was a foolish, ambitious man, of more pretension than his father and brother, though with none of their abilities. The Khalif being childless and exceedingly fond of him, he obtained the promise of being made heir to the throne—thus curiously playing the part of Harold towards Edward the Confessor. Now the Khalif was supposed to be the lineal representative of the Prophet, and therefore a sacred personage, and the admission of a new family outraged all Moslem feeling, more especially as there was no lack of men of Ommeyad descent, since most of the previous Khalifs had large families who had lived together in all peace and amity. The appointment, though made in the secrecy of the harem, was whispered abroad, and Mahommed-a-ben-Abel-al-Djahar, a grandson of Abd-el-Rhaman III., hastened to Cordova to assert his rights. He obtained possession of the person of the unfortunate Haschem, forced him to abdicate, and put to death by the cross the unfortunate and foolish Abd-el-Rhaman, after a ministry of only five months.

Poor weak Haschem was spared at the entreaty of his servant Wadha, but he was kept in a secret dungeon, while obsequies were celebrated for a man who much resembled him, and who had been strangled on that account. The new Khalif still mistrusted the Zenetes, or guard of honour, instituted by the first Abd-el-Rhaman, recruited from Barbary, and always on guard at the palace, and he tried to break them up. They fought hard; the citizens of Cordova took part against them, and there was a terrible street fight, ending with their being expelled, and the head of their leader thrown to them over the walls. They elected his cousin, Suleiman-ben-al-Hakem, the ferocious Berber we saw at Tormès, and marched off to Toledo, where they allied themselves with Sancho, Count of Castille, and with his aid and support fought a tremendous battle at Quintos. Mahommed gained the victory, and pushed on to Cordova. Once more, though only as allies, did the Spanish nobles behold the towers of Cordova. They were only admitted as far as the suburbs, and thence returned home with their mules loaded with plunder, and with the promise that six cities should be added to the Castilian territory.

The Berber Suleiman—no son of Ommeyad—was proclaimed Khalif; but Mahommed had made his retreat good, and called in the assistance of another Christian ally, Ramon, Count of Barcelona. Again there was a great battle, in which the Berber was defeated. Finding himself unable to hold Cordova, he went off to the lovely Al Zohra palace, and pillaged it, mosque and all, of its splendid ornaments and treasures, meaning to carry them off to Africa. Mahommed hurried after him to recover the spoil, but coming up exhausted, was defeated so completely that he had again to shut himself up in Cordova, where, finding all the people against him, as a last hope, released the deposed Haschem from his dungeon. Suddenly in the Khalif's place, in the great mosque, was seen the true prince, who had for two years been thought to be dead. The Cordovans hailed him with ecstasy. The usurper threw himself at his feet with abject entreaties for life, but all in vain; and presently Suleiman received the head of Mahommed on the point of a lance, with the message that such was the fate of traitors.

Suleiman, on his side, made use of the head. He embalmed it in camphor and sent it to Obeid-Allah, the son of the late usurper, with the message: "This is the head of thy father, Mahommed. Thou seest how Haschem recompenseth the man who restored him to the throne. If thou wouldest have safety and vengeance, Suleiman will be with thee."

Haschem's servant, Wadha, made his way to Castille to obtain support against Obeid-Allah and Suleiman.

Sancho was ready to change sides. "Six cities were given me by Suleiman," said he; "but if thou wilt offer the like, I had rather serve the Khalif than the usurper." The Castilian forces enabled Wadha to overcome Obeid-Allah, who was made prisoner and crucified.

The humane and generous customs of the Moors had been lost in this deadly civil war. Suleiman and his Berbers acted like true barbarians. Encamped on the banks of the Guadalquivir, they ravaged and desolated Andalusia like a conquered country, cut off the supplies from Cordova, and reduced the city to all the horrors of famine and pestilence. The citizens cried out that it was the consequence of Allah's wrath at their unholy alliance with the Christians. Haschem—wretched, cowardly, and foolish—put to death his only true friend, Wadha, as the instrument of this alliance. The whole city was in confusion, though the new hajib, Hairan-al-Ameri, was a brave man, who resolutely defended the walls. A general assault was commanded by Suleiman. Hairan fought to the last at the head of the Khalif's guard—a gallant band, which perished to a man on the steps of the palace. Hairan, senseless and desperately wounded, was found among the slain by a poor man, who hid him in his house, while the city was sacked for three whole days by Suleiman and his savage Berbers. The exquisite mosques and the Aljama college were not spared, and great numbers of the scholars, philosophers, and poets perished in the massacre, the beautiful houses and the costly treasures being destroyed, and many of the great old Arab families being exterminated. The unfortunate Khalif Haschem was never seen again, and no doubt was killed without being recognised. His fatal reign thus ended in 1013.

Suleiman tried to strengthen his usurpation by giving six Berber chiefs lands to hold as fiefs, on the condition of serving him in war, after the example of the northern nations. The Arabs, however, hated this Berber dominion, and Hairan, recovering from his wounds, cleverly obtained the stronghold of Almeria, and made it a rallying-point. His brother, or kinsman, Ali-ben-Hamoud, wali of Ceuta, came to join him with an Arab reinforcement from Africa; and in a battle near Seville, fortune turned against Suleiman, who was taken in his flight, and, with his brother and his old father, the governor of Cordova, was brought before the victor.

"Old man," said Ali, "what have you done with Khalif Haschem? These heads are called for by vengeance."

"Strike me alone!" said Suleiman; "the others are not guilty."

Ali, however, swept off all the three heads with his scimitar. Search was everywhere made for Haschem, and, when he could nowhere be found, Ali was proclaimed Khalif. In his jealousy of Hairan he forgot his gratitude, and sent him off unrewarded to his old province of Almeria. There, of course, Hairan stirred up a fresh revolution, finding another Ommeyad to proclaim as Khalif. He counts as the fourth Abd-el-Rhaman, and gained the allegiance of the south-east, but was defeated by Ali, who cut off Hairan's head with his own hand, as he had cut off Suleiman's. Still the love of the Ommeyad, as the right heir of the Prophet, was so strong that the usurper could not be endured, and Ali was smothered in a bath immediately after his return to Cordova.

But in this miserable time, the destruction of one pretender only seemed to multiply parties. Al Kasim, Ali's brother, was elected by his soldiers; and when Yah-yah, son of Ali, came over from Africa, one reigned at Cordova, and the other made war on Abd-el-Rhamam IV. After about four years, in 1022, Al Kasim was overthrown and imprisoned for life; and soon after Abd-el-Rhaman was killed in battle with Yah-yah. Another Abd-el-Rhaman, of the Ommeyad dynasty, was elected; but he was one of the stern, ascetic, and devout class of Moslems; and his troops, demoralised by the long civil war, declared that he was only fit to be sheik of the dervishes in the desert. They murdered him after he had reigned only forty-seven days, and set up his cousin, Mahommed. Feeling that all depended on these soldiers who had become a perfect Prætorian guard, he pampered and flattered them to the last degree, and taxed the people heavily to supply their demands; but all in vain—he was poisoned at the end of sixteen months. Yah-yah soon after perished, and the last of the Ommeyads, Haschem III., was chosen. He was a timid and gentle person, much distressed at this perilous elevation, and tried in vain to win the hearts of his people by mildness. When a new tumult arose and they demanded his deposition, he quietly gave thanks to Allah, laid aside the ensigns of royalty, and left Cordova. Thus, in 1031, ended that grand dynasty which had ruled southern Spain for two centuries. As long as great men succeeded one another it had prospered, but with the first weak sovereign it collapsed altogether; one lawless captain after another seized the power, and the discordant elements of Arab and Berber fell apart, the walis gradually becoming independent sovereigns, with little courts of their own.

It would be only confusion worse confounded to try to trace their wars and entanglements. A Khalif was elected at Cordova, 1031, Djehwar-ben-Mahommed, who did much to restore order and good government, and bring back the sciences and arts for which it had been so famous before these thirty years of anarchy.

But his power was greatly diminished, and the *Emirs*, as the governors of provinces were called, were like the great crown vassals of France and Germany, scarcely under the yoke of the sovereign. Seville, Toledo, Malaga, Granada, Jaen, Carmona, Zaragoza, Medina-Sidonia—each had its own emir. The great peninsular khalifate had become a set of mere fragments—some retaining the Arabic traditions of culture, others little more than nests of Berber savage marauders. The old fable of the bundle of sticks was worked out; the ruin of all was only a matter of time.

CHAPTER XIV.

THE UNION OF CASTILLE AND LEON.

WHY did not the Christians profit more by the divisions of the Moors? Ultimately they gained; but they were far too unsettled and disunited to make any great effort in the common cause. Indeed, they were not unwilling either to hire out their swords to the Moors, or to obtain Moorish aid against their enemies; and both religion and morals were at a low ebb amongst them. The difference was that Islam had done its very best in forming such civilisation as that of the Ommeyad; while Christianity, though at a low ebb in the Spanish mountains, had infinite possibilities.

The kingdom of Leon had prospered under the regency of Elvira, the widow of Bermudo III., who bred up her son, Alfonso V., to much excellence. He rebuilt Leon, fortified Zamora, and hoped to take Viseo; but while reconnoitring without his armour he was killed by an arrow from the walls, when only thirty-four years old, in 1027, leaving two children, Bermudo III. and Sancha, both very young.

Castille had likewise a young count. That Garcia who had been typified by Al Mansour's stag, had left a son named Sancho. Of him a strange story is told

—that he fell in love with a Moorish lady, and his mother, the Countess Marioña, wishing to prevent the marriage, prepared a cup of poison for him. Another version says that it was Doña Marioña herself who wanted to marry a Moor, and tried to poison her son for fear he should hinder it. As to the fact, both are agreed that he guessed her intentions, and insisted on her drinking off the potion herself; whence, say the Spaniards, arose the custom of the lady being the first to pledge the gentleman in a cup. Probably the eastern habits of keeping women in the background led to this desire to account for a custom inherited from the more courteous Goth.

In expiation for his mother's death, Sancho founded a great double monastery in a lovely valley, watered by four tributaries to the Ebro, of which the Oca is the chief. The dedication was to San Salvador; but it was called Oña, after the countess; and Sancho's daughter, Doña Frigida, was the first abbess. He extended his borders during the wars of the Moors; sometimes, as has been seen, by hiring out his alliance for so many fortresses, sometimes by conquest; and he was besieging Sepulveda, when he died of a short illness in 1022.

He left an only son and three daughters. The eldest was the wife of Sancho IV., king of Navarre, who took under his protection the young Don Garcia Sanchez, Count of Castille, a very promising boy of fourteen. A marriage was arranged between him and Sancha of Leon; but the poor boy had incurred the resentment of the three sons of the Count of Vela, probably because his brother-in-law had tried to break up a sort of outlaw settlement in the Castle of Monçon, where some of the family were living by connivance of the Moors. At any rate, the very evening the young bridegroom arrived at Leon, he was stabbed to the heart in the street on his way to church, in the midst of all the Leonese nobles. The assassins made good their escape to Monçon, but were pursued thither, taken, and burnt alive by the King of Navarre.

He was the last male of the line of the Counts of Castille founded by Garcia Fernandes; and his eldest sister, Elvira (or Nuña), carried the inheritance to her husband, Sancho IV. of Navarre, called *el Mayor*, the Great. Indeed, he really was by far the greatest of contemporary kings of the Peninsula, and for a time it seemed as if Navarre might unite all the little realms under one head; for the line of early kings of Aragon had failed, and that district was only governed by a count, as vassal to Navarre. The eldest daughter of Sancho and Elvira of Castille married Fernando III. of Leon, but her only child died a few days after its birth; and Fernando, the second son of the King of Navarre, was betrothed to Doña Sancha, the only sister and heiress of Bermudo, the intended bride of poor young Count Garcia of Castille.

More wild stories are here told. Sancho was hunting on the borders of Leon, when his prey, either a boar or a deer, took refuge in a cave or vault in some old ruins. Out came a hermit to protect the hunted creature; and when the king would have struck it he found his arm powerless; but on his humbling himself it was restored at the prayer of the hermit, a Frenchman named Antholin. Sancho found that the spot was the site of an ancient monastery called Palencia, and vowed to restore it. It became a palace and also a school of learning, where St. Dominic's education was begun. The well of St. Antholin is still shown, and the water is thought to work cures.

Palencia was on Leonnese ground, and Bermudo considered Sancho's buildings as an aggression. A war was threatened, and was only prevented by Sancho's engaging that his wife Elvira's inheritance of Castille should pass to his second son, Fernando, the husband of Sancha of Leon, instead of to his eldest son Garcia, the heir of Navarre.

Another strange romance is here brought into account for the disfavour of the firstborn. It is said that while King Sancho was absent, Garcia wanted to use his father's favourite horse, and that he had obtained consent from his mother to his riding it, when Don Pedro Sese, the Master of the Horse, assured her that the king would not trust it with the youth, and she withdrew her sanction. Don Garcia, in savage fury, made the vilest accusations against his mother and Don Pedro; and his brother Fernando, when appealed to, neither affirmed nor denied her innocence. She appealed, like all queens in romance in such a predicament, to the ordeal of battle; but no one cared to descend into the lists with the heir of the kingdom; and she was in danger of the stake, when a champion rode forward and undertook her cause. He proved to be Don Ramiro, an illegitimate son of the king himself, a brave youth, who could not bear to see an innocent queen perish by the slander of her own son. No sooner was his name proclaimed than a monk rushed between the half-brothers, and addressed such burning words to Garcia, that the lad, overwhelmed with shame, fell at his father's feet and declared that the whole accusation had sprung from his anger. D[on] Sancho, bitterly grieved and angered, declared th[at] Doña Elvira must mete out the just punishment to h[er] sons, and it was she who deprived Garcia of her i[n]heritance of Castille, and gave it to his less guil[ty] brother Fernando. She also begged that Rami[ro] might be made equal to her own sons; and he ther[e]fore received the county of Aragon.

There is no doubt that, whatever the cause, Sanc[ho] the Great broke up his dominions on his death, leavi[ng] Navarre and Biscay to Garcia, Castille to Fernand[o], Aragon to Ramiro, and Sobreira and Ribagorça [to] Gonzalo, the youngest. This was in 1035, and all too[k] the title of king. Gonzalo was soon after murdered b[y] one of his servants on the bridge of Monçon, and h[is] small kingdom was immediately absorbed into Arago[n].

A fresh quarrel broke out between Fernando I. an[d] his brother-in-law, Bermudo of Leon. Garcia assiste[d] his brother, and in a battle near Carrion, Bermudo wa[s] killed by the thrust of a lance in 1037. Fernando too[k] possession of his kingdom, and the Christian territorie[s] were in the hands of the three Navarrese brothers.

Garcia and Ramiro spent most of their strength i[n] wars with one another; but Fernando I., whose king[dom] was by far the strongest, was in condition t[o] make real advances against the Moors. He was [a] man full of devotion of the fervent Spanish descriptio[n], which regarded wars with the Moslem as sacred; an[d] the Moors, after a short breathing-time, were in a stat[e] of utter confusion, the emirs all attacking one another and the khalifate the prize of the ambitious, until, i[n] 1060, the last bearer of that illustrious title, Abd-el Malek, was murdered at Cordova.

Fernando's first exploits were the sieges of Viseo and Coimbra. The Spaniards have a legend that a Greek bishop, who in his own country had derided the Spanish stories of Santiago, and said St. James was a fisherman of Galilee, was visited in a dream by that great champion of Christendom with a bunch of keys in his hand, who said: "These are the keys of Coimbra. I am about at this very hour to deliver it into the hands of the Faithful." The bishop set out for Spain, found that the city had surrendered at the very hour of his dream, and became a most devout votary of Santiago. (So saith the "Chronicle of the Cid.")

Fernando is said to have called himself Emperor, and thus brought on himself the displeasure of both Emperor and Pope. A legate was sent into Spain, who viewed the old Gothic liturgy with great jealousy and dislike, but could not prevail on the Spanish Church to discard it. The devotion of Fernando and his Queen Sancha was, however, unquestionable. The Queen built a church at Leon, to which she meant to remove the corpse of her brother from Oria. Wishing for some relics to hallow it, she recollected two virgins, Justa and Rufina, who had been martyred at Seville; and sent Avito, Bishop of Leon, to demand their bodies from Ben Abed, Emir or King of Seville. The emir made no objection, except that nobody had the least idea where to find the corpses of the martyrs. While, however, the inquiry was going on, Bishop Avito had a vision of the great Bishop of Seville, St. Isidoro, who said: "I am the Doctor of the Spains. Mine is the body to be removed!" and further disclosing the very spot where it was to be found.

It was removed to Leon, miracles being worked to

attest its reality, and a church founded wherever it rested for a night. The king and queen went out in the midst of a great procession to meet it, and San Isidoro became almost as much a champion of Spain as Santiago himself.

He appeared to Fernando himself in the middle of a successful campaign to foretell his approaching end. The king did in fact come home very ill, went to the church of the saint, performed humble penance for his sins, then, becoming worse, died on the 27th of September, 1065. The benefits of union were so little perceived that he again split up his kingdom, giving Castille to his eldest son, Sancho; Leon to the next brother, Alfonso; Galicia to the third, Garcia; and the cities of Zamora and Toro to his two daughters, Urraca and Elvira.

CHAPTER XV.

RUY, MI CID CAMPEADOR.

WE have reached the central figure of Castilian song and story—the national champion—Rodrigo Diaz de Bivar, commonly called The Cid. We will tell his story first as Spain has sung and told it ever since the thirteenth century; and then, alas, we must put it into the crucible of modern criticism and comparison of authorities.

In the time of King Fernando I. there dwelt at Burgos an old hidalgo named Diego Laynez, Lord of Bivar. A strife arose between him and the Lord of Gormaz, Count Gomez, and he received a blow which he was too feeble from age and infirmity to repay. He returned to his house broken-hearted at the insult, all the more because Gomez was a mighty warrior, and his elder sons durst not avenge his honour in the combat. His youngest son was Rodrigo, a mere lad, as yet untried, but his heart so burned within him at his father's grief that he took down a sword from the wall—the very sword of Mudarra, the avenger of Lara—and went forth to defy the count.

> Weeping sore, Diego Lainez
>   At the board was seated,
> Bitter tears of sorrow shedding—
>   Of his shame he treated.

At the meal the old man sat,
  His heart with sorrow swelling ;
On a thousand questions nice
  Of punctilio dwelling.

When his son Rodrigo entered,
  And by the hair he bore
Count Gomez' severed head, and held it,
  All ghastly, dripping gore.

From a swoon his father waking
  To a joy so sweet :
" Here the evil weed thou see'st ;
  Eat, my father, eat.

" Open father, ope thine eyes,
  Lift thy face," he said ;
" See thine honour safe—its life
  Is risen from the dead.

" Every stain is washed from off thee,
  Right from his pride is wrung ;
The hand that hurt thee is no hand,
  The tongue, no more a tongue."

  * * * * *

" Sit down to eat, my noble son,
  Above me," Lainez said ;
" For he who yonder head has brought
  Is of this house the head."

Diego died soon after, and Rodrigo did many exploits against the Moors in the service of the king. When the king, Fernando, next held his court, a lady came before him. She was Ximena, daughter of Count Gomez, and her prayer was that the king would give her to wife to Rodrigo de Bivar, because she knew he would be greater than any man in Castille, and she could then pardon him with a good will.

So he came to Palencia, and plighted his troth to Ximena most willingly; but he placed her with his mother, vowing that he would not take her to his own house till he should have fought five battles against the Moors. Of course he fulfilled his vow; and afterwards he made a pilgrimage to Compostella. In the midst of this journey the Ballads give one of those acts of devotion which so strangely blend with the ferocious pride of the age. A poor leper called to Rodrigo for aid from the midst of a quagmire. He not only set the man on his own horse, but, on reaching an inn, ate with him at the same table and lay down to rest in the same bed. In the middle of the night he missed the leper, and, after searching for him in vain, he beheld a man in robes of white, who declared that he was indeed St. Lazarus, who had appeared under the form of a leper, and went on to promise him victories and blessings untold.

Rodrigo was knighted by King Fernando, and did good service in his wars. The names of Cid and Campeador were then given him. Cid the Spaniards consider equivalent to *Al Said*, the Arabic for chief; Campeador, his chronicler says, means the person who chose the place for encamping, though it is also explained to mean Champion. Quarrels soon broke out among the children of Fernando I. after his death. Sancho, the eldest, thought himself injured by the division, and attacking Alfonso, defeated him and shut him up in the convent of Sahagun, whence he escaped to the protection of Al Maimon, the Moorish king of Toledo. Garcia was in like manner subdued and imprisoned at Luna, then Elvira was deprived of Toro, and lastly Sancho attacked Zamora. Urraca would not yield her inheritance without a struggle, and, in the midst of the siege, Sancho was treacherously slain by a knight in his own army, named Vellido Dolfos, in 1073, who escaped into the city, and whom Urraca would not give up.

She sent at once for her brother Alfonso, her especial favourite, and he was readily accepted as king; but a large number of persons, with the Cid at their head, suspected that Doña Urraca and Don Alfonso had been concerned in the murder, and at the coronation Rodrigo insisted on the king and his knights clearing themselves by oath, which oath was to be taken on the bolt of the gate of Zamora and on the crossbow staff.

> At Santa Agueda of Burgos
>   Did the hidalgos* swear,
> Of brother's blood, the clearing oath
>   Alfonso must take there.
>
> The good Cid tendered it—
>   That good Castilian brave—
> Upon the iron bolt,
>   And on the arblast's stave.
>
> With holy Gospel books
>   And Crucifix he stood ;
> So strong and stern his words,
>   They awed that monarch good.
>
> "May villains slay thee, king—
>   Villains, not men of birth—
> No lords of Oviedo's forts,
>   Nor of Asturian earth.

* *Filio, fijo-dalgo, hijodalgo, hidalgo*—son of a Spanish gentleman—the term for somebody.

> "Pierced by no lance or dart,
>   May thy base life be spilt
> By mere horn-handled knives,
>   And not by daggers gilt."

Many curious particulars followed as to the dress of these low-born murderers, who were to wear green leathern hose, and not boots, and hempen, and not holland, shirts, and to ride asses instead of horses or mules. Then the Cid continued to the king, who was much overawed by these minute threats.

> "May they take out thine heart
>   Alive, and never rue,
> Unless to what I ask thee now
>   Thou giv'st an answer true.
>
> "Wert thou, or wert thou not,
>   Of Sancho's death aware?"
> So awful was the oath,
>   That the king would not swear.
>
> Then up and spake a knight,
>   One to the king most near:
> "Come, take the oath, good king,
>   And take it free from fear.
>
> "Ne'er yet was king a traitor,
>   Nor Pope 'scommunicate."
> And now the king hath sworn himself
>   Free of his brother's fate.
>
> But then in haste and wrath
>   The king thus spake his will:
> "Ill hast thou sworn me, Cid—
>   Cid, thou hast sworn me ill.

"Since thou hast put me to the oath,
  When thou should'st kiss my hand,
A bad knight art thou proved, O Cid;
  Go forth, then, from my land.

"Nor here return again
  Till from this day a year."
"Well pleased am I, then," quoth the Cid,
  "Well pleased and glad my cheer.

"For I'm the first in all thy reign
  To bear commands from thee;
Dost banish me for one year's space?
  For four I banish me."

Then sped the good Cid forth,
  And with him went away
Three hundred horsemen brave,
  Hidalgos all were they.

The Ballad makes the banishment the immediate penalty of the exaction of the oath, but the Chronicle puts it on an accusation that he had broken a truce with the Moorish king of Toledo.

The Cid had to depart in nine days' time. To provide means for his journey he sent his nephew, Martin Antoninez, to borrow nine hundred marks of two Jews, leaving them in pledge two chests, iron-bound and locked with many locks, which were supposed to contain valuables, but really were full of sand. Jews were considered as fair game, so that this shocked no one. He left Doña Ximena and her little children in the monastery of San Pedro de Cardeña, and with his friends Alvar Fanez and Martin Antoninez led a wild outlaw life, the theme of endless ballads, which represent the Spanish ideal of devotion, loyalty, courage, and courtesy, though dashed at times with terrible ferocity.

The Chronicle and the Ballads make him live rather as David did at Ziklag, making war only on the enemies of his religion, except when attacked. Ramon Berenguer, the Count of Barcelona, thus fell on him to take away his spoil, but was defeated and made prisoner. Then, says the story, "A great supper was prepared for my Cid Campeador;" but Count Don Ramon would not eat. "I will taste no meat for all Spain. I will lose my life, since such wretches have conquered me in battle."

My Cid heard him. "Eat, count, eat this bread, drink this wine; so shalt thou cease to be a prisoner."

Finally, the generous conqueror prevailed, and the count's supper was his ransom. He was set free with many fair gifts of horses and furred mantles.

Rodrigo reconciled himself to the king, coming creeping to his throne with a saddle on his back; but he always dwelt beyond Alfonso's dominions, and finally won Valencia, whither he brought his wife and children, and reigned, only doing homage to the king for the rest of his life. He had an ivory chair in the Cortes, and he and his good steed Babieca were always in the forefront of the battles, where he wielded one or other of his bright swords, Colada and Tizona.

The Cid lost his only son, Don Diego Ruiz; and his daughters, Elvira and Sol, were viewed as heiresses. The two sons of the Count of Carrion, Ferdinand and Diego Gonzales, sought them in marriage, and by favour of the king obtained them. Rodrigo gave them, not only his daughters, but much wealth, and his two beloved swords, Tizona and Colada; and for two years they lived with him in Valencia.

Now the Cid kept a lion, with which he was wont to amuse himself. One day, at dinner-time, there was an alarm that Moorish ships were seen in the offing. Rodrigo said he was very glad, for it was three years since he had had a stroke at a Moor. He gave all his orders, and then fell asleep in the noonday heat. In the alarm, the door of the lion's den had been left open, and the beast made his appearance in the castle-hall, to the extreme terror of the Infants of Carrion. Fernando crept under the Cid's couch; and Diego, crying "I shall never see Carrion again," rushed out through a postern-door, and fell into a wine-press, where he was stained by the lees. The warriors stood round the couch to defend the Cid, and the noise they made awoke him. As he saw the lion coming towards him he quietly said: "What's this?" The lion stood still at the sound of his voice, and he took him by the mane as if he had been a mastiff, and led him back to his den.

The two Infants came forth from their hiding-place, and were much laughed at for their cowardice. They showed an equal want of valour in the attack of the Moorish ships that followed; and finding themselves altogether in disgrace and looked down upon, they desired to take their wives and return to their home in Castille, meaning to have a base and cowardly revenge.

The mother, Doña Ximena, was so uneasy that she begged that Rodrigo's nephew, Feliz Muñoz, might follow her daughters and watch them. Well it was she did so; for when the Infants had reached the great oak-wood of Corpes, they encamped for the night, and in the morning sent all their attendants on before them. Then they fell upon the two poor ladies, tore off their furred velvet mantles, beat and kicked them with their spurred heels, and left them for dead, saying: "Lie there, daughters of the Cid. It is not fitting that ye should be our wives, or have dower on the lands of Carrion! We shall see how your father will avenge you, and we have now avenged ourselves for the shame he did us with the lion." Wherewith Fernando and Diego rode away, leaving their two young wives swooning on the grass, where their cousin found them. He covered them with his cloak, fetched them water, and tried to revive and console them; and presently found a good peasant, who took them to his cottage, and gave them shelter, while tidings were sent to their father.

The companions of the Infants of Carrion had been shocked at their treatment of their wives, and had turned back and searched for the poor ladies in vain. The king was greatly displeased, and when the Cid's complaint came, he held a Cortes for the trial of the two recreants.

The Cid appeared, and the first demand he made was that, since the Infants had renounced his daughters, they would give him back his swords, Colada and Tizona. Hoping this was all, they brought the swords, which were so bright that the whole court shone with their light. He kissed them, and said: "Ah, my swords, Colada and Tizona; I gave ye in keeping to the Infants of Carrion that they might do honour to my daughters with you. But ye were not for them!

They kept you hungry, and did not feed you with flesh as you were wont to be fed!"

After this grim congratulation Rodrigo demanded that all the treasure he had given the Infants with his daughters should be restored. With much difficulty they were made to refund this; but thirdly, he demanded satisfaction for the honour of his daughters. Fernando had the assurance to declare that, the lineage of the Cid not being equal to that of Carrion, the marriage was unequal, and ought to be broken; but all that came of this was a challenge to him and his brother to fight hand-to-hand with the terrible Cid and his nephew, Martin Antoninez. The king forced them to accept it; and, lest they should avoid it, came to Carrion in person to see it fought out. It could end in only one way: Fernando was killed, and Diego —driven ignominiously out of the lists—and his father were banished, and the lands of Carrion forfeited to the king; while Doña Sol and Doña Elvira obtained noble husbands in the Infants of Aragon and Navarre.

When the time came for the Cid to die, the Moors were threatening a great attack on Valencia. He knew it could not be held out without him, and he therefore charged his wife, Doña Ximena, that no crying nor lamentation should be made when he expired, but that the trumpets should sound and bells should ring. Then should his embalmed corpse be clad in armour and set, fastened upright, on his good steed Babieca, and that Tizona should be bound to his hand and his banner borne before him, while his warriors formed in battle array, with the women, children, and sumpter beasts in their midst, and thus should every Christian pass out of Valencia and give battle to the Moors.

Thus then it was done, and thus, as a dead man, did Ruy Diaz de Bivar win his last victory, and guard his wife and his followers back to Burgos. Never man mounted Babieca again after that wonderful ride!

The Cid was placed on an ivory chair at the church of San Pedro at Cardeña, where he remained till a Jew ventured to pluck his beard, when the dead hand struck down the sacrilegious intruder. After this he was buried in San Pedro.

Such is the outline of the story told in the "Cronica del Cid" and in his "Cancionero," containing one hundred and fifty-four popular ballads on this favourite hero, whom Spanish fancy has made up to its own fantastic standard of devotion and loyalty, though far from being unmixed with darker traits.

Alas! by the test of charter and veritable history, and by what can be gathered from the Arab chroniclers, it is plain that the fancy of a more chivalrous age has adorned the rudeness of a fierce outlaw with many borrowed graces.

Rodrigo de Bivar—or, as the Moors called him, Al Sayd Rouderik-al-Kambythour—seems to have early become a leader of free lances, and to have hired himself out first to Ben Houd, Emir of Zaragoza—an ally of Fernando I. Then he passed into the service of King Sancho the Strong, and married Ximena, daughter to the Count of Oviedo. When Sancho perished, at the siege of Zamora, Rodrigo distrusted Alfonso, and returned to his former roving habits of hiring himself out to fight the battles of Moorish chiefs, feeding his band upon plunder alike of Moor and Christian.

Valencia was still Moorish, but the emir, Al Kadir,

paid tribute to Alfonso, and had admitted a Christian bishop. Al Kadir was a tyrant, and exacted such heavy imposts, especially on barley, that the very dogs were said to bark at the words "give barley."

Discontent was great, and Alvar Fanez—the friend and comrade of the Cid—was invited to fight the emir's battles, while another Christian soldier from Barcelona was called in by the malcontents. Al Kadir was successful, and, being unable to give Alvar Fanez any pay, he presented him with a castle, where all sorts of lawless people collected and lived by plunder, accompanied by horrid cruelties. They made prisoners all who fell in their way, whether Mahommedan or Christian; and, if no ransom were brought for them, cut out their tongues, put out their eyes, and hunted them with dogs.

Al Mostain, Emir of Zaragoza, proposed to the Cid to overthrow Al Kadir, when the Moor was to keep Valencia itself and the Christian be paid by plunder; but ere the attack began Al Kadir had an interview with the Cid, and bribed him not only to refuse to continue the war with one who paid tribute to Castille, but to pass into his own service, levying huge sums as black mail from the cities which he did not plunder. During an illness of Al Kadir he managed the affairs of Valencia; but, so far from holding it for his native prince, he made it independent. Alfonso besieged Valencia; Rodrigo harried Castille to call him home. Finally, while Rodrigo was at Zaragoza, there was a rising against Al Kadir, and the Almoravid chief, Ibu Djahhaf was admitted by the people. Al Kadir fled, carrying in his bosom a necklace of precious stones which had belonged to Zobeideh, the wife of the great Khalif Haroun-al-Raschid. He was pursued, slain, and his head thrown into a pond.

There then followed a war between Al Mostain, assisted by the Cid, and Ibn Djahhaf, ending in a siege. After a long blockade, some of the citizens opened the gates, and a frightful slaughter ensued; only those being saved who could ransom themselves, or were worth being sold for slaves. Ibn Djahhaf was taken, and, after having given up the necklace and all the rest of the spoil, was burnt alive in revenge for the death of Al Kadir.

Murviedo was also taken by the Cid by treachery, and cruelly used. The Arab records say that a Moorish army defeated Alvar Fanez, and that Rodrigo, who was already ill, died of grief. Then the Moors besieged Valencia. Ximena held out for seven months, till the King of Castille came to bring succour. Finding the place no longer tenable, he escorted away all the Christians and set it on fire. Rodrigo's body was brought home and buried at San Pedro de Cardeñas. His two daughters, whose real names were Maria and Christina, married the Infants of Navarre and Aragon.

Two generations seem to have built up the wonderful superstructure of romance on the life of one who probably had much brilliance, courage, and dignity, but who evidently was really only the fierce partisan warrior of Spain, not by any means the perfect Christian hero. However, the "Cronica del Cid" has so many actual bits of history in it that his feats have been accepted as genuine. Corneille made his marriage the theme of a drama; and when the French invaded Spain in 1808, they fell into raptures over the tomb that Chimène shared with her lord, and removed it to the public promenade at Burgos. It was afterwards restored to Cardeña, but the remains of the Cid were taken from his tomb and placed in a walnut urn in the museum of Burgos.

CHAPTER XVI.

THE ALMORAVIDES AND THEIR CONQUEST.

To complete the story of the Cid, it has been necessary to anticipate the great changes produced by the disunion of the Moors and the increased strength of the Castilian kingdom under Alfonso VI.

He was an able man, not very scrupulous, who kept his brother Garcia in prison till his death, and neglected no chance of extending his frontiers. He kept the peace with the Moors as long as his friend Al Maimoun lived; but when that emir died, he allied himself with Mahommed Aben Abed of Seville against his son, and besieged Toledo in 1074.

After holding out with true peninsular constancy, the city surrendered, on condition that such Moslems as left it should carry away their property, and those who remained should freely exercise their religion and retain all their mosques. Thus Alfonso, after three hundred years, re-entered the capital of the Goths, and obtained the city where the unhappy Rodrigo, last of the Goths, had reigned.

He was the first Castilian king who had been important enough to wed beyond the Pyrennees. His wife was Constanza of Burgundy, granddaughter of

Robert the Pious of France. She came full of the revival that had taken place under that devout monarch, and bringing with her Bernard, a monk of Cluny, bred up under the vigorous and devout rule that favoured our Lanfranc and Anselm. They were shocked at the laxity of Spain, both in morals and in doctrine, and they had already obtained that a synod should be held for a reformation of the Church. They were unable to understand any Christianity save what was like that which they had left at home; and the Mozarabic liturgy was a sore trial to them, though its orthodoxy had been approved by a legate from Rome. Castille was as yet so isolated that all its culture came from the Moorish schools; and though physical science was there infinitely more advanced than anywhere else in the West, and learning and poetry had revived under the late emirs of Seville, such studies seemed suspicious to the northern monk and his devout queen. They were displeased at the king's friendly intercourse with his Moorish vassals, and were shocked at the toleration with which Moslem and Christian lived side by side in the cities which owned either a Moorish or a Spanish master.

And when "the crown of Spain," Toledo, on the seven hills above the Tagus, was gained, and Bernard was made its first Archbishop, they could not brook that the Alfaqui the noblest building in the city, should remain a Moorish mosque. No sooner had the king left the city than at night the queen gave authority to Bernard and his monks of Sahagun to open the doors, hang bells, erect altars, set up crosses, and summon the Faithful to mass in the morning. The king returned, greatly angered, and threatened punishment, but the

Moorish inhabitants, satisfied by his indignation, begged him to pardon the monks. The day of reconciliation was consecrated to Our Lady of Peace, and the Alfaqui became the cathedral, but little that is Moorish remains about its architecture.

Constanza and her Archbishop continued to struggle for the substitution of the Roman liturgy, and the national clergy were as strongly against it. At last it was decided to try the two service-books by ordeal. A great pile was erected in the market-place of Toledo for the most harmless *auto da fé* that ever took place there. King, queen, court, and all the magistrates of Toledo looked on, as well as the two parties of clergy, while, with prayer that God would show whether of the two He had chosen, the two books were committed to the flames. The heavy bindings and parchment leaves would not be very easily consumed, and the Gothic liturgy came out little injured, while the Latin was found to be illegible. But the superiority of St. Gregory's ritual was too firmly fixed in the minds of the northern ecclesiastics for them to allow that this trial had been decisive. They demanded a trial by battle; champions were appointed on either side, and did battle in the lists, and again with success to the national party, and without submission from the strangers, who finally so far prevailed that all newly-founded or conquered churches should start with their ritual, though the elder ones were not to be disturbed in the Mozarabic use.

Alfonso's conquest of Toledo startled the Moors. The Spanish frontier had advanced first to the Ebro, then to the Douro, and now to the Tagus; and Castilian knights had become superior in prowess to the Moors.

L

The schools of Cordova and Seville still educated men in science and literature. Geometry, algebra, natural history, and poetry were studied, and the houses and gardens of the Moors were still exquisite; but their fiery courage and steady endurance were gone, their emirs were disunited, and every dispute among them was the occasion of fresh advances to the Christian. The Castilian knights made forays up to the very walls of Medina-Sidonia; and when the emir of Seville, Mahommed Aben Abed, sent to Burgos to complain, Alfonso replied by sending his treasurer, a Jew, with five hundred knights as escort, to demand tribute. So much enraged were the Moors that they slew the whole, an act so unlike the gentle poetical Aben Abed that it was probably the work of some popular rising.

The danger thus incurred was such to the whole Mahommedan power in Spain that a divan was held at Seville, to which each emir came in person, or sent a kadi to represent him, and the proposal was there brought forward of calling in the aid of their African brethren.

In times beyond the ken of history the Lambounab tribe had migrated from Yemen, or Arabia Felix, and had taken up their abode in the desert of Western Africa, between the Atlas mountains and Senegambia, where they lived a wandering life, like their forefathers in Arabia; not mingling with other tribes, but wearing camels' hair, and driving their flocks wherever pasture was abundant.

Somewhere about the middle of the eleventh century the faith of Mahommed was brought to them by an imaum from Fez, named Abd-Allah-ben-Yasim, who came as a missionary to bring the Koran and all its supposed revelations to the sons of Ishmael. He had been bred in the schools of Cordova and Seville, and was a man of much ability. Seventy sheiks became his pupils, and were by him awakened to a sense of the glories and joys destined for their race. Those who were thus taught by Abd-Allah took the name of *Al Morbethyn*, or devoted to Allah. The western form of this word is *Marabouts*; but the tribe is usually called Almoravides. Abd-Allah was lost while crossing Mount Atlas, but the impulse he had given continued; and the Almoravides, like the Saracens before them, were impelled, in the freshness of their conversion to Islam, to become great conquerors.

Yousuf-ben-Tashfyn, under this first impulse, led their bravest warriors from the desert, and, overcoming the wild nations on the west of Africa, founded, in 1070, the city of Marrakash, or, as we call it, Morocco, where he built the chief mosque of bricks moulded by his own hands. He was one of those brave, temperate, high-spirited men who were the best type of Moslem; and he subdued Mequinez, Fez, Tangier, Ceuta, Algier, and Tunis—in fact, all the Berber portion of Africa between the Senegal river and the site of ancient Carthage.

It was to this Yousuf that the dejected emirs proposed to apply for aid. There was only one dissentient voice—that of the wali of Malaga—who said: "Let us be united, and we shall be strong enough to overcome the Christians; but let us not call into the delicious plains of our Andalusia the lions and tigers of the burning sands of Africa. They will only break the chains of Alfonso to give us chains that we cannot break."

The civilised man's instinct against his more wild and savage neighbours was not shared. The emir of Badajos was charged to go and ask the aid of Yousuf against Alfonso. The Arabic historians have preserved the actual letter of invitation:

"To the most mighty Emir, by the favour of Allah Imaum of the Moslems, Prince of the Almoravides, Yousuf-ben-Tashfyn, with the light of whose splendour Allah illuminates all parts of the earth, with whose perfection Allah adorns all creatures.

"We, the Arabs of Andalusia, have not preserved our illustrious tribes: we have dispersed and intermixed them, and have long had no fellowship with our tribes and families who dwell in Africa. Want of union has divided our interests; disunion has led to discord, and our natural enemies are prevailing against us.

"Each day becometh more unbearable—the fury of King Alfonso, who, like a mad dog, enters our lands, takes our castles, makes Moslems captive, and will tread us under foot unless an emir from Africa will arise to defend the oppressed, who behold the ruin of their kindred, their neighbours, and even of their law.

"They are no more what once they were. Pleasures, amusements, the sweet climate of Andalusia, delicious baths of fragrant waters, fountains, and dainty meats have enervated them, so that they dare not face the toils of war.

"We dare no longer raise our heads; and since thou, great lord, art the offspring of Homayr, our forefather, we turn to thee in hope, entreating thee to hasten to Spain to overcome our faithless and treacherous foe, who seeks to destroy our law. He has just written us a letter, full of thunders and lightnings, that we may yield our castles and towns and leave him our mosques, that he may fill them with his monks, set up his crosses on their minarets, and sing his mass and requiem where prayer is made!

"Allah has made for thee, O king of true Believers, an empire whose increase he blesses. He has made thee his messenger, that thou mayest uphold his law and share the brightness of his divine light.

"If thou art moved by desire of earthly wealth, here wilt thou find rich carpets, jewels of gold and silver, precious raiment, delicious gardens, and clear springs of flowing water. But if thine heart seeks only to win eternal life in Allah's service, here is the opportunity, for never are wanting bloody battles, skirmishes, and fights. Here has Allah placed a paradise, that from the shadow of weapons thou mayest pass to the everlasting shadow, where he rewards the deserving."

Yousuf was not insensible to the various inducements held out to him. He required only that the Green Isle—*i.e.* Al Gesira—should be placed in his hands, and then immediately crossed, bringing with him an enormous host of Almoravides, Berbers, and negroes.

Alfonso, at the same time, rallied all his forces from all his kingdoms, and obtained help from Aragon and Navarre. The two armies were encamped on either side of the river of Badajos, at a place called *Al Zalakah*, or, the slippery.

Here Yousuf wrote to Alfonso, offering him his choice of three measures—either to become a Moslem, to be his vassal and pay tribute, or to give battle.

Of course Alfonso chose the last, and he further wrote to fix the day, saying, like Bermudo at Tormès, that the morrow was Friday, the Moslem holyday; Saturday was the Sabbath of the Jews, of whom there were many in both armies; and Sunday was the Christian feast; —therefore the battle had better take place on the Monday. To this Yousuf agreed; but Aben Abed did not in the least believe in the king's sincerity, and fully expected a sudden attack, so he caused watch to be kept all night and morning. Unfortunately he seems to have been right, for, on Friday morning, while he was at morning prayer, his scouts hurried in, saying: "*Muley* (prince), the enemy is in motion, with an innumerable crowd like swarms of locusts."

Aben Abed sent word to Yousuf, and called an astrologer, who drew a magic figure, and said: "Muley, this will be an unlucky day if the Moslems begin a battle in this hour." Aben Abed would not, however, tell the other emirs, for fear they should think him cowardly and superstitious.

Alfonso, on his side, had dreamt that he was riding on an elephant and beating a huge kettle-drum, and, to explain this augury, he summoned, first, all the bishops and priests, then all the Jewish rabbis, and lastly, an Arab fakir. None of them gave favourable answers, so that it is the more surprising that he should have thus unfairly hurried on the battle, if indeed it was not an accident caused by the encounter of the light troops on either side.

Yousuf had been up all night, and was quite ready for battle when Aben Abed's message reached him. He sent his chief general, Daooud-ben-Aischa, with a great troop of archers and a vanguard of Almoravid cavalry; and these were met by the *campeadors*, or foremost champions of the Spaniards, who gained the advantage. Each party then drew up in battle array, and Aben Abed caused his astrologer again to consult the heavenly bodies, and this time heard that it was a favourable conjunction. Being an Arab poet himself, he sent Yousuf these four lines:

> Allah's wrath is on the Christians,
> By thy sword shall they fall;
> The heavens foretell victory,
> And a blessed day for the Believers.

Yousuf then took courage, mounted his horse, reviewed his men. Daooud-ben-Aischa first led his troops to meet the onset led by Alfonso. The lances broke in the shock, and they fought with swords, apparently without much advantage on either side. The other half of the Christian army, under Count Garcia Ramirez of Aragon, fell on Aben Abed's Andalusians, and covered them " as the shades of night cover everything," and put them to flight in the direction of Badajos, no one keeping the field but the horsemen of Seville, with Aben Abed in the midst of them, all fighting like wounded lions. Hearing of their need, Yousuf sent to their assistance his reserve of Berbers, and himself led his best Lamtounahs, other Almoravides, to fall on the Christian camp, which they plundered and set on fire. This brought back Alfonso, who had thought the day his own, and there a most terrible fight ensued. Yousuf had two horses killed under him, but went on assuring his men: " Allah has counted the Infidels and lessened them. Paradise awaits you! The slain are already enjoying it!" His enthusiasm and generalship prevailed. Alfonso was driven out of his camp. A negro slave wounded him with a scimitar, and seized his bridle; but his knights made in to his rescue, and with five hundred of them he at length at nightfall galloped off from the unfortunate slippery field. Aben Abed, lying wounded in his tent, sent off a few lines under the wing of a carrier pigeon to his son at Seville, where there were great rejoicings. The slaughter had been frightful. A great lance was planted in the middle of the plain, and Christian heads were heaped round till it disappeared. The skulls were divided between the chief cities of Moorish Spain to serve as grisly trophies, a ferocious trait new in the history of the Arabs, and probably derived from the new-comers from Africa.

Yousuf took the title of Chief of Believers, called by the Spaniards Miramamolin; soon after the battle of Zalakah he was recalled to Morocco by the death of the son whom he had left there to act for him; but he left a large body of men under his Bey, Syr-ben-Abi-Bekr. The victory proved to have been of little benefit to the Moorish cause. There was no central point of union; the emirs were "each man for his own hand;" and the Almoravides in Algesiras, which had been ceded to Yousuf, were only a fresh element of confusion, and pillaged the whole of the west.

Alfonso had rallied his forces most vigorously after his crushing defeat, and sent to entreat aid from the kindred of his wife, Constanza, who had lately died, leaving him a daughter, Doña Urraca. Raymond, Count of Burgundy, nephew to Constanza, led a considerable force of knights, and also brought a great number of clergy and monks to fill the churches and convents that lay along the banks of the Tagus. The Moors were attacked on all sides, and Aben Abed was so distressed that he went to Morocco to entreat Yousuf to return to the succour of Andalusia.

He came in 1088, and collected the emirs to besiege the fort of Alìd and concert operations; but they disputed so violently that he saw there was no hope of getting them to act in concert; dismissed them in haste on the approach of the Castilians, and hurried home, almost like a fugitive, but having in truth made up his mind to subdue them all, and reign as absolute master of Andalusia.

He came in 1090, at the head of a huge host of all the chief Berber tribes; and as Algesiras was already in his hands, he effected a landing easily, and began at once by deposing the Emir of Granada, on a charge of alliance with the Castilians. The other emirs were then attacked one by one. Aben Abed in his distress entreated the aid of Alfonso, and even offered him his daughter Zaida in marriage. She was a Christian in heart, having been converted, said the Castilians, by a dream of St. Isidoro. Her father gave her the cities of Cucuça, Ucles, and Huate, as her portion; and she was conducted to Toledo, where she was baptised as Maria Isabel, and married the king. She only lived to give birth to his only son, who was named Sancho.

Alfonso sent an army to assist his father-in-law, but it was defeated, and its overthrow brought on the fall of Aben Abed. He capitulated in 1091, and was taken to the castle of Aginât in Africa, with his wife Zaida Cubra, and her daughters, for his sons had been killed in battle. Their maintenance was so scanty, that the ladies had to spin to eke out their subsistence, while the fallen emir tried to solace himself with poetry and literature. The daughters all quickly pined away and died in their exile from their lovely home, and Aben Abed followed them to the grave after four years' captivity.

Meanwhile Yousuf's two Beys, Syr and Daooud, had reduced all the other emirs to the east and west, and not one of the former chiefs was spared except Ahmed Abu Djafar, of Zaragoza, who was left to serve as a sort of breakwater against the Christian force, though still only as tributary.

This Almoravid conquest was really the Moorish or African conquest. The first had been by true Saracen Arabs, with a comparatively small admixture of Moorish or Berber tribes, and Arabs had been the dominant race, though there had been a continual immigration from Africa to supply the Berber guard till these had in many parts overpowered the Arab element. But when the kingdom of Yousuf swallowed up the emirs, the true Moorish dominion began in 1094, the year of the Council of Clermont.

Yousuf, though he had begun life as a wild Moor, encouraged the scholarship of his Andalusian subjects. At this time lived at Cordova the great man of science, Abd Abdallah Ibu Rosha, whose fame became so world-wide as to have been transmogrified into the more classical sounding Averroes, and who was the first person to make Aristotle's writings known in the Middle Ages. At Cordova was found a writing which was said to contain a promise from the Jews that, if their Messiah did not appear within five hundred years of Mahommed, they would accept the Prophet of Islam. Yousuf threatened to make them fulfil their promise, but let himself be bought off by large tribute; and altogether the Jews fared much better in

Spain than anywhere else, both among Moors and Castilians.

Yousuf lived a temperate hardy life, which lasted till his hundredth year, when he died in 1107. The popular songs of Algeria still exalt his fame. He left his dominions to his son Ali, of whom a poet had said:

> Ali, last in age,
> First in worth,
> As the least finger
> Wears the most precious ring.

He was by nature gentle and merciful—like his father, who had never condemned any man to death; but the Almoravides were, as a people, much ruder and more violent than the Arabs, and craved for constant war. In the first year of his reign Ali then sent out an expedition against the Castilians. Alfonso VI. was too ill to take the command of his army; but he sent his only son Sancho, then eleven years old, under the care of Don Garcia de Cabra, his best captain, to relieve the city of Ucles, which had been part of the portion of the inheritance of the boy's Moorish mother, Zaida. Young Sancho fell early in the battle; his guardian, Garcia, died defending his corpse; and the Christian loss was so severe that this was called the Battle of the Seven Counts.

Alfonso was left much in the condition of his contemporary, Henry I. of England, a little later: his only male heir dead, and nothing left him but an unsatisfactory daughter and several illegitimate children. The daughter—Urraca, child of Constanza—had been married to Raymond of Burgundy, and early left a widow with one son, Alfonso. The Castilian nobles wished her to marry Count Gomez of Candespina, with whom she was herself in love, and the Jewish physician Cidelio hinted the plan to the king; but Alfonso was so indignant that he banished the Jew, and at once gave his daughter to Alfonso, the brother of Pedro I., king of both Aragon and Navarre. The death of Pedro brought the bridegroom to the throne of that kingdom in 1104; and on the death of Alfonso VI. in 1108, Castille, Navarre, and Aragon were again for a short time united; the more direct line of Aragon from Garcia having been set aside.

national spirit was disposed to rally; but in the universal confusion, Ali, King of Cordova, advanced with the Almoravides in 1110, sacked Talavera, Olmos, Guadalujara, and Madrid, and tried to take Toledo, but was repulsed by Alvar Fanez, the old comrade of the Cid. The next year the Almoravides again besieged the place; but the citizens held out so gallantly as to repulse them, though neither king nor queen sent to the aid of the capital. They were quarrelling too hotly to attend to anything else. Alfonso had imprisoned the queen, and she had made her escape, but the Castilians would not support her; and the Gallicians, declaring that a marriage between first cousins was altogether invalid, renounced both her and her husband, and charged the Archbishop of Compostella to crown her son, Alfonso Ramon, and, further, to anoint him—the first time that this symbolical rite had been used in Spain.

Pascal II. sent a legate, who pronounced a divorce; whereupon Castille and Aragon, not only fell apart, but went to war. With punctilious loyalty, Peranzuelas came before Alfonso to be freed from his oath of allegiance, clad in scarlet, riding a white horse, and with a halter round his neck. It was jealousy of Aragon, not love for their queen, that edged the swords of the Castilians. Two, the Counts of Lara and Candespina, each hoped to marry her; and her conduct towards them so disgusted her son's guardian, the Count of Portugal, that he deserted her cause, and at the great battle of Espina in 1112 Lara fled, Candespina was killed, and Aragon triumphed. After a few more years of desultory and fruitless warfare, Alfonso wisely gave up the attempt to subdue Castille; and Urraca, failing to

CHAPTER XVII.

DON ALFONSO, THE BATTLE-FIGHTER OF ARAGON

URRACA, the new queen of Castille, was in Aragon with her husband when her father died. Her heart was still with Don Gomez, and she hated Alfonso so much as to be deeply offended that his name should have been placed before hers in the letters sent by her father's minister, Peranzuelas, to inform her of her accession.

Setting out to take possession of her new dominions, Urraca confiscated the estates of Peranzuelas, and took Gomez into favour that shocked her subjects. Everything was in confusion. Alfonso of Aragon arrived, undid all that she had done, and kept her in restraint, filling the fortresses with Aragonese governors. This greatly offended the Castilians, for the nobles of these little kingdoms were apt to hate one another worse than they did the Moors; and this was probably the reason that they always fell apart after each attempt at uniting them. Urraca's illegitimate sister, Teresa, had married Henry, a son of one of the Dukes of Lorraine, whom the late king had made Count of the North of Portugal, and who was the guardian of the son of the queen's first marriage with Raymond of Burgundy. Round this boy the secure any support, consented to resign her crown to her son, Alfonso Ramon, and ended her unhappy and disgraceful life so obscurely that the date of her death is uncertain.

Alfonso *el Batallador*, or the Battle-fighter, is the title given to her divorced husband, the first of his name in Aragon, and a man of considerable ability, who was able to take advantage of the death of Aben Houd, the Arab emir of Zaragoza. Amâd-el-Daoulah, the son of that prince, was beset on the one hand by the Almoravides, who had regained Valencia on the death of the Cid, and on the other by the Aragonese; but the city held out for four whole years against the Batallador with the same constancy as afterwards made its name a proverb, until, in 1117, when half the people were dead of hunger, Amâd surrendered on the same terms as had been granted to Toledo. Zaragoza was supposed to have been the spot where the Blessed Virgin had appeared to St. James, standing on her pillar of jasper; and of course the pillar was discovered (though it had been a dream pillar), and is extant still. Thus the city became the favourite Aragonese shrine and place of pilgrimage, though never equal in fame to Compostella; and Alfonso removed his court thither, so that it became a city of tall castellated houses, each capable of making a defence on its own account. Catalayud was soon after taken; and thus, in 1120, Alfonso was master of all the lands forming the present province of Aragon.

Ali had in the meantime been called to Africa by an insurrection in Morocco. In his absence the Cordovans, unable to bear any longer the insolence of the Almoravid garrison, rose against them, killed a great many, and drove the rest out of the city. Ali hurried back, laid siege to the place, and, when it surrendered, showed himself a wise and merciful man by merely requiring from the inhabitants compensation to the Almoravides for the plunder of their houses, and then placing these rude warriors under stricter discipline. He then again crossed the strait, for he was threatened by great dangers in Africa.

A Berber dervish, named Mouhamed-Aben-Ald-Allah-ben-Thoumrout, who had studied in the most noted Arabic schools of Syria, Egypt, and Spain, had begun to preach in the streets of Morocco, inveighing against the luxury and oppression of the rich and the vices of the imaums, and accusing them of having departed from the doctrines of the Koran. He said there was no doctrine but the unity of the Godhead, and that there ought to be no prayer save this: "Allah El Allah, the most merciful of the merciful, Thou knowest our sins—pardon them; Thou knowest our wants—supply them; Thou knowest our foes—defend us from them. This is enough with Thee, our Lord, Maker, and our Support."

The imaums were furious against him, and Ali, who had long refused to punish one whom he viewed as a mere crazy fanatic, yielded at last to their persuasions, and banished him from the city. He betook himself to the world of tombs beyond the walls, and crowds resorted to him, becoming so enthusiastic that the emir became alarmed and sent men to put him to death. Warned in time, he fled to the deserts of Mount Atlas, accompanied by his more devoted followers, and gathered round him the fierce Berber tribes, who hailed him as the *Mâhdy*, or guide. He appointed ten special companions and fifty counsellors, and at the head of a great multitude, collected in the Atlas deserts, he burst upon Morocco just as Ali returned from Spain. Three terrible battles took place, in all of which the new fanaticism was too much for the older. The followers of the Mâhdy were called *Al Monahedyn*, or Unitarians—or, more shortly, *Al Mohides*; and for three years they dwelt on an almost inaccessible mountain belonging to the Atlas range. Descending again, they made another attack on Morocco; but six out of the ten chief companions were killed, the army broken, and the remnant only saved by the skill of Abd-el-Mounem, whom, as a lad, the Mâhdy had singled out for his intelligence and vehemence. At the same time, the Mozarabic Christians and the Jews, finding the Almoravid yoke much heavier than that of the Ommeyads or the emirs, entreated Alfonso el Batallador to come to their aid. He collected a large army—including volunteers from France—and marched through Andalusia; but though many Mozarabic Christians joined him, they could not put any important place into his hands. He had vowed to fish in the Mediterranean sea at Malaga, and this he accomplished, for Ali's orders were to keep within the fortresses and let him march on, and thus he had to return without having gained a single castle. The only effect of his expedition was that the Christians were forced by Ali to leave the cities near the borders and dwell in the interior of Andalusia. Those who had actually joined Alfonso were deported to Africa, for Ali, like his father, never uttered a sentence of death.

Alfonso el Batallador now called himself Emperor, meaning that he was chief of the other kings of the Peninsula, as Edgar the Peaceable had been Emperor of Britain. He might well be called the Battle-fighter, for he had fought twenty-eight battles with the Moors, and kept them in such a state of alarm that they proclaimed the *Azala* of Fear. This meant the worship in time of danger, when all the prayers and preachings were shortened, and men were allowed to attend the mosques without the regular ablutions, and in their armour. Alfonso el Batallador never married again after his unfortunate experiences with Urraca of Castille. He was a devout prince, and of high and honourable character, and he was much attached to the two great religious orders of knighthood, the Templars and Hospitallers—who viewed a campaign against the Moors in Spain as accordant with their vows as the doing battle with the Saracens in Palestine.

In the last of his inroads into the Moorish territory he besieged Fraga, on the borders of Catalonia, a strong city with the rapid river Cinca before it, and a steep mountain behind. Here the Almoravides attacked him in great force, assisted by reinforcements from Morocco, and, after a desperate combat, his troops were overpowered by numbers, and a terrible slaughter took place. He cut his way out with seven hundred knights, and made his way back to Aragon a broken-hearted man. He would not enter Zaragoza, but turned aside with ten of his knights to the Count of San Juan de la Peña, where, at the end of a week, he died of grief, in the year 1134.

He had left his dominions by will to the Knights of St. John and of the Temple; but his subjects would not endure to be thus disposed of. Navarre found Garcia Ramiro, a descendant of Garcia II.; and Aragon took, from a convent in Narbonne, Ramiro, the youngest brother of the Batallador. A dispensation was obtained from the Pope, and the monk-king was married to Agnes—or, as the Spaniards call her, Iñes, daughter to the last Count of Poitiers, and sister to the lady who, some years later, created a great scandal by being divorced from Louis VII. of France, and immediately being married to Henry Fitz Empress, Count of Anjou, and soon after second of his name in England. The claim of the knights was bought off, with the Pope's sanction, with large grants of lands, and the right to the homage of a vassal from each of the three nations—Mozarabic, Jew, and Moor—in each freshly-conquered city.

The monk-king did not turn out satisfactory. He was unable to defend his kingdom against the Moors, and he was very harsh at home. The Aragonese told of him, and of his former abbot, the old story of the advice to Sextus Tarquinius about cutting off the heads of the poppies; and it is also said that he told his turbulent nobility that he would make a bell that should ring throughout his dominions, and fulfilled the threat by showing the city of Huesca a bell-frame garnished with fifteen heads of hidalgos. It was the desperate effort of a helpless man made savage by terror, and he soon gave up the struggle. He betrothed his baby-daughter, Petronila, to Ramon, Count of Barcelona; and, giving up his crown to them, retired into the chapter of Huesca, in 1137.

The death of the Batallador had not deprived the Christians of all their gallant champion kings, for the two cousins, Alfonso Ramon in Castille, and Alfonso Henriquez in Portugal, were both brave and victorious. Alfonso Ramon was crowned emperor, with the consent of the Pope, by the Archbishop of Toledo. His wife was Berenguela, the sister of the Count of Barcelona, a lady of great beauty and of a high spirit. In 1139, while her husband was absent on an expedition into Andalusia, a body of Moors appeared and laid siege to Toledo. The queen came forth on the ramparts, and, calling for the Moorish chiefs, upbraided them with coming to besiege a woman when their swords were needed at home. The chiefs owned that her reproach was just, lowered their lances in homage to her beauty, and filed away from beneath her walls. Some time after, when two heads of Moorish chiefs were brought home and fixed to the palace gates, Berenguela expressed her horror at the barbarity, caused them to be taken down, embalmed, and sent in mourning chariots to the families. Alfonso Henriquez had succeeded his mother, Teresa, in Portugal, after she had had a career far too like that of her sister, Urraca, in Castille. He obtained the assistance of a band of French and English knights, who put in at Oporto, on their way to the second crusade in 1139, and, mustering all his forces, marched towards the Guadiana. The Moors had obtained accessions of force from Africa and, when the two armies came in sight of each other at Campo d'Ourique, the Portuguese troops were far outnumbered. It is said that Alfonso was much encouraged by opening a Bible at the defeat of the Midianites by Gideon, and that a hermit visited him and promised him a sign of victory. In truth, at daybreak, as the matin-bell sounded, there was such a luminous Cross in the sky as had been seen by Constantine; and an assurance was given him that he should be king, and that his children, to the sixteenth generation, should reign on the throne of Portugal.

His army did in fact salute him king ere the battle, and he rode forward on a white horse, followed by enthusiastic troops, who won a most brilliant victory. Portugal became a kingdom. Its shield was a white field with five lesser red scutcheons arranged in the form of a cross, in allusion to the Five Sacred Wounds; and in 1147, its capital, Lisbon, was won by the aid of William Longsword, Earl of Salisbury, on his way to the Holy Land. The first Archbishop of Lisbon was an English priest named Gilbert, whom the king persuaded to settle there instead of pursuing his crusade.

The emperor, Alfonso VIII., died in 1157, again breaking up his dominions, giving Castille to his eldest son, Sancho, and Leon to the second, Fernando.

CHAPTER XVIII.

THE BROKEN CHAINS OF NAVAS DE TOLOSA.

THE Almoravides had always been viewed as rude tyrants by their own fellow Mahommedans in Andalusia, and in *Al Garb* (the west), now called Algarve, a dervish named Ahmet-ben-Kossay, holding the same form of doctrine as the Almolides, raised a revolt which drove them beyond the Guadiana.

His success filled the Andalusians with hope. Cordova, Valencia, Murcia, Granada, Ronda, Xerez, all revolted, and chose their own leaders, till nothing was left to the Almoravides but Seville. In Africa they were faring equally ill. Ali was dead, and his son Tashfyn, after many defeats, was shut up in Oran on the seashore. He tried to escape at night, but was killed by a fall from the rocks.

Morocco was taken after a long blockade, and Fez, where the last Almoravid emir, Ali, had taken refuge, was attacked. The river that flows through it was dammed up by the Almoravides, till a great body of water was collected as in a reservoir. Then they destroyed the bank, the flood rushed forth, did in one moment the work of a hundred battering-rams, and made the place their own, on the very morning that the unfortunate young emir was celebrating his wedding.

Abd-el-Moumen, now the leader of the Almoravides, had no sooner gained Africa than he pursued his career of victory into Spain. The Almoravides tried to stand by allying themselves with the Christians, but this proved a vain expedient; and by the year 1157, all had been exterminated except a few who had taken refuge in the Balearic isles, while Andalusia was brought under the dominion of the new Miramamolin, Abd-el-Moumen. He had invented a new coinage, square, and bearing the inscription, "Allah is our Lord; Mahommed our Apostle; the Mâhdy our Imâm." He was therefore called the Master of the Square Coin.

Abd-el-Moumen was a man of taste and culture; but his Almohides were the Puritans of Islam, and their barbarism added to the ruin wrought by the Almoravides. Just as Roman became a term for the down-trodden and oppressed after the Teutonic conquest, so an Arab was now in disgrace; and the proud old families carefully concealed their lineage and sheltered themselves under the title of Moors. It was not the fault of the Miramamolin, who tried to foster the arts for which the Spanish Arabs had been so celebrated. The schools of Cordova and Seville were encouraged, and produced books of science, philosophy, and poetry as of old; the fields and gardens were again cultivated; and Alhas Yahix of Malaga must have been a most ingenious mechanic, for he not only constructed warlike engines, but mills, and also a wonderful pulpit and royal pew for the chief mosque. Both were made of aromatic wood, wrought with scrolls and flowers, and with fastenings and hinges of gold; moreover, a foot on the steps of each made their doors open noiselessly, and more curious still, they both moved to their places, smoothly and without sound, when the prince took his place. He also fortified Geb-el-Tarik, or Gibraltar.

The Christians had meantime been prosperous. Each of these African invasions always left a margin of forts unsubdued, which were sure to fall in process of time into the hands of the steadily-advancing Spanish power. Calatrava was one of these. It was taken by Sancho el Desirado, King of Castille, eldest son of Alfonso VII. He gave it at first to the Knights Templars, but they were hopeless of defending it from the Moors. Then the Cistercian Abbot Raymond came forward, and offered to keep it if he might make his monks knights like those of St. John and the Temple. The king consented. Raymond made good his word; and thus arose the Order of Knights of St. Julian, or Calatrava, at the same time as, in Portugal, arose another similar order of chivalrous monks of Avis; and in 1162 Fernando, King of Leon, made a branch of the Augustinian Order into Knights of Santiago de Compostella, with a red sword for their badge. These orders of knights, with commanderies on all the dangerous points, and without families or personal estates, were a most valuable standing army of trained warriors, and supplying garrisons against the common enemy; and, as long as the wars with the Moors lasted, were far from being a mere complimentary order of knighthood.

Sancho was a youth of much promise. He was married to Blanca of Navarre, and her death in the first year of his reign was the more unfortunate that he survived her only two months, dying in 1148; so that his three-year-old child, Alfonso IX. was an orphan, and a mark for the ambition of his nearest kindred. His nobles quarrelled about him; his uncle, Don Fernando of Leon, claimed the custody of him; and the citizens of Burgos were driven so hard that they were obliged to undertake to yield him up. But on the way to the hall where he was to be given to his uncle, the child, then five years old, cried bitterly, struggled hard, and clung to the knight who was carrying him. To pacify him he was taken into a house, where was Don Pedro Muñez of Fuente Almega, one of the nobles who most distrusted the King of Leon. He wrapped the little fellow in his cloak, and rode off with him, too discreet it seems to cry again, and took him to San Esteban; whence he was carried to the strong castle of Avila, where he was safely kept till his eleventh year, though Fernando had obtained the rest of the country. The faithfulness of the men of Avila became a proverb in the country.

Almeria had fallen under a chief named Maimu, whose galleys infested the Mediterranean with their piracies. It was so rich that the saying was that the streets were pearl, the dust gold, and the gardens paradise, and Granada was only a sort of farm to it. The Genoese, then the chief merchants of the western Mediterranean, offered their aid to the Count of Barcelona, regent of Aragon, to root out this nest of pirates, and it was besieged and taken in 1147. The Genoese accepted no part of the plunder save a great cup, called of emerald, but probably malachite, which they believed to be the same with the Saint Greal of the north, the Cup of the First Communion. Almeria could not, however, be kept by the Christians, and was again fortified by a Moorish garrison.

The Count of Barcelona died soon after; and as there was only a widowed queen in Aragon, and a baby-king in Castille, with half his realm usurped by his uncle, Abd-el-Moumen deemed it a fit time for an attack on the Christians; and collected such a host that the Arab historians say it numbered three hundred thousand men, that the earth shook beneath their tread, and that the camp covered the hills, the valleys, and the mountains. In the midst of his preparations, however, Abd-el-Moumen died in 1163; and his son, Syd Yousuf Abou Yakoub, dismissed the army, having to attend to the revolts that were made by his brothers. Yakoub was a great builder. He finished the splendid mosque at Seville which his father had begun, and which is now, by the name of the Giralda, the most magnificent and unique of cathedrals. He also built a grand *alhama*, or court-house, and quays, and aqueducts; so that Seville began to equal, if not to surpass Cordova, which never recovered its greatness after the fall of the Ommeyads.

In 1170, the young Alfonso IX. being of age, Esteban de Illan, one of the chief men of Toledo, built a tower and dedicated a church to San Romano, where he set up the standard of the castles of Castille in honour of their young king. The whole country responded to the call, and the yoke of Leon was shaken off without an effort, and Alfonso found himself king of all Castille. He asked and obtained the hand of Eleanor, the eldest daughter of Henry II. of England and Eleanor of Aquitaine, who is said to have brought him the appanage of Gascony, and who bore him thirteen children—of whom all the sons died early except Ferdinand and Enrique. Some years later Eleanor's brother, Richard Cœur de Lion, married Berenguela of Navarre.

In 1179 the five Christian kings of Spain had a conference, in which they agreed to unite their forces and drive Mahommedanism beyond the Straits, proceeding to fix what territory each should have; but this dividing of their bearskin before they had killed the bear naturally led to disputes, and the Kings of Leon and Portugal began one war with each other, and those of Navarre and Castille another, instead of attacking the Infidel. When Sancho of Navarre was wasting the lands of Cardeña, the priest of the church of San Pedro came out with the banner of the Cid, and such was the honour in which that champion was held that the Navarrese at once desisted from the attack and restored the plunder. The quarrels were, however, pacified; and while Syd Yakoub was absent, putting down a rising of the Almoravides in Africa, the Castilians, under Don Martin de Pisuerga, Archbishop of Toledo, foraged Andalusia to the confines of Algesiras, and Alfonso sent the following challenge to the Miramamolin:

"Since thou canst not come and attack me, send me ships and I will come and seek thee where thou art."

The emir replied with a verse of the Koran:

"Allah, the All-powerful, hath said: 'I will turn them back by armies that they have not seen, and that they cannot escape, and I will grind them to powder.'"

The challenge and reply were read in all the mosques, and the *ghazouah*, or holy war, was proclaimed, after which Yakoub crossed the Straits, with numbers such that, in oriental terms of magniloquence, the streams could not quench their thirst. Alfonso of Castille advanced to meet him without the support of the other kingdoms, and met him at Alarcos, on the 19th of July, 1195. Before the battle Yakoub dreamt of a warrior on a white steed unfurling a green banner, and his success was equal to the promise of the vision. The Castilians were inferior in numbers, and were totally routed, the knights of Calatrava being cut off almost to a man, and the king himself escaped with difficulty. The Moors ravaged up to the very walls of Toledo, and retook Calatrava and many other places, after which they granted a peace for twelve years, and the emir released all the captives—twenty thousand in number—to the great discontent of his Berbers, who expected to make slaves of them.

When Yakoub died shortly after, in 1197, he said this release was one of the three things he repented of. With him the Almohid crescent began to wane. His son Mahommed was one of the weak harem-bred princes, who always are the ruin of oriental nations. However, his vizier, Abou-Sayd-ben-Ghames, a fierce treacherous man, much hated, after driving the remains of the Almoravides out of the Balearic isles, proclaimed, in 1210, the *ghazouah*, and collected another immense rabble host from Africa, swearing to root out the Christians from Spain. The troops took three months in the transport, and are said to have numbered four hundred and sixty thousand fighting men.

The delay had given the Spaniards time to prepare. The five kings—Alfonso IX., the Noble, of Castille; Fernando II. of Leon; Pedro II. of Aragon; Sancho IV. of Navarre; and Alfonso II. of Portugal—laid aside all their feuds and resolved to unite. The Bishop of Segovia was sent to Rome to intreat the Pope to proclaim their resistance a Crusade, and grant indulgences for those who should die in it; and the Archbishop of Toledo went to seek for succour in France. Great numbers of knights were willing to join the Christian host, and the rallying place was Toledo. In the year 1219 King Alfonso knighted his eldest son Fernando in the cathedral of Burgos, and sent him to deserve his spurs by an expedition with the knights of Calatrava, who were very anxious to regain the city whence they took their name. The foray did not succeed, and Don Fernando came home with a fever, of which he died in a few weeks.

There was no time to grieve, for the troops had to be gathered in and measures taken for the defence. Ten thousand horse and forty thousand foot of the Ultramontanes, as the Spaniards called their allies from beyond the Pyrennees, had come in; but so narrow was the faith of the thirteenth century under Innocent III., that these Crusaders were scandalised at the different rites used by the Mozarabic Christians of Toledo, and were so desirous of beginning by a Crusade against these supposed heretics, and likewise the Jews and the tolerated Mahommedans, that the King of Castille was fain to send them out on a foray under Don Diego Lopez de Hara, to keep them from ravaging his capital. They besieged Calatrava, and their fierce intolerance was greatly displeased at the merciful terms offered by Don Diego. So determined were these fanatics to exterminate the Moors that he was forced to escort the inhabitants himself with his Spanish troops to a place of safety, when the Crusaders were so indignant that they turned back to the Pyrenees, alleging, perhaps with truth, that the summer heats made the campaign dangerous to their northern constitutions, leaving only two leaders— Arnold, Archbishop of Narbonne, and Thibaut Blacon —behind them.

The kings of Castille, Aragon, and Navarre united their forces at Salvatierra, and decided to cross the Sierra Morena with the thirty thousand lances which formed their army. The Moors had in the meantime lost the opportunity of securing the passes by useless sieges. Moreover the captains of the garrison of Calatrava had been publicly put to death for yielding, by the savage vizier, Aben Ghamea; and this had so offended the Spanish Moors that they had drawn off into a separate camp, and left the Africans to fight alone. The whole has been closely described by Rodrigo, Archbishop of Toledo, who was beside the king all the time.

On the 12th of July, 1212, the Christian host was at the base of the Sierra Morena, or brown mountains, a range of round-backed hills overgrown with aromatic shrubs and gigantic thistles, and separated by deep defiles. The higher portions are covered with pine-woods, and the whole chain is fitted for a barrier. The Moors held most of the passes, but Don Diego Lopez drove them from that of Muradae. This, however, was too narrow for it to be safe for the whole army to pass, and the three kings were in consultation whether they must after all retreat, when a shepherd offered to show them a new and safer passage. Some distrusted him, but Diego Lopez and Garcia Romero offered to follow him and reconnoitre. He led them to a broad but winding valley, which has ever since been called the Puerto Real, or Royal Gate; and thus by the 14th of July the army had reached a broad open space called the Plains of Navas de Tolosa, full in sight of the enemy. Mahommed's red tent was in the centre upon a knoll, his green banner above it, and around it was a great square mass of Almohides and negroes, secured by heavy iron chains drawn round a palisade, which were supposed to render them impenetrable.

Again and again the Castilians charged, but in vain. Alfonso, trying to rally them, and intending to throw himself on the enemy, cried: "Here we must die." "No, señor," said the Archbishop, "here we conquer." Therewith his cross-bearer rushed into the enemy. The Castilians flew to save their cross, and just then the Spanish Moors, who hated the African tyranny, wavered and fled before the Aragonese and Navarrese. Then the King of Navarre, Sancho the Strong, succeeded in breaking through the chains with his best troops, and fought a way to the negro guard of Mahommed. All this time the Moramamolin had sat still on his shield in front of his tent, repeating a verse of the Koran, till an Arab chief made his way to him, saying: "What dost thou, commander of the Faithful? The will of Allah is done; the Faithful are conquered!" Mounting a fleet mare, Mahommed fled, and there was a frightful slaughter of the lightly-armed Africans. When the chase was over, Rodrigo chanted *Te Deum* on the plain with all his clergy. It is said that two hundred thousand of the enemy perished, and only fifteen hundred Christians. The scattered arrows and lances were so many that they served for two days as firewood to the whole Christian army; and thirty-five thousand horses were taken. The King of Navarre decorated the shield of his kingdom with gold chains in honour of this exploit, and the day of the battle was consecrated a holyday as the Triumph of the Cross. The kings ravaged as far as Ubeda, but then returned to their kingdoms; and Mahommed, after cruelly putting to death the Andalusian chiefs, fled to Morocco, where he died the next year; and as his son was a child, a horrible and ferocious time of anarchy set in; so that, though the Christian kings did not at the time follow up their victory, the battle of Navas de Tolosa was in fact the deathblow to the dominion of the Almohides. The sports with which the victory was celebrated by the kings were certainly not so elegant as those of the Moors. Among other amusements, there was great diversion caused by turning a pig into the lists among a set of blind men armed with clubs. He who killed it was to have it as a prize; and there was infinite sport in watching the blows dealt at the beast and to each other.

The very civilisation of the Moors seems to have acted unfavourably on the Spaniards. The more worldly and the merely intellectual might be attracted by the pomp, beauty, riches, and learning of the south, but the religious only withdrew into greater bareness, sternness, and severity.

A very remarkable set of warriors among them were termed *Almogavars*, a name by some said to mean men of the earth. They slept, winter and summer, on the bare ground, herded only together, seldom spoke, and wore only leathern garments. Their arms were pike, sword, and dagger, and sometimes a club; but no breastplate or shield. Their eyes sparkled with ferocity when a battle was coming on, and they stood with the butt end of their pikes planted against their feet so as to meet the charge of the Moorish horsemen, by spitting the animal in the breast, and then cutting down the rider as he fell. In the next generation, one of these men was made prisoner by the French, who looked at him as a curious wild animal. His dress was a short frock, girt round him with a rope; a cap of undressed leather, with buskins and sleeves of the same. He was lean and sunburnt, with bushy black hair and beard; and the French knights laughed at him; but he challenged anyone of them to fight, provided he might have his liberty if he were the victor. A young knight mounted his horse and charged him; and in an instant he had pierced the chest of the horse and cut the lace of the knight's helmet in preparation for the death-blow, but he was withheld.. The promise was kept—he was set free; and his master, the King of Aragon, released ten Frenchmen as making up his equivalent.

These were the men who made up the dense bodies of Spanish foot, savages in life and habits, and scarcely living save for the deadly frontier warfare which flowed onward ever a little farther south. A professed Almogavar could have been little better than a beast of prey; but to have served among these men for a season or two was considered a needful qualification for a complete Spanish warrior.

An *adalid*, who was a sort of captain, and had the command of these men, was always to have been one of them, and he could only be appointed by the king or count after twelve adalides had declared upon oath that he had the four great qualifications of an adalid, namely, wisdom, courage, common sense, and loyalty. The king then presented him with garments, a sword, and a horse. Then a noble, or *rico hombre*, girt him with the sword-belt; the king put the sword into his hand, and he was raised, standing on a shield, by some of the adalides, with his face to the east. He waved his sword in the air, defying all enemies of his king and of the Faith; then struck downwards, and then across, describing in the air the sign of the cross; and he repeated the challenge to the four quarters of the world. Then he was lowered, the king placed a pennon in his hand, and he thenceforth ranked as an adalid. The ceremony and the title are both Gothic, the word evidently being *adel*, noble.

Twelve adalides chose an *Almoçaden*, an Arabic term, which gave him a higher command; and there was another officer also elected by jury called an *Alfaqueque*, who was a sort of herald, charged with the arranging for the exchange or ransom of prisoners, and who thus had close relations on both sides, and had to be a man of much weight and worth.

CHAPTER XIX.

THE CONQUESTS OF SAN FERNANDO AND JAYME EL CONQUISTADOR.

EVERYONE remembers how King John of England detached Philippe Auguste of France from supporting the claims of Arthur of Brittany, by offering his eldest son, Louis the Lion, the hand of one of the daughters of Eleanor, the eldest English princess, Queen of Castille. The rights that this lady might have brought with her, seem, from an English point of view, hardly valuable enough to be a temptation at the time, though as it proved they almost gave Louis the crown of England; but probably what Philippe thought most of at the time was the great Acquitainian inheritance in the south. His ambassadors were sent to fetch the bride from among Alfonso IX.'s daughters. The two elder were equally fair and good, but one was named Berenguela and the other Blanca; and the messengers, with true French hatred of an unpronounceable name, took the lady whom they could call Blanche, and carried her home to become one of the noblest and best of queens of France.

Philippe must have regretted the selection, for Berenguela was soon the nearest to the crown of Castille. The peninsular kings, being all descended from Sancho II. of Navarre, were closely related, and their families could not intermarry without falling under the stern discipline of Innocent III. Alfonso, King of Leon, began by marrying Teresa, the daughter of the King of Portugal; but after she had borne him two daughters the marriage was annulled by the Pope, and Teresa, going into a convent, lived so holy a life that she was canonised. Alfonso then wedded Berenguela of Castille without asking a dispensation. For nine years they remained together, but at last the threat of laying the kingdom under an interdict forced them to separate, after they had had two sons and two daughters, whose legitimacy, however, was fully allowed. Berenguela returned to her father's court, and was so highly esteemed, that at his death in 1214, only two years after the battle of Navas de Tolosa, he left her regent for her young brother, Enrique I.; and her mother, the English Eleanor, dying of grief shortly after, he was left entirely to her care.

Pedro II. of Aragon, grandson to Queen Petronila, had married Maria of Montpellier, whose mother was a Greek princess of Constantinople. Only one son was born of this marriage; and Maria, anxious that he should have an apostolic patron, yet uncertain how to choose, arranged, by the advice of her confessor, Bishop Boyl, that twelve tapers should each be consecrated to an Apostle, and that the child should be called after him whose candle should burn the longest. Southey has thus depicted the suspense:

> The tapers were short and slender too,
>   Yet to the expectant throng,
> Before they to the socket burnt,
>   The time, I trow, seemed long

The first that went out was St. Peter,
　　The second was St. John,
And now St. Matthias is going,
　　And now St. Matthew is gone.

Next there went St. Andrew,
　　Then goes St. Philip, too;
And see, there is an end
　　Of St. Bartholomew.

St. Simon is in the snuff,
　　But it is a matter of doubt
Whether he or St. Thomas could be said
　　Soonest to have gone out.

There are only three remaining,
　　St. Jude and the two Saints James;
And great was then Queen Mary's hope
　　For the best of all good names.

Great was then Queen Mary's hope,
　　But greater her fear, I guess,
When one of the three went out,
　　And that one was St. James the Less.

They are now within less than quarter inch
　　The only remaining two,
When there came a thief in St. James,
　　And it made a gutter too.

Up started Queen Mary,
　　Up she sate in her bed:
"I never can call him Judas,"
　　She clasped her hands and said.

"I never can call him Judas!"
　　Again did she exclaim.
"Holy Mother, preserve us!
　　It is not a Christian name."

> She opened her hands and clasped them again,
>   And the infant in the cradle
> Set up a cry, a lusty cry,
>   As loud as he was able.
>
> "Holy Mother, preserve us!"
>   The Queen her prayer renewed,
> When in came a moth at the window,
>   And fluttered about St. Jude.
>
> St. James had fallen in the socket.
>   But as yet the flame is not out;
> And St. Jude hath sing'd the silly moth,
>   That flutters so blindly about.
>
> And before the flame and the molten wax
>   That silly moth could kill,
> It hath beat out St. Jude with its wings,
>   But St. James is burning still.
>
> Oh, that was a joy for Queen Mary's heart,
>   The babe is christened James;
> The Prince of Aragon hath got
>   The best of all good names.
>
> Glory to Santiago,
>   The mighty one in war;
> James he is called, and he shall be
>   King James the Conqueror.
>
> Now shall the Crescent wane,
>   The Cross be set on high,
> In triumph upon many a mosque,
>   Woe, woe to Mawmetry!

The boy was called Jayme—the Aragonese form of Jacobus or James—instead of the Castilian Diego. Poor Maria was not "as fair as she was good," and Pedro neglected and wanted to divorce her. She went to Rome to plead her cause with the Pope, and little Jayme was placed in the care of Simon, Count of Montfort, to whose daughter, though only three years old, he was contracted. It was at the bidding of the Pope, whose vassal Pedro had made himself in his early youth, when he had received the surname of The Catholic—a title he was strangely to bely at the end of his life. The war against the Albigensian heretics was raging when Pedro returned after the battle of Navas de Tolosa. Montfort and the Archbishop of Narbonne were driving them and all their abettors to the last extremity. There was an appeal made to Pedro, who was considered as the natural head of the romance-speaking nations around the Eastern Pyrenees; and he, fired by the accounts of the harshness of Rome towards Toulouse, Beziers, and Carcassonne, and angered at the Pope's opposition to his divorce, eagerly took up their cause. He crossed the Pyrenees with an army, and laid siege to Muret, one of the cities then occupied by the Crusaders. There Simon de Montfort surprised him, and he was slain in his thirty-sixth year, on the 12th of September, 1218.

Little Jayme, then six years old, was, by command of the Pope, placed in the hands of his subjects, who gave him into the keeping of the Grand Master of the Knights Templars, from whom he received an excellent education. He was a boy of wonderful ability; and perhaps no other prince—except William of Normandy —ever showed such ability in his nonage, followed up by so glorious a life; and, curiously, both bear the surname of Conqueror.

The boy-king of Castille, Enrique I., was killed in 1217, by a tile falling on his head while he was at play. His sister, Doña Berenguela, now queen in her own right, instantly sent for her son, Don Fernando, to Leon ; but, fearing that his father might detain him and set up a claim to reign in her right, she bade her messengers conceal the death of her brother, and only ask for a visit from him. He was eighteen years old, gallant, devout, and winning ; and as soon as he arrived his mother presented him to her Cortes, who raised him on their shields and proclaimed him king. Shortly after, her youngest sister, Leonor, was married to King Jayme of Aragon, but only to raise fresh troubles on account of their relationship ; and Berenguela avoided these entirely for her son by obtaining for him the hand of Beatriz, daughter of the Emperor Philip of Suabia.

Jayme, when a captive in the hands of Simon de Montfort, had—mere baby as he was—made a vow that, when he should be a man and a king, he would endeavour to do something for the redemption of captives. So, before he was a man in age, he instituted another religious order of knighthood, called La Merced, which added to their other duties that of collecting alms and using them for the ransoming of captives to the Moors.

Miserable indeed was the state of the Moors. The young Miramamolin, Yousuf, soon died, and then began a desperate civil war in Morocco among his relations, during which the Spanish walis of Baeza, Murcia, Valencia, and Seville, asserted their independence. The two young kings of Castille and Aragon were not slow to avail themselves of the disunion of their enemies : Fernando, the eldest of the two, was the first. He set forth from Toledo in 1224, accompanied by Don Alvar Perez de Castro, an able captain, who had served among the Moors, and Rodrigo Ximenes de Rada, Archbishop of Toledo, a great scholar, who understood six languages, had been at the great Lateran Council, and became the chronicler of the reign. Baeza was the first place attacked, and the wali, being unsupported, offered to become tributary, gave up his two chief cities, and retired to Cordova. There Al Maimoun—who had succeeded in winning the throne of Morocco—came across the Strait to the defence of Andalusia, and was welcomed by the Cordovans with the head of the recreant wali of Baeza.

Fernando retreated, but Jayme, or *Jacom*, as the Moors called him, was preparing a fleet against the Balearic isles, which had become a nest of Moorish pirates, who preyed on the shipping and harassed the coasts of all the western bay of the Mediterranean. Sancho the Wise, the old King of Navarre, was so delighted with the prowess of young Jayme that he not only greatly assisted him in fitting out his fleet, but adopted him and promised to leave him Navarre, to the exclusion of the rightful heir, his sister's son, Thibault de Blois, Count of Champagne. By another arrangement, the Balearic isles, which were supposed to be a fief of the county of Urgel, were ceded to him, if he could conquer them. Two campaigns gave him first Majorca, and then Minorca and Yvica, while the Almohides retired to add to the confusion in Africa.

The King of Leon on his side besieged and took Merida, and defeated an army of Moors which came to its relief. It was his last campaign. He died the next year, 1230, on his pilgrimage of thanksgiving to the shrine of St. Isidoro, leaving his kingdom to the two daughters of his first marriage. However, his two discarded wives—Berenguela of Castille, and Teresa of Portugal—being both women of wisdom, piety, and public spirit worthy of a better lot than had been theirs, met and agreed that it was for the good of the Christian cause that Castille and Leon should not be separated again, but that Berenguela's son, Fernando, should inherit them both. Nor were they ever again divided.

Fernando was a good and pious man, in many points resembling his cousin St. Louis; and he, too, bore the like title of Saint, being pure in life, just, upright, and single-minded like him; and he was devoted to his wife, Beatriz of Suabia, who died at Toro while he was absent at the siege of Ubeda, in 1233. His heart was almost broken, and he did not take the field for a whole year. He was on the whole, however, a harder and narrower man than Louis; and Spanish intolerance began to set in from this time. The Albigenses, who had taken refuge in his dominions, were hunted down, and, when they were burnt, it was the king himself who laid the first flaming faggot on the pile. The Mozarabic Christians were also discouraged, though they were perfectly orthodox, and the Moors who remained in conquered cities received much less favourable terms.

Much of this was no doubt owing to the influence of the Popes, who made the granting of indulgences for crusades against the Infidels contingent on uniformity. At the Council of Tarragona, in 1230, the Inquisition had been introduced, the reading of the Spanish version of the Scriptures forbidden, and the presence of heretics at church prohibited. Sancho of Navarre died that same year, but the Cortes being unwilling to accept Don Jayme, the crown passed to the Count of Champagne, and from that time Navarre became more connected with French than with Spanish interests.

The Pope, Gregory IX., induced Jayme to marry Violante, daughter of Andrew, King of Hungary, to whom he became fondly attached, and, unfortunately, he took a dislike to his eldest son, Alfonso, who had been sent to Castille with his mother, Leonor. Fernando and Jayme were watching to advance step by step upon the Moors. On the death of Al Maimoun at Morocco, in 1232, confusion had become worse confounded. A new tribe, called Beny Merques, came down from the Atlas, and ruined the Almohides; the connection between Morocco and Andalusia was broken; and, if the Spanish Moors no longer had to dread irruptions of savage Berbers, they also ceased to have any foreign assistance in repelling the Christians.

Again, walis and kadis set themselves up as rulers of their governments, each acting independently, and therefore all those on the border speedily fell before the three powerful Christian monarchs.

The three most really able and worthy of these walis were, at Valencia, Djomayl-ben-Zeyan; at Granada, Aben Houd; and at Jaen, Mouhamed Aben-al-Hamar, and if they had united they might have long kept back the Christians; but they were bitter rivals, always at war with one another, whereas the three Christian kings kept the peace towards one another.

In 1235, just after the summer campaign, when King Fernando had returned to his capital, the governor of the newly-conquered city of Andujar,

Diego Muñoz, learnt that the inhabitants of Cordova reckoned on the inaction of the Spaniards, and were keeping careless watch. He therefore set forth with the bravest men of his garrison, and on a winter's night scaled the walls of the little fortified suburb of Al Scharkya, which was cut off from the rest of the city by the Guadalquivir, and actually made himself master of it, thence gaining the honourable surname of De Cordova, which became the most illustrious in Spain two centuries later. He sent tidings to Alvaro Perez de Castro, general, or *adelantado*, of the army of the frontiers, who hurried to his aid with provisions and reinforcements. Another messenger set out and overtook the king at Benavente. Fernando sent to muster all his troops, and riding off himself with only thirty knights, arrived at the newly-gained suburb and set up his camp.

The inhabitants of Cordova had sent intelligence to the wali, Aben Houd, and he arrived with an army about the same time as Fernando. He could hardly believe that the Christians were actually laying siege to the Moorish capital with such a mere handful of men; and he sent a Castilian deserter, Lorenzo Suarez, who had been banished on account of his crimes, to act as spy, and ascertain the true numbers of Fernando's force; but he proved himself a double traitor, for he went to Fernando, and purchased his pardon by undertaking to advise the Moors to defer the attack, thus giving the Spaniards time to collect their forces from all parts. Meantime, an entreaty came from Valencia for aid against Jayme of Aragon; and Aben Houd, thinking that the attack in that quarter was the most dangerous to his own dominions, set out to relieve it, but was assassinated on his way by an emissary of the wali of Jaen.

The Cordovans, suffering at once from hunger and from mutual dissensions, and with no hope of relief, were forced to surrender, though on terms much harder than the former kings had imposed on the conquered cities. Fernando had no toleration for Islam, and the Moors were expelled ruthlessly from their beautiful city, taking with them no property but what they could carry in their hands. The gloriously beautiful Aljama mosque was purified and consecrated; and the bells of Compostella, which were found reversed among the lamps, where they had been hung by Al Mansour, were taken down and sent home to Santiago on the shoulders of Moorish prisoners. The beautiful Al Zohra palace and the magnificent library of Abd-el-Rhaman were both plundered and destroyed, though how much of the desolation was owing to the Berbers and how much to the Christians is not certain. Fernando, a much better man in morals and in piety than his forefathers, had none of their admiration for Arabian learning and science, and had no mercy where misbelief was concerned. He drove the Moors so entirely out of the surrounding country, that rich as is the soil round the Guadalquivir, there was such a famine that he was forced to send corn to supply the garrison of Cordova.

Jayme of Aragon was determined to have Valencia, and obtained the assistance of the Archbishop of Narbonne, as well as of a number of Crusaders returning from the sixth Crusade. He bound himself by a vow before the altar of Santa Maria de Puch not to return to his home till he was master of Valencia; and in 1236 appeared before the walls of the city, raising a fortress to protect his camp. Aben Zeyen, wali of Valencia, implored for help from Africa, but no one but the wali of Tunis attempted to send him ships or provisions, and these were intercepted by the Catalan fleet. Aben Zeyen offered to capitulate, and Jayme was less hard to deal with than Fernando, and allowed the Valencians either to carry away their goods or to remain with free exercise of their religion, and no heavier burdens than the Christians, while Aben Zeyen was to retire beyond the river Xucar, which was to become the boundary. Thus did Jayme the Conqueror win the city which the Cid had held for a brief time, and whose valleys were so rich and fertile that the Arabs called them the Orchard of the Charms of Spain.

Seven years' truce was granted; but before they were over, in 1239, while Jayme was at Montpellier, his knights had broken the truce, and were foraging the lands across the Xucar. Their master blamed them, but kept the conquests, and followed them up, so that by the end of the seven years, he had seized all the banks of the Xucar. Then he further broke his engagement by expelling all the Moors who had remained at Valencia on the strength of the treaty. He was a high-minded, honourable man in his dealings with Christians, but the whole public opinion of the century was unfortunately against keeping faith towards the Infidel, and toleration was regarded as a sin.

The Moslems took refuge in the provinces of Murcia and Granada; and Aben-el-Hamar, called the Pillar of Islam, who was wali of Jaen, made himself master of Cadiz, Loja, Alhama, and Granada, and was endeavouring to take Murcia. The wali preferred to yield to a Christian rather than to his rival, and offered to pay tribute to the King of Castille, who sent his eldest son, Alfonso, to place garrisons in Murcia and the other dependent cities. Carthagena and Lorca were also taken, and the Spanish troops actually encamped for a few days before Granada; but it was too late in the season to begin the siege, and Fernando retreated.

The next year, however, 1245, Fernando besieged Jaen, and there was much hard fighting round the walls. It was on the point of being taken by assault, when Aben-el-Hamar took the desperate resolution of going alone and unattended into the Castilian camp to speak face to face with Fernando. He was led to the royal tent, where he bent his knee and kissed the king's hand in token of homage. Fernando raised him and treated him with kingly courtesy, and it was agreed that Jaen should receive a Spanish garrison, but that Granada should be secured to Aben-el-Hamar, though only a tributary to Castille. The prince thereof was to have a seat in the Cortes, like the *ricos hombres* or peers of Castille, was to pay a tribute of one hundred and fifty thousand doubloons every year, and to furnish troops to the army of his suzerain.

Seville was under an Almohid wali, Seyd Abou Abd Allah, and therefore was not included in this convention. Thus, in 1247, Ferdinand attacked that province, and Aben-el-Hamar brought five hundred picked lances to serve in the Christian army. With them he surprised the fort of Alcala de Guadaira, where the garrison did not suspect that their national dress and weapons could belong to an enemy. It was a grand fort, crowning a hill above the river, with a mighty wall defended by nine bastions, and with granaries excavated beneath the donjon tower, so that it could have held out for months. The possession of this fortress decided Fernando to besiege Seville itself. He hurried to Biscay to collect ships, and sent them round the coast to the mouth of the Guadalquivir, while he mustered the whole of his forces for the land attack, including all the nobles called *de pendon e caldrera* (of the pennon and the caldron—*i.e.* those who could gather their vassals round their pennon, and feed them from their boiling-pot.) The caldron is a frequent bearing in Spanish heraldry, and is akin to the kettle, which is so often found in northern nomenclature. He further made up all threatened disputes with Aragon by marrying his son Alfonso to Jayme's daughter Violante, and thus concentrated his full strength against the lovely city.

His al emir, or admiral, Don Ramon Bonifaz, forced the mouth of the Guadalquivir, taking or sinking all the Sevillian ships, and thus cutting off all hopes of aid from Africa. On each side of the stream the Castilians established an entrenched camp, where they spent the whole winter, continually reinforced by volunteers from all quarters, even by whole convents of monks, who came to take their share in the victory.

The city of Seville stands on both sides of the river, and the only connection between the two portions was by a bridge of boats. Within, as the old wali could not venture out, the command was given to the wali of Niebla, Abou Djafar, under whom the Mozarabic Christians fought, even as the Granadine Moors were fighting under Fernando. It was a time of chivalrous encounters, as the Christians lay encamped beside the river. Single knights, or small bodies of men, rode forth and broke lances together, and another cycle of ballads has gathered around the siege of Seville. The prime knights of all were the two brothers, Don Garcia and Don Diego Perez de Vargas, the latter of whom was called el Machuca, or the bruiser, because at the siege of Xeres, when his lance and sword were broken, he had defended himself with the trunk of a young tree torn up by the roots. They came from Toledo, and were unrivalled for prowess. Garcia and another knight were riding forth, when they saw a party of Moors. We must let the ballad speak in Lockhart's translation.

King Ferdinand alone did stand one day upon the hill,
Surveying all his league and the ramparts of Seville ;
The sight was grand, when Ferdinand by proud Seville was lying,
O'er tower and tree, far off to see, the Christian banner flying.

Down chanced the king his eye to fling, where for the cause below
Two gentlemen along the glen were riding soft and slow ;
As void of fear each cavalier seem'd to be riding there,
As some strong hound may pace around the roebuck's thicket fair.

It was Don Garcia Perez, and he would breathe the air,
And he had ta'en a knight with him that had as lief be elsewhere ;
For soon this knight to Garcia said : "Ride, ride we, or we're lost !
I see the glance of helm and lance—it is the Moorish host."

The Baron of Vargas turn'd him round, his trusty squire was near,
The helmet on his brow he bound, his gauntlet grasped his spear;
With that upon his saddle-tree he planted him right steady :
"Now come," said he, " whoe'er they be, I trow they'll find us ready."

O

By this the knight who rode with him had turn'd his horse's head,
And up the glen in fearful trim unto the camp had fled.
"He's gone," quoth Garcia Perez. He smiled, and said no more,
But slowly with his esquire rode as he rode before.

It was the Count Lorenzo, just then it happened so,
He took his stand by Ferdinand, and with him gazed below.
"My liege," quoth he, "seven Moors I see ascending from the wood;
Now bring they all the blows they may, I trow they'll find us good;
But it is Garcia Perez, if his cognizance they know,
I guess it will be little pain to give them blow for blow."

The Moors from forth the greenwood came riding one by one,
A gallant troop with armour resplendent in the sun;
Full haughty was their bearing, as o'er the sward they came,
While the calm Lord of Vargas, his march was just the same.

They stood drawn up in order, while past them all rode he,
For when upon his shield they saw the red cross and the tree,
And the wings of the black eagle that o'er his crest was spread,
They knew it was Garcia Perez, and not a word they said.

He took the casque from off his head and gave it to the squire.
"My friend," quoth he, "no need I see why I myself should tire."
But as he doff'd his helmet he saw his scarf was gone;
"I've dropt it, sure," said Garcia, "when I put my helmet on."

He look'd around and saw the scarf, and still the Moors were near;
And they had pick'd it from the sward, and loop'd it on a spear.
"These Moors," quoth Garcia Perez, "uncourteous Moors they be!
Now by my soul the scarf they stole yet durst not question me.

"Now reach once more my helmet." The esquire said him nay:
"For a silken string why should ye fling perchance your life away?

"I had it from my lady," quoth Garcia, "long ago,
And never Moor that scarf, be sure, in proud Seville shall show."

But when the Moslem saw him they stood in firm array;
He rode among their armed throng, he rode right furiously.
"Stand, stand, ye thieves and robbers, lay down my lady's pledge,"
He cried, and even as he cried they felt his falchion's edge.

That day when the Lord of Vargas came to the camp alone,
The scarf, his lady's largess, round his breast was thrown.
Bare was his head, his sword was red, and from his pommel strung
Seven turbans green, sore hack'd I ween, before Garcia Perez hung.

Another story declares that a knight who bore the same coat of arms as Vargas, disputed Garcia's right to it. The next time there was a sally of the Moors this gentleman fled, while Garcia stood and defended the outpost. When next they met he said: "Certes, señor, you show more honour to these bearings than I do; since you have kept yours bright and clean, while mine are all dinted and defaced." Whereat the gentleman was much ashamed.

Don Ramon Bonifaz was anxious to break through the bridge of boats so as to cut off the communication between the two parts of the city; and preparing two ships, he sent them full against the centre, when wind and tide were both favourable, and broke through the chains, scattering burning pots of grease and pitch, which destroyed the boats around. After this the two chief suburbs were taken, and the inhabitants became much straitened for provisions, so that, after a defence of eighteen months, they offered to surrender. Fernando gave them favourable terms, giving those who wished to leave the place means of transport for their property, and promising toleration to those who remained. No less than three hundred thousand persons migrated from Seville to Africa, and the king entered the city in triumphant procession—

> With many a cross-bearer before
> And many a spear behind.

The magnificent mosque was purified and consecrated in the name of our Lady. It did not acquire its name of Giralda till three centuries later, when the revolving figure of Faith became its weathercock. The saying about the Castilian churches was—

> La de Toledo la rica,
> La de Salamanca la fuerte,
> La de Leon la bella,
> La de Sevilla la grande.

Aben-el-Hamar took leave of Fernando and returned to Granada, unwilling to witness the division of Sevillian estates and riches among the Christian knights and clergy. Fernando had now made himself master of both the great capitals of the Moors, and indeed of all the cities dependent on them, except those around Granada. His cousin St. Louis sent him warm congratulations, and relics to consecrate the newly-won mosques. After arranging the affairs of the country he had gained, he was about to pursue his conquests into Africa, and Ramon Bonifaz had just cleared the seas by a great naval victory, when the good king, the saint of his line, died of dropsy, on the 30th of May, 1252. He was a very noble and devout person, a lawgiver and statesman as well as a warrior, never erring save by harshness towards misbelief, which was the flaw in the religion of the age.

Eleanor of Castille, the beloved and excellent wife of Edward I., was the daughter of St. Fernando, and was given to him when a mere child by her brother Alfonso X., the Wise, in 1254, when he received knighthood from the Castilian sword. The charter given at her marriage is still extant in the British Museum, signed by Aben Hamar as a member of Cortes. It is a Spanish chronicler who tells the story of her sucking the poison—another Spanish princess named the holy Sana Sancha, the daughter of Jayme of Aragon, who went thither in disguise and became a nun of the Holy Sepulchre.

The other great conqueror, Jayme el Conquistador, brought troubles on himself in his latter days by endeavouring to make Catalonia a separate kingdom for his favourite son Don Pedro, the child of Violante. His people would not tolerate a fresh division, and rebelled under his eldest son Alfonso, whom he had always disliked, and peace was only restored by his son's death.

His private life was also stained with much of the licence too common in Spain, coupled with much devoutness of a certain kind. Yet he had many kingly qualities, is said never to have been guilty of an act of cruelty, and deserved to belong to an age wonderfully fertile in great sovereigns, producing as it did St. Louis, St. Fernando, Jayme of Aragon, Frederick II., Alexander III. of Scotland, and contemporary, though somewhat later, Edward I., and Rudolf of Hapsburg.

Jayme excelled in all kingly qualities and had few rivals in personal prowess. He was of great height, beautiful in person, inured to hardship, never had an illness, and was vigorous and active to the end of his life. He had taken the cross, intending to join St. Louis and Edward of England in their crusade, and meant to have been at the rendezvous at Carthage, where his Moorish experience might have been of use; but a tempest dispersed his thirty ships, and drove him into a small French port, where he learnt the tidings of the French king's death. He was his own chronicler, and kept up his active life till, in 1376, he was much grieved by a defeat his sons received from the Moors. Falling ill, he resigned his crown to his son Pedro, and assumed the Cistercian habit, made public confession of his sins, and lamented his ill example, and died on the 25th of July, having lived seventy-six years and reigned seventy. No one save Louis XIV. ever had so long a reign, and no one ever so long a period of personal government, since Jayme took the reins into his own hands at twelve years old.

CHAPTER XX.

THE CREAM OF THE WEST.

A NEW era had begun in the fortunes of the Moors. Reft of their two magnificent capitals at Cordova and Seville, they had gathered into the extreme south, under the able and beneficent rule of Aben-al-Hamar, who, though a tributary to Castille, termed himself Sultan and Emir of the Faithful, and is usually called King of Granada.

Karnattah, as the Arabs had named it, meant the Cream of the West. The Spaniards in later times, deceived by the likeness of the word to *Granada*, a pomegranate, fancied it to have been thence named, and took the fruit as its emblem. The kingdom was a mere fragment, and did not even reach to the Straits; for *Algesira*, the green island, and its great fortresses, belonged to the Africans; and it had in it elements of no small danger, containing as it did the remnants of no less than thirty-two Arab and Moorish tribes, many of them at deadly feud with one another, and divided by their never-ending national enmities. The two great tribes of Abencerrages, or sons of Zeragh, and the Zegris, or refugees from Aragon, were destined to become the most famous of these.

The king himself, Mohammed-Abou-Said, was of the old Arabian tribe of Al Hamar, by whose name he is usually called. He was of the best old Arabic type—prudent, just, moderate, temperate, and active, and so upright as to be worthy to belong to this age of great kings, and his plans for his little kingdom were favoured by the peace in which his Christian neighbours left him; while Alfonso X. of Castille was vainly endeavouring to become, not Emperor of Spain alone, but Roman Emperor.

The Almohides of Algarve obeyed neither Alfonso nor Al Hamar, and they united to subdue them. Ten cities were surrendered by the governor on condition that he should enjoy the estates of the King's Garden at Seville, and the tenth of the oil of an oliveyard. There was still a margin of petty walis who preferred a brief independence to a secure tenure of existence as tributaries, and these one by one fell a prey to the Castilians, the inhabitants of their cities being expelled, and adding to the Granadine population.

Al Hamar received them kindly, but made them work vigorously for their maintenance. Every nook of soil was in full cultivation; the mountain-sides terraced with vineyards; new modes of irrigation invented; the breeds of horses and cattle carefully attended to; rewards instituted for the best farmers, shepherds, and artisans. The manufacture of silk and wool was actively carried on, also leather-work and sword-cutlery. Hospitals and homes for the sick and infirm were everywhere; and in the schools of Granada the remnants of the scholarship of Cordova and Seville were collected.

Granada itself stood in the midst of the Vega, around two hills, each crowned by a fortress: Albayzin, so called by the fugitives from Baeza; and the Alhâmra, or Red Fortress. The wall was extended so as to take in its constantly increasing population, and the king began to render the Alhâmra one of the strongest and most beautiful places in existence. Though begun by Al Hamar it was not completed for several generations, each adding to the unrivalled beauty of the interior; for, as usual in Arabian architecture, the outside has no beauty, being a strong fortification of heavy red walls.

The entrance was by a large, square, gateway-tower, which still bears inscriptions showing that here, according to Oriental custom, the king "sat in the gate" to do justice. Beyond it lies a court, with a cloister around it of horseshoe arches on palm-tree columns; the walls are covered with a sort of enamelled plaster, called *azulejo*, with inscriptions in Arabic, some from the Koran, some complimentary to the king. In the middle of the court, surrounded by beds of flowers and walks, between two rows of orange trees, was a long marble basin, filled with running water, for the ablutions of the inferior servants.

Beyond was the exquisite place called the Court of the Lions. It is surrounded by a cloister of one hundred and twenty-eight marble columns, either in threes or twos, wonderfully slender and graceful, the pavement blue and white, the *azulejo* showing a wonderful harmony of scarlet, azure, and gold, in semi-natural patterns, like those on a cashmere shawl, or sentences from the Koran, written so that each letter was an ornament, the spaces between the arches filled with lovely marble filagree. Two beautiful cupolas closed the cloister, and in the centre is an alabaster cup six feet across, supported on the backs of twelve dignified but exceedingly conventional lions. Four centuries of injury and neglect have not utterly destroyed the magic beauty of this wonderful place, though much has been ruined. The halls and saloons were still more gorgeous. The Hall of Music had a fountain in the centre, round which the court sat on carpets, while the performers were in tribunes above them. The seraglio shows how through a perforated marble slab the odours of sweet perfumes came up from the vaults where they burnt beneath, and the arrangement for light and ventilation show a skill that it would be well if modern science could recover. The dados were of richest mosaic, the gates and partitions of the most delicate and graceful brazen lattice-work, the ceilings wondrous efforts of mathematics and carpentry. They are combinations of triangles, in the lesser chambers rising into conical linings to the cupolas, in the larger halls forming stalactites or pendants, all in the most delicate colouring, touched with gold. Some of the chambers had natural subjects on their wall-paintings, hunting ones chiefly, but also figures showing the exploits of their kings. The view from the terraces over the city to the Vega and the snowy-capped mountains is still enchanting; and the gardens, now called the Generalife (a corruption of *Jemma-l'arif*, the gardens of the architect), were also marvels of beauty, with fountains, groves, and flowers, though little is left of their old glory but a few gigantic cypresses and myrtles.

There was also a splendid mosque of the Alhâmra, considered by the Moors a masterpiece, but now vanished. Even in its decay this wonderful palace is like a dream of loveliness, and in its full beauty must have seemed a thing too exquisite for earth. It was as perfect in its way as the Parthenon had been, and like that, it lacked the one thing that Christian art possesses, the suggestion of something higher, the yearning for what is beyond.

As the heavy columns and low-browed vaults of the Aljama of Cordova were of the age of the Byzantine pillar and circular arch, so the delicate horse-shoe arch and palm-tree shaft of the Alhâmra is contemporary with the pointed arch and slender clustered column of the earlier decorated style; but it stopped short with the minaret; it never pointed upwards in the spire.

Mohammed Aben-Al-Hamar died 1273, and his son Mohammed II. followed in his steps. There was an alarm that a new Berber invasion of the Beni Merinys was about to take place, and as this would have been almost as dreadful to the Andalusians as to the Spaniards, Alfonso and Mohammed formed an alliance against it. Mohammed came to Seville, and was lodged in the palace, and splendidly entertained. But when all the Christian kings were gone to the Council of Lyons, the natural inclination of a Moor to his fellow believers, led Mohammed to hope for the recovery of some of the Moorish dominions, and to ally himself with Abou Yousuf, chief of the Beni Merinys and Emir of Morocco, and open to him the ports of Algesiras.

Again there was a great African invasion, and the first battle was fought by Don Nuño Gonzalez de Lara, who was overpowered by numbers, and slain. Mohammed had been on terms of kindly intercourse with him, and when his head was brought in, wept over it, and said: "Alas my friend, thou hast not deserved this from me!" He sent the head embalmed, and in a silver urn, to be buried with the body.

Another army was led by Don Sancho, a son of

Jayme of Aragon, who was titular Archbishop of Granada. He was defeated and made prisoner, and there was a great struggle between the Africans and Andalusians, each of whom wanted to secure him for their own chief, until Aben Nazir, a kinsman of Mohammed, rode up, crying: "Shall true Believers slay one another for an Infidel dog," transfixed the unfortunate prelate with his spear, and cut off his hand. This was the grief that broke the stout heart of his father.

Alfonso X. had hurried home from Lyons to collect his troops, but on the way he was detained by the illness and death of his eldest son, Fernando, called *de la Cerda*, or, of the bristle, because he had been born with a hairy chest. Though only twenty-one, he had been two years married to a daughter of St. Louis, and left two infant sons. In the meantime the Biscayan fleet had come round to the Mediterranean, and the Beni Merinys, not wishing to have their retreat cut off, came to terms with Alfonso, and peace was restored. Three years later, however, Alfonso tried to take Algesiras, which was still held by the African Moors, but was defeated. Though not unjustly called *al Sabio*, or the wise, Alfonso was one of those men whose very talents injure them; and his vacillations as to whether his crown should be left to his infant grandson or to his eldest surviving son, Sancho, led to a great revolt. Alfonso, by beheading his own brother, Don Fadrique, and causing a powerful and popular noble to be burnt alive, alienated almost all his vassals, among them Mohammed of Granada, and after seeking in vain the aid of the Kings of Aragon, Portugal, and France, entreated that of the Emir of Morocco, who was then at Algesiras superintending the rebuilding of the fortifications.

Now there was at Algesiras, a young Castilian knight, Alonso Perez de Guzman, the illegitimate son of Don Pedro de Guzman. The popular word for persons thus born was *de ganancia,* or of gain; and at a tournament a year or two before, when the king had asked who had borne off the prize, the answer had been Don Alonso Perez de Guzman—"Which?" asked the king.

"*Mi hermano de ganancia,*" answered his legitimate half-brother, in a tone that roused the youth's ire; and when the king tried to pacify him, he vowed never to return to Castille till he could be indeed called "hermano de ganancia." Like all disaffected Castilian heroes, he took service with the Moors, though his chronicler declares it was with the proviso that he was never to serve against Castille. In his distress, when no city was left to him but Seville, Alfonso X. resolved to make this young man his intercessor with the emir, and sent him all the crown jewels to offer in pledge, together with a piteous letter dated from "Seville, my only loyal city, in the thirtieth year of my reign, and the first of my troubles."

Yousuf was much affected by the letter. He sent Guzman back at once with six thousand gold doblas, and promises of further aid; and thus Guzman kept his oath of returning when he could truly be called "de ganancia." The king rewarded him with the hand of Doña Maria Coronel, a Sevillian heiress, and set out with him to meet his new ally.

They met at Zara, in the Moorish camp, where Aben Yousuf received the fallen sovereign with lavish tokens of honour, making him ride on horseback into his magnificent pavilion, and placing him in the seat of honour, with the words: "Sit there, thou who hast been a king from thy cradle, while I have only been a king since God made me one."

Alfonso, in the same grand Eastern style, replied: "God gives nobility only to the noble, honour only to the honourable, and kingdoms only to such as deserve them; and thus God gave thee a kingdom for thy deserts."

"Give me an adalid" (a sort of guide or quartermaster), said the Moor, "to lead me to the lands that do not obey thee; I will lay them waste, and bring them back to thine obedience."

Alfonso did so, after having charged his adalid to take him where he could do least harm.

Then a strange war began, in which the Andalusian Moors fought in the cause of the son, and the Africans in the cause of the father. It was ended by both princes falling ill, when Sancho, in terror of death, implored his father's forgiveness; and Alfonso granted it, confirming the choice of the Cortes, which, in accordance with old Gothic custom, gave the kingdom to the most effective member of the royal family. Sancho recovered, but Alfonso died in the year 1281.

Alfonso's wisdom was somewhat of the same type as that of our James I., more erudite than practical; but he had much real ability. He completed the code of laws begun by his father, San Fernando, and had them published, not in Latin but in Castilian, by the name of "Las Partidas de Don Alfonso." Their preface showed that he had the true Spanish faculty of making proverbs, such as—"The tyrant uproots the tree, when the wise king prunes it." He also wrote the history of his time, and was an intense admirer of the Cid, whose monument he built at San Pedro de Saldanha.

He was also a great astronomer, profiting, of course, by the labours of the Arabs, but giving much attention to the drawing up of tables of calculations of the courses of the heavenly bodies, and he was no mean proficient in mathematics. A translation of a scientific treatise of his from Arabic into Spanish is extant; and his mind was so convinced of the awkwardness of the Ptolemaic solar system that he shocked the pious by saying, that if he had been present at the making of the universe, he could have given the Creator some good advice.

In chemistry and medicine he was also skilful; his works still remain, and the vulgar believed that he had been a Frankenstein, and had actually constructed and animated a human creature. Of course, his astronomy connected itself with astrology, and his chemistry with alchemy, and there still remains a Book of the Treasure, namely the recipe for the Grand Arcanum, the philosophers' stone, which he learnt from an Egyptian sage, and recorded in thirty-five octavos of cyphers, which no one has ever been able to read.

Two more books of his are preserved at Toledo; the words and music of a set of hymns to the Blessed Virgin, and the Libro de Querelas, or laments, after his son had rebelled. They are dignified and pathetic, worthy of a king who could do everything—except reign. He also caused the Scriptures to be translated, and was enlightened enough to avail himself of the aid of learned Jews in elucidating the text.

Guzman followed Yousuf into Africa, and there remained till Sancho IV. invited him to return in 1291; and soon after, a naval victory over the Berbers encouraged Sancho to lay siege to Tarifa, one of the most important seaports, and one which was often a landing-place of the Moors from Africa. It was taken by assault after six months; but it was so exposed, and so far from succour, that it was thought to be impossible to keep it. However, the Grand Master of Calatrava undertook to defend it for a year, and after that Don Alonso Guzman took up the defence, carried his family thither, repaired the walls, filled the stores, and established himself there as Alcayde.

The only one of his family who had been left behind was the eldest son, whom the king's brother, Don Juan, had undertaken to carry to Portugal, there to become one of the king's pages. But Don Juan, a turbulent, worthless prince, quarrelled with his brother, went to Tangier, and offered his services to the King of Morocco, taking young Guzman with him. An attempt on Spain was at once to be made, beginning with Tarifa, and Guzman had been so much connected with the Moors, and so often at enmity with the king, that great hopes were entertained of buying him over. But he was one of those men whose personal word was inviolable, and to all their offers, he replied, that " Good knights neither buy nor sell victory." Then Don Juan thought of another expedient, which he is said to have employed once before with success. He led his charge, a boy of ten, before the walls, and called out to the father that he should be slain unless Tarifa were instantly surrendered.

Guzman stood on the walls white and resolute. "I

did not beget this son," said he, "to be my country's foe. I gave a son to my country to withstand its enemies. If Don Juan slays him, he will give to me honour, to my son true life, and to himself eternal infamy in this world, and condemnation after death. And to show how far I am from yielding the place, and failing in my duty, there goes my knife, in case he needs a weapon for his cruelty."

So saying, Guzman left the walls and sat down to table with his wife, commanding his countenance so that she should guess nothing. Presently there was a great shouting of horror and dismay. He rose, but presently came back saying: "I thought the Moors were in Tarifa." But he had seen the bloody head of his firstborn. The Moors were however horrified, and likewise hopeless of overcoming such a man. They raised the siege, and all Spain rang with praise of the loyalty of Guzman, who has been ever since known as *el Bueno*, or the good. He was the founder of a noble family from whom sprang the Dukes of Medina-Sidonia. His constancy was sung in ballads, and he became one of the great examples of Spanish loyalty.

CHAPTER XXI.

THE BATTLE OF SALADO.

SANCHO THE BRAVE died in 1295, leaving the regency to his widow, Maria de Molino, since his eldest son, Fernando IV., was a young child. She was the only queen-regent who ever obtained the title of Great, and she had a hard task, for the Infants de la Cerda, now grown to man's estate, put forward their claim, and the wretched Don Juan gave her much trouble ; but she met all perplexities with manlike wisdom and courage. She does not seem, however, to have been equally successful in educating her children, for her son grew up weak, violent, and distrustful of her.

Meantime Aragon was fully engaged. Pedro III. had married the daughter of Manfred of Sicily, and it was to him that the glove was carried which Conradin threw down among the people as an appeal to the justice of his cause, when he, the last of the Hohenstanfen, was perishing by the axe of Charles of Anjou. Pedro bided his time till the brutality of the Provençals had occasioned the revengeful massacre known as the Sicilian Vespers, and then accepted the invitation of the Sicilians to become their defender. The great Jayme had diligently fostered the navy at Barcelona and Valencia, and under Don Roger de Lauria, the greatest man of his time, Sicily was gained, and Aragon became a great maritime power.

Juana I., heiress of Navarre, had married Philippe IV. of France. For two generations the kingdoms were divided, and as Navarre had long ceased to have any Moorish border, it wholly ceased from concerning itself in these wars. Portugal had likewise long ago made up its frontier, and the Moors of Granada were left at peace both by their Spanish neighbours and the Africans. In 1298, Mohammed III. was able to purchase Algesiras from the Emir of Morocco, and thus reigned over the whole country to the south of the Sierra de Comares, between Carthagena and Almeria. He was said to have been the handsomest man then in existence, until he injured his eyesight by studying through the greater part of the nights, and became too blind to carry on the government at any critical moment.

When young Fernando IV. of Castille came of age, he called on Jayme II. of Aragon to unite with him in a grand attack on the Moors. Jayme besieged Almeria, and Fernando attacked at the same time Algesiras and Gibraltar. The importance of the latter place depending on the use of cannon commanding the Straits, it had not then been so fortified but that Fernando was able to take it by surprise, and according to the Castilian fashion, expelled all the inhabitants. One poor old man, who had been driven from his home twice before, stood lamenting in the streets before the young conqueror. "Woe is me! I am banished again in my old age. Thy great-grandfather Fernando drove me out of Seville, and I fled to Xeres. Thy grandfather Alfonso banished me from thence even to Tarifa. Thither came thy father Sancho, and with my people I fled from him hither as to a place of distant refuge; but thou hast found me out, and in the latter days of my life, where must I again seek a home?" "Cross the sea," was all the king answered.

Fernando was pressing on the siege of Algesiras, when his brother, the Infant Don Juan, on some offence left the camp, carrying off a number of nobles, and so weakening the army that Fernando consented to accept a large sum of money from Mohammed for the ransom of the town. This mode of saving the city was viewed by the Granadine chiefs as a disgrace, and rising against their blind king, they dethroned him in favour of his brother Al Nassir, who had just forced Jayme of Aragon to raise the siege of Almeria. The Moorish revolutions were seldom bloody, and Mohammed was allowed to retire to one of the lovely palaces on the slopes of the Nevada, where he used to wander about the gardens with poets and scholars, listening to their compositions or reciting his own, until, venturing to cross the gardens without a guide, he fell into one of the marble basins of water, and was drowned.

Those sworn foes of Islam, the Knights Templars, were at this time under the cruel persecution of Philippe IV. of France, and his miserable tool, Pope Clement V. In 1311, the peninsular sovereigns received the papal mandate, commanding that the Templars should be arrested, their property confiscated, and their persons tortured, to make them confess the horrible crimes laid to their charge. The Spaniards were by no means inclined to carry out this dreadful decree. The Templars were their fellow-soldiers and brave champions, and many were of the noblest families in the Peninsula. Besides, the Cortes of Aragon had declared torture to be unworthy of any Christian country; and so, though in obedience to the Pope, a council was held at Tarragona, to which the knights were cited, none of them were put to the rack. A few of the more fierce and lawless members of the order were put to death to save appearances, but the others were allowed to enjoy their estates till they died out, when the property was divided between the crown and the local military orders. In Portugal, Dom Diniz formed the knights into a new Order, which he called that of Christ.

It is well known that when in 1314, three years after the murder of the great body of the Templars, their Grand-Master, Jaques de Molay, was led out to execution, he appealed to the tribunal of Heaven, and summoned both Pope and King to meet him there, and that both died at the very time he mentioned. Two years previously such an awful summons had been made to Fernando of Castille, and he had obeyed it.

One of his favourite nobles had been assassinated while leaving his chamber at Palencia, and the suspicion of the guilt had fallen on two brothers named Carvarel. They had, however, joined the army with which the Infant Don Pedro, brother to the king, was besieging the Moorish town of Alcandera, and there Fernando found them. Enraged at their insolence, he commanded that they should be hurled from the top of a precipice; and though they protested their innocence, and demanded a fair trial, the cruel sentence was carried out. Their last words were a summons to Fernando to meet them within thirty days before the Judgment-seat. He treated it lightly at first, but when after a few days he fell ill of a fever, his spirits gave way; and though he was revived by the surrender of the town, and an offer of peace from the Moors, he died on the thirtieth day from the summons, when his attendants had left him asleep on his couch, on the 17th of September, 1312. The Spaniards distinguish him as Don Fernando el Emplazado, or the summoned. He was only twenty-eight years old, and his son Alfonso XI. was but two; and after a few struggles the old queen, Maria the Great, resumed the government of Castille.

The Granadine Moors were a turbulent race, always dangerous to their sovereign; and when Al Nassir's vizier was too despotic to please them, they demanded his dismissal. When the king refused, his sister's son, Ismael Ben Farady, headed a revolt and besieged him in the Alhâmra. He sent to ask aid from Castille, and Don Pedro set forth to his assistance, but came too late, for he had already been forced to surrender, and had resigned his throne and retired to Cadiz. Thenceforth there was a divided interest between the lines of Al Hamar and Farady.

Pedro continued his friend, and sent him a present of provisions with so large an escort, that Ismael's suspicions being aroused, he sent troops to intercept it. They were beaten off with severe loss, and Pedro continued to make forays on the Moorish dominions, surprising and taking many lesser forts, and at last, with his brother Juan, appearing beneath the very walls of the Alhâmra. The spirit of the Moors was aroused; Ismael reproached them with their supineness which had allowed the Christians to make so much progress, and led them out to battle. It was on St. John's Day, 1319, that the great combat took place in the Vega of Granada, in which the Castilians were routed, with the loss of both their Infants, though, by the Spanish account, neither died by a Moorish scimitar; but when Don Juan sent to his brother for reinforcements, Pedro, after trying in vain to make his horsemen move, was so enraged at his failure and exhausted by his efforts that he dropped dead from his horse; and the tidings, being carried to Juan, had an equally fatal effect upon him. Be that as it may, the corpses of the two brothers were found on the battle-field, and the Castilians were forced to ask a truce of three years.

At the end of that time Ismael became the invader, and attacked Baeza, with what his Arab chronicler calls "engines which projected globes of fire, with great explosions, in all respects like the thunder and lightning of the tempest." The powder was brought from Damascus. The like engines were used many years later by Edward III. at Crecy. They however failed to take Baeza, and Ismael went on to attack Martos, where he was more successful. In the partition of the spoil, one of his kinsmen obtained a beautiful maiden, but not until she had been seen by the king, who caused her to be carried to his harem. She proved a very Briseis, for her disappointed master revenged himself by poniarding the king in the midst of the rejoicing for his victory; and the crown fell to a young child, Mohammed IV.

At fifteen this young king made his first campaign by attacking Baeza. In a combat before the walls, he pierced a Spaniard with his lance, the handle of which was set with gold and precious stones; but he could not withdraw the weapon, and the man rode off with it sticking in the wound. "Hold back!" cried the king to the attendants, who would have given chase to recover the lance; "we will leave him the means of paying for his cure."

Baeza was taken, and likewise Gibraltar; but the Beni Merinys were again casting jealous eyes on Spain; and the Emir of Fez, Aboul Hacem, claimed the rock and put in a garrison. In 1330 the Castilians besieged it by land and sea, until Mohammed brought relief to the Beni Merinys, and drove the Christians back. Proud of his prowess, the young king boasted that the Castilians had been courteous to their countrymen of Granada, coming to break a lance with them and to leave them the honours of the field. His wit affronted the savage Africans, and they murdered him as he was riding up the face of the hill to visit Aboul Hacem.

That emir resumed Algesiras, and treated Yousuf Aboul Hedjaz, the new king of Granada, as his vassal. In an inroad upon the Christian territory, a favourite son of the emir was killed, and his fall brought upon Spain a tremendous invasion. In 1310 Aboul Hacem, swearing vengeance, collected an enormous host from the wild tribes of Fez and Morocco, and transported them across the strait in two hundred vessels, which plied between Gibraltar and Ceuta, bringing not only the warriors but their wives and families, since the emir intended not conquest merely but settlement.

The alarm of the Christians was great. A crusade was proclaimed, and the three kings of Castille, Aragon, and Portugal mustered their forces, and were joined by many of the clergy, with the Archbishops of Toledo and Compostella at their head, as well as by all the knights of the military orders, and likewise by a little band of Scots under the good Lord James of Douglas, on their way to lay the heart of Robert Bruce in the Holy Sepulchre. As there was no fighting to be had at Jerusalem, and they had learnt, on putting in at Lisbon, that so grand an opportunity of striking a blow at the Infidel was to be had, they thought that to join in the combat was an excellent mode of fulfilling their vow.

Pedro IV. of Aragon, remained in reserve, but the two Alfonsos—the Eleventh of Castille, and the Fourth of Portugal—united their forces and marched to relieve Don Juan Alonso de Benavides, who had for five months been holding out Tarifa with constancy worthy of Guzman el Bueno himself, and detaining the enemy before the walls, in spite of the cannon of the Moors brought from Damascus, and of the loss of many of the Castilian ships, which had been taken by the Africans, while endeavouring to bring him provisions.

The city is on a rocky islet, between which and the mainland flows the river, called El Salado, from its brackish waters. On the farther side were encamped the Moorish host; and on the 29th of October, 1340, the two Christian kings endeavoured to force their passage to the beleaguered city. The ford was defended by the troops of Granada, who fought so bravely that the Castilians were driven back; and James of Douglas, thinking all was lost, took from his breast the case containing the heart of Bruce, and crying "Go first, as was thy wont," flung it into the thickest of the foe, dashed after it, and fell, lying over it, so as to cover it with his body.

Meantime two brothers, Garcias and Gonzalo

Leisso, had found a little bridge, by which they led another division of the army across the river, and attacked Aboul Hacem and the Beni Merinys. While they were engaged, Don Alonso de Benavides saw his opportunity, made a sally from the town, and fell on the unguarded camp. This decided the fortune of the day. The Africans turned headlong from the fight to protect their camp, but were not in time to save the harem of their emir. Their confusion broke up the resistance of the Granadine Moors, and the rout became total. Spanish historians reckon their slain enemies at two hundred thousand, and only twenty on their own side. The first number is probably mere hyperbole; the second, no doubt, means twenty gentlemen, and these being sheathed in armour, were not very pervious to Moorish weapons; while the Berbers were lightly clad, and closely massed together, so that those who could not gain their ships, were penned in like sheep for the slaughter. Still the number is probably much exaggerated. James Douglas was found among the few of the Christians who fell, and his companions had no spirits to pursue their pilgrimage, but carried the heart back to Scotland.

Aboul Hacem reached Gibraltar, and took ship for Africa that same night. Yousuf fled to Algesiras, with the victors following close on his heels to lay siege to the city. The king escaped by sea, and the Alfonsos, finding that the place was too strong to be taken by an immediate assault, returned to Seville. The rejoicing was ecstatic; processions of all the dignitaries—ecclesiastical and secular—came forth with banners displayed, the streets were hung with tapestry and illuminated at night, and the two kings were greeted as defenders of the Faith and preservers of their country. Of all the spoil, Alfonso of Portugal would accept nothing but some Moorish trappings, swords and spurs, with which trophies he returned home; while Alfonso XI. sent an embassy to Avignon to present the Pope with the horse he had ridden in the battle, the standard of the emir, twenty-four Moorish banners, and a hundred richly-caparisoned steeds, each with a helmet and shield hung from the saddle-bow. All the cardinals came out in procession to meet the ambassador, and the Pope himself sang the mass of thanksgiving.

The Christians might well rejoice, for so important a battle had not been gained since Navas de Tolosa. Alfonso was resolved to profit by his success to endeavour to cut the Granadine Moors off from reinforcements from Barbary. He summoned the Cortes to ask for supplies, and their enthusiasm was such that they granted him a larger amount than he chose to accept, saying that he only took as much as was required for his necessities and left the rest for them. The money was raised by an impost called the *alcavala*, on every article of food consumed in the kingdom. His first attack was on Alcala de Benazyde; and Gil de Boccanegra, brother to the Doge of Genoa, brought a large fleet to his assistance, and kept watch in the Straits to hinder succour from being sent from Morocco. Yousuf attempted to relieve the city, but failed, and it surrendered on honourable terms. Several other successes were gained, and Yousuf began to sue for peace, but Alfonso made it a condition that he should again become a vassal to the crown of Castille, and renounce his alliance with the Emir of Morocco; and to this he would not consent.

Aboul Hacem was preparing another armament to come to his relief, but Gil de Boccanegra totally defeated the whole Berber fleet, and destroyed twelve galleys in his very port. All Europe was beginning to take an interest in the Moorish war, and as the wars around the Holy Sepulchre had ceased, many knights satisfied their desire for a crusade by coming to the support of the Spanish Christians. These warriors carried their swords to the assistance of Alfonso, among them Henry, called Wryneck, Earl of Derby, of the English blood-royal, and William Montague, Earl of Salisbury, husband of the fair Katharine, the supposed heroine of the Garter. Froissart mentions the siege of Algesiras, or, as he terms it, "the strong town of Africa;" and in one of his illuminations, cannon are represented as firing at the walls. They are wonderful things, constructed of bars of iron, with a large ball coming out of each of their mouths in the midst of a great star of flames.

Alfonso had a great entrenched camp, almost another city, blockading the place, while the King of Granada hovered about endeavouring to bring it relief; and the emir also was striving to collect forces, but was hindered by the rebellion of one of his sons. Alfonso found his means run short, and sent orders that all his plate should be melted down and coined. This so moved his subjects that the large cities at once subscribed a great sum to prevent it, and he also received aid in money from the Pope and Philippe VI. of France; and Philippe Count of Evreux, the husband of Juana II., Queen of Navarre, joined the army with a body of her subjects.

Chains and booms were thrown across the harbour,

but still the place held out. The foreigners were wearied out, and the Genoese threatened to go home if the siege were not soon ended. At last it was discovered that on dark nights, about once a month, a clever Moorish seaman was wont to conduct into the harbour fifty small boats laden with provisions, and had thus enabled the place to hold out for a whole year. On this the king closed the harbour more completely, and the fleets of Aragon and Portugal came up and cut off all hope of succour by sea. But the winter rains had brought disease into the besieging camp, and the Counts of Foix and Evreux both died, so that Alfonso was the more willing to listen when Yousuf, by order of Aboul Hacem, offered to yield the place on condition of all the inhabitants being allowed to march with their property.

A truce for ten years was granted, and Alfonso returned to Seville in triumph, when the first thing he did was to send all the ladies of the emir's harem, whom he had taken at Salado, back to Fez, splendidly equipped with robes and jewels, an act of courtesy which Aboul Hacem requited with magnificent gifts.

Yousuf spent the interval of peace in further decorating his beautiful city of Granada, and furthering all arts and sciences, as well as in arranging the government on the system which continued to the end of the Moorish rule in Granada. Mechanics throve as much as ever, and the great astronomer, Abu Abdallah Ben Aracam, made curious clocks, and drew up astronomical tables, while experiments were made on the polarity of the magnet, and the use of the mariner's compass established.

Before the truce was over there was a great civil

war in Morocco, between Aboul Hacem and one of his sons; and Alfonso XI. thought this the fit opportunity for making himself master of Gibraltar. It was an unfortunate moment for assembling an army, for it was in 1350, the year of the pestilence called the Black Death, which raged all over Europe. The young Queen of Aragon died of it, also Joan, daughter to the English Edward III., on her way to marry Pedro, the son of Alfonso; and in Tarragona the deaths were said to be at the rate of a hundred a day. When Alfonso had been a whole year engaged in the blockade, and had almost starved out the garrison, the deadly scourge appeared in his camp, and he was strongly advised to break up his army. "No," he said; "Gibraltar had been lost in his nonage, and he was bound to recover it; besides, the pestilence could strike him in the court as well as in the camp."

It did seize him in the camp, and he died on Good Friday, March 26th, 1350. He had been a gallant soldier, and his generous enemies put on tokens of mourning, and abstained from all hostilities while the mournful plague-struck army broke up and escorted the corpse of their king to its burial-place at Cordova. Alfonso el Justiciero, or *el Cortese*, was only thirty-eight years old, and had been one of the ablest and most upright, as well as the bravest of Castilian kings, stained only by one defect—that licence of morals so frequent in Spain. When a mere lad of seventeen he had first loved the beautiful Doña Leonor de Guzman, of the same family as the great Guzman el Bueno. Though only a year older than himself she was already a widow; and though the policy of his grandmother had decreed that he must marry the Infanta Maria of

Portugal, he never gave her his heart. When for three years she remained childless, he had almost made up his mind to plead his kinship with her and obtain a divorce, but was dissuaded by Leonor herself. Even when two sons were at last born to the queen, the other lady remained far more truly the head of the court, and the prime source of influence. She even established a sort of order of merit, marked by a red ribbon, whence its members were called Caballeros de la Banda. It was for the promotion of courtesy, for it seems that the habits of the Castilians were still rough and rude; and the ceremonious Arabs declared that they were brave men, but they had no manners, and entered each other's houses freely without asking permission.

In twenty years Leonor had borne ten children; but after the battle of Salado, though her charms were unimpaired, Alfonso was induced to repent, and to part with her forever. He gave her the strong city of Medina-Sidonia, and endowed her children richly. Of the two eldest, one had died, and the other was imbecile; but the twins, Enrique and Fadrique, who were nearly of the same age as his only surviving legitimate son Pedro, were endowed, as mere boys, with the county of Trastamara and the Grand-Mastership of Santiago, and provision was made for all, so as much to impoverish the royal patrimony.

Alfonso's Warden of the Marches deserves mention. He was Don Juan Manuel, the grandson of St. Fernando, and husband to a daughter of one of the Infants of La Cerda. Though for twenty years he was fighting with the Moors, he was able to find time to make a considerable collection of stories and apothegms, which he put together in a book called "Count Lucanor," in which that nobleman is supposed to ask advice of his friend Patronio in all emergencies, and to receive it couched in the truly Eastern form of proverb or anecdote. Here is a specimen :

> Quien te alabare con lo que non has in ti,
> Sabe que quiere relever lo que has de ti.

> He who praises thee for what thou hast not,
> Wishes to take from thee what thou hast.

"There was a Moorish king at Cordova called Al Hakem, who thought his kingdom prosperous enough, and cared not to do anything honourable or famous, as kings ought to do; for kings are not only bound to guard their realms, but to do some great deed, for which they are made famous in their lives and after their deaths. But this king cared only to eat, drink, and sport, until one day he heard a man playing an instrument called *albogon*, which is much esteemed by the Moors. The sound was not good, so the king took the *albogon* and made another hole in it opposite to the other, so that the sound came out better. It was a good invention, but not worthy of a king. The people commended in scorn, and used to call any slight improvement '*Vahedezes Alhakime*,' meaning Al Hakem's invention. The king heard of it, and was grieved. As he was a good king, he did not punish those who spoke thus, but he resolved to do something which should win worthy praise from them. The Mosque of Cordova was not finished, and he caused it to be completed; so that it was the most beautiful and noble mosque that the Moors had in Spain. Praise be to God that it is now a church, and called Santa Maria de Cordova, for it was offered by the holy King Don Fernando to St. Mary when he won Cordova from the Moors. And when this was done, the proverb was altered; and when an addition is made which is better than the thing itself was before, the Moors call it 'Al Hakem's' addition."

CHAPTER XXII.

THE AGE OF TYRANTS.

THE unfortunate Peninsula was afflicted in the middle of the fourteenth century with a combination of the worst set of kings who ever reigned at one time.

With Pedro el Cerimonioso of Aragon, a fierce but upright man, this history has little concern, and still less with Charles the Bad of Navarre, whose wickedness was chiefly displayed in France. Over the strange wild romance of Iñes de Castro, which seared the heart and crazed the intellect of her husband, Pedro the Severe of Portugal, we must also pass; but the stories of Pedro the Cruel of Castille, and of Ismael of Granada, must be dwelt upon.

Maria of Portugal had bred up her son in the bitterest hatred to her rival, and in schemes of vengeance to be carried out as soon as the power should be in his hands. His father's death, when only thirty-nine, placed him on the throne at sixteen, and at once the mother and son took their measures. Leonor was invited to Seville to attend to the interests of her children. Two noblemen pledged their honour for her safety; but she had scarcely entered Seville before she was made a prisoner, and her son Enrique received timely notice that he was to be arrested, and fled into the Asturias.

The unfortunate Leonor was dragged about after the court to Burgos, and then sent to Talavera, still called *de la Reyna*, because it was an appanage of the queen-dowager, by one of whose servants she was strangled.

There Maria would have rested. She had no ill-will to the sons of her husband, and she instructed her son to treat them as brothers; but she did not know what a tiger she had nurtured on plans of revenge. He was fair and handsome, and (like Tiberius), had a profusion of beautiful flaxen hair; but after this taste of blood his savage cruelty soon became utterly unbridled.

Pedro's first love was his cousin Juana, the daughter of Don Juan Manuel, the author of "Count Lucanor;" but the maiden, who was good, wise, and fair, already knew enough of him to fear him, and was besides in love with his half-brother Enrique, Count of Trastamara. In secret the young pair were married; but Juana was instantly thrown into prison, while her bridegroom made the best of his way to Portugal.

Most likely the queen-mother and her father were glad of this marriage, for they made Pedro recall Enrique, and arranged for him a marriage with Blanche, daughter of the Duke of Bourbon, and sister to Jeanne, wife to Charles, the heir of France. But while Blanche was being fetched from her home by his brother, the Master of Santiago, Pedro fell in love with a bright-eyed dark girl, Doña Maria de Padilla, one of the well-born damsels who attended on Doña Isabel de Albuquerque. So passionate was his admiration that he was by some held to be bewitched, and he could hardly be persuaded to leave her to go to Valladolid, where his ill-starred wedding with Blanche took place with great pomp. The two other brothers, Enrique and Tello, walked on either side of the bride's palfrey, and figured in the ensuing tournament; but Fadrique was absent, and it seems that Pedro, being resolved to get rid of his unhappy wife, had fixed on him the imputation of acting like Sir Tristrem towards Yseulte, and having gained her affections on the road.

Popular fancy declared that poor Blanche had obtained from a Jewish sorcerer a belt, which she was told would bind the love of the wearer to her, but that this wizard had been bribed by Maria de Padilla, and as soon as the king put it on it became a serpent, and that his hatred to Blanche was thus caused by terror. There were, however, numerous legends and ballads about the tragedy of the poor lady's history; and all that is certain is that a few days after his marriage he rode back to Montalvao, where Maria was, and left Blanche alone. Don Alfonso of Albuquerque, who had first made the lady known to Pedro, tried to take her away; but this roused the king's savage temper, and a secret warning from the Padilla herself to her former lord and his friends just enabled them to escape death by flying into Portugal.

This seems to have caused a quarrel with her royal lover, who returned to his wife at Valladolid; but after two days quitted her, declaring that nothing should ever induce him to see her again. He had taken a fresh passion for Doña Juana de Castro, who was foolish enough to let the marriage ceremony pass between them on his oath, before two bishops, that he had made a secret protest against Blanche, and that the wedding was therefore invalid. However, he left

Juana the next day, and never came near her again, though he gave her the city of Dueñas, and let her call herself Queen for the rest of her life.

He then returned to Maria de Padilla, who seems to have been nothing but a helpless frightened being, fluttering in the hands of the savage who had fastened his brutal affections on her. He afterwards declared he had married her before his wedding with Blanche; but this was probably to legitimatise her children, for no one could believe his word. Meanwhile, Blanche was sent as a sort of prisoner to the Alcazar of Toledo; but on the way she asked leave of her escort to pay her devotions in the cathedral, and when there, she claimed the privilege of sanctuary, and refused to leave it with her guards.

The clergy would not give her up; the ladies flocked round her and brought their husbands. The old mosque with its heavy arches and large columns was a wonderful scene, as the young French queen, not yet twenty, stood on a step, telling them of her cruel wrongs and imploring succour, while ladies wept for her under their black veils, and men's swords flashed, and oaths were taken to uphold her cause. She was taken to the Alcazar in triumph, and there soon hastened to her Don Alfonso of Albuquerque, and the twin-brothers; Fadrique, bringing seven hundred knights of his order to her aid, and swearing to devote his sword to her. After rifling the treasury, they all repaired to Medina del Campo, and sent their terms to the king—namely, that he should take back his wife and dismiss Maria de Padilla and her relations. He made no answer; but his mother and half the kingdom joined them, so that he was forced at last to put himself into their hands.

For four years he was kept somewhat as the barons kept the English Henry III. and his son, and was never allowed to take the air without a guard of a thousand men; but at last, when out hawking, he took advantage of a heavy fog to elude his guard and ride off to Segovia. There he sent to his mother for the great seal, declaring that if she refused it, he had metal to cast another. She sent it; and the nobles being all scattered to their estates, he was able to deal with them separately. Terrible executions took place, and the whole country was in a state of deadly terror. The queen-mother, with Enrique and Fadrique, tried to hold out Toro against him, but finding it impossible, and distrusting the citizens, Enrique retired into Galicia, and Fadrique threw himself on Pedro's mercy, coming forth to him with a few attendants, while the citizens delivered up the place, the queen-dowager taking refuge in the Alcazar with Enrique's wife.

Her son summoned her to come forth, and when she endeavoured to stipulate for the lives of the gentlemen who were with her, he replied that come out she must, and he would do what seemed best to him. She came down, endeavouring to protect them by walking between two, leaning on their arms; but no sooner were they in the court than Pedro made a sign to his ballestero men, who immediately fell upon them, and despatched them with their clubs, so that their blood was spattered on the queen's dress, and she fainted away. Indeed, one was reported to be her lover; and she was held in very low estimation. On her recovery, she uttered frightful curses against her son, of which he took no notice, except to order her to be removed.

She soon repaired to Portugal, where her life was so disgraceful that her father, Pedro the Severe, caused her to be privately put to death. Yet Pedro had spared his brother Fadrique, and another younger one who was in the city; but every year was adding to his ferocity, and his cruelties were terrible.

In Toledo he commanded the massacre of all the Jews, but finding it dangerous to proceed, stopped it after one thousand had perished—ordering, however, the execution of several knights and twenty-two citizens for having favoured the rebellion. One was an old goldsmith of eighty. His son of eighteen offered to die in his stead, and was accordingly led out to execution, amid the tears and sobs of all the people.

The next brother, Don Tello, had married the heiress of Biscay, and to him the Count of Trastamara had fled, trusting to the mountains for defence; but finding himself in danger there, he escaped to France, where he served in the army of Du Guesclin against the English, until, a war breaking out between Aragon and Castille, he accepted the invitation of the king of the former country to join him. He was anxious about his wife, Doña Juana Manuel, who had been in prison almost ever since their hasty secret marriage. No one could tell what Pedro might do if further provoked; and one of his friends, Pedro Carillo, undertook to bring her to him. Going to the king, he promised to bring his brother to him, dead or alive, if he might have the command of a troop of horse. With this troop he entered Toro, and obtaining access to the imprisoned countess, disguised her, and took her safely with him to her husband in Aragon. The successes of the Castilians, however, alarmed Enrique into the fear that he might be given up on the making of peace, and he fled with his wife to his old friends in France.

On this Pedro grew more violent against his unfortunate family. He invited the Master of Santiago to keep Easter at Seville with him, and Fadrique arrived with many of his knights, who kissed the king's hand. The king received him affectionately, and asked if he had met with good inns; to which the Master answered that he had only come from Cantilena, five leagues off, and did not know if the inns were good. The king gave orders that his suite and mules should be lodged in the inns, and that he alone should be in the Alcazar, and he then went to visit Doña Maria de Padilla and her little children. She looked very unhappy, knowing what was intended, but not daring to warn him. On going into the court, he found that all the mules had been sent away, and this alarmed one of the few knights who were still with him, who advised him to escape at once by an open gate; but at that moment he was told the king was calling him, and entered the dining-hall, followed by the Master of Calatrava and four knights. There stood the king with his ballesteros, or body-guard of club-men, of whom Pedro Lopez de Padilla, Maria's brother, was the leader.

"Pedro Lopez, take the Master."

"Which?" said Padilla.

"The Master of Santiago," said the king.

"Be taken," said Padilla, laying his hand on the Grand-Master.

"Ballesteros, kill the Master!" then cried the tyrant; and as they hung back, one of the chamberlains cried out: "Traitors! do you not hear? The king bids you kill the Master."

But as they advanced with their maces, Fadrique

broke from Pedro Lopez, and rushing out into the court, tried to draw his sword; but the handle was so entangled in his tabard that he could not succeed, so he could only run from one end of the court to another, trying to escape by the closed doors, till the ballesteros came up with him, knocked him down with a blow on the head, and despatched him. His attendants were also pursued and slain, though one of them ran into the very apartment of Doña Maria, and catching up her little daughter Beatriz, held her up before him; but the king snatched the child away, and struck him with a dagger before his ruffians came up.

Other murders ensued, and Pedro then set forth for Biscay; but Tello, getting timely warning, embarked at Bermeo. Pedro, following close upon him, pursued; but the sea was rough and the king was forced to land, while his brother safely reached Bayonne, and he could only murder the wife, who had been left behind.

There is a ballad on Fadrique's death, describing Maria de Padilla as looking on with fiendish delight, and throwing his head to the dogs; but this was only from the spirit of popular execration. The poor woman was most miserable, and died that very year, 1359, of a broken heart, leaving four young children—a son, who died shortly after; Beatriz, who took the veil; Constanza, and Maria. It was the very year of poor Blanche's death, in her prison at Medina-Sidonia, though whether she died by Pedro's cruelty is uncertain. A touching ballad, which of course makes her die by the hand of a ballestero, makes her say:

"The crown they put upon my head was a crown of blood and sighs.
God grant me soon another crown, more precious, in the skies!"

Granada was not much better off. Yousuf had been murdered while praying in the mosque, in 1350; his eldest son, Mohammed V., was dethroned by another brother, Ismael, and escaped with difficulty in the disguise of a slave of the harem. Ismael, in his turn, was dethroned by Abou Sayd, one of the other race—that of Al Hamar—and murdered with his young brother.

Mohammed V. had fled to Africa, and thence came to implore the aid of Castille. Pedro lent him some troops, but they were so savage that the Moorish prince, unable to bear the sight of the devastation committed by the Almogavars, dismissed these ferocious allies and retired to Ronda, intending to live in disguise rather than ruin his country. His arrival, however, had led to a universal revolt against the tyranny of Abou Sayd. Malaga rose on behalf of Mohammed, and Abou Sayd, finding himself in danger of being deserted by everyone, resolved to throw himself on the favour of the King of Castille, whom he hoped to buy over by splendid gifts of high-bred horses, rich robes, jewels, and gold.

With a splendid train he arrived at Seville, and thus addressed Pedro: "King of Castille, blood enough has been shed in the quarrel between the Ben Farady and the Al Hamar. Judge between us which ought to be king. If the Ben Farady, let me return safely to Africa; if myself, receive my homage and aid me to obtain my lands."

Pedro received him courteously and entertained him at a banquet; but that night he had him arrested, together with thirty-six noble Moorish cavaliers. They were placed on asses and driven out to the tablada meadow, where they were tied to olive-trees. Abou

Sayd himself was paraded half-naked all over the city, and then taken to the same place, where he beheld them all murdered by the ballesteros, and finally was killed himself by the king, uttering these last words of reproach: "Oh Pedro, Pedro, what a deed for a knight!"

Pedro's thirst for blood had become a passion, like nothing but the frenzy of the Cæsars at Rome; and like them, his cruelty was chiefly directed towards the nobles, so that he was not hated by the populace, as might have been expected from his savage nature.

After hearing of the slaughter of his twin-brother, Enrique of Trastamara resolved no longer to leave the tyrant unmolested on his throne. It was a favourable moment, for the peace of Breteuil had lately been made with England, and thousands of free companions were roaming over France, the pest of the miserable country. The great Breton knight, Bertrand du Guesclin, offered King Charles V. to relieve the kingdom of them, by leading them to avenge the misery of the queen's sister, and to set Don Enrique on the throne of Castille.

Froissart has told the story of their march. The first tidings brought Pedro's savage cruelty on the only two of his brothers still within his reach—boys of fourteen and ten. These he murdered; and then, before a Cortes at Seville, declared that he had been married to Maria de Padilla, and caused her boy Alfonso to be declared heir to the throne; but the child died soon after, and Pedro found his nobles falling fast away from him.

They, with the knights of Aragon, had repaired to Calahorra, where Enrique of Trastamara, arriving with

Sir Bertrand du Guesclin and the English Sir Hugh Calverley, and all their free companions, was proclaimed king, second of his name, in 1366. He marched towards Burgos, and Pedro fled to the south, whence he made his way with his daughters through Portugal to Galicia. At Compostella, the archbishop kindly received the fugitives; but partly because he rebuked the crimes that had caused their misfortunes, and partly because of his riches, Pedro had both him and the dean murdered, and then made his way to Bordeaux.

When apart from his own kingdom, where he could not employ his ballesteros in slaughter, Pedro could comport himself like a knight and a king, and he warmly interested the Black Prince in his cause. To Edward his was the cause of legitimacy against illegitimacy, and of the ally of England against the *protégé* of France; and Pedro had moreover brought a great amount of treasure, the prey not only from Compostella, but from many a murdered and rifled Jew, especially an unhappy old merchant of Toledo, one Samuel Levi, whom he had tortured to death. Nor indeed had he been a bad king as far as the citizen and artisan class were concerned; he had done them even-handed justice, and improved their condition, and it was only the Jews and nobles, and his own kindred who had suffered from his savage violence, which had almost the character of a monomania. His servants were attached to him; and there was much about him to lead Edward to regard him rather as the victim of plot and calumny, than as a wild beast deserving to be hunted down.

To tell the story which has been minutely and perfectly told by Froissart would be vain; so it will be enough to follow King Enrique, instead of tracking the steps of the Prince of Wales across the Pyrenees. Enrique had been crowned at Las Huelgas, and had rewarded his allies by giving Du Guesclin his own county of Trastamara, and bestowing on Sir Hugh Calverley the old title, dear to romance, of Count of Carrion; but no sooner did Sir Hugh and all his free lances hear that their favourite leader, the Black Prince of Wales, was going to take the field against him, than they immediately set off to join in the invasion. Bertrand du Guesclin—or, as the Spaniards called him, Mosen Beltran Claquin—however, stayed by Enrique, and tried to persuade him to follow the tactics of Charles V., and let the climate reduce the strength of the English before giving them battle. Enrique, however, was afraid of the desertion of his troops, and decided on giving battle between Najara and Navaretta, where, chiefly through Tello's impetuosity, his army was immediately broken, and he himself obliged to fly—first into Aragon and then into France—while Du Guesclin and many other persons of high rank were made prisoners.

Pedro began to butcher his captives till prevented by Edward, and then left his allies to waste away in their unwholesome camp, without paying them the sums he had promised, till they returned in despair, the Prince bearing with him the seeds of his lingering but fatal malady. Still, with a view to future claims, his two brothers, John of Gaunt and Edmund of Langley, married Pedro's two younger daughters, who both appear to have been good and gentle women, especially the Duchess of Lancaster. The eldest girl,

Beatriz, had been left in Portugal, where she became a nun.

Enrique had by no means resigned his hopes. He made his way to Avignon, where the schismatical Pope did all that in him lay to remove the stain of his birth, and he obtained promises of aid from France and Navarre. He is even said to have gone to Bordeaux in disguise, and to have had an interview with Du Guesclin, whose ransom he partly paid with some of the money granted him by the French king. Meanwhile Pedro was proceeding in his old course— destroying all whom he viewed as partisans of his brother, of however high rank or influence they might be, and even killing a noble lady because he could not seize her son. All this was but preparing the way for Enrique, who had assembled an army, chiefly of free companions, in the south of France, and entered Spain through Aragon. There, in order to be safe with both parties, the king sent to deny him a passage, but not till he was nearly beyond the domains of Aragon. No sooner had he crossed the Ebro, and found himself once more in Castille, than he fell on his knees and gave thanks for his return. The nobles flocked to his standard, Burgos opened her gates to him, and he was welcomed with delight throughout the north.

The south, however, held out for Pedro, and his vassal Mohammed V. came to join the Castilian army, and made ample reprisals for what had been done by the Spaniards in his cause by destroying Jaen and Ubeda. Disgust at his proceedings sent further supporters to Enrique, who laid siege to Toledo, where Pedro had a strong garrison. Marching from Seville to relieve them, the king still expected safety, for a soothsayer had told him that it would be from the tower of Estrella that he would go forth to die, and he knew of no such tower. The brothers and their armies met at Montiel, and as Du Guesclin was always victorious whenever he was not opposed to the English, Pedro was routed and forced to shut himself up in the castle of Montiel, which was closely besieged by the whole of his brother's army.

Seeing that his fall was only a question of time, Pedro caused one of his knights, Men Rodriguez de Sanabria to call to Du Guesclin over the walls and offer him five cities and a huge sum of money if he would enable the king to escape. Du Guesclin's answer was: "I am the vassal of France; I have been sent to uphold King Enrique, and as a knight will I do so in a knightly manner."

But after making this public refusal, either he treacherously listened to these proposals and warned his king, or—what, considering the honourable characters of both himself and Enrique, is more likely— Pedro expected more mercy from him than from any Spaniard; for at night, when the castle was reduced to extremity for want of water, the unhappy king came forth with three attendants, and rode towards the tent marked by the Du Guesclin eagle. It is said that as he left the castle he looked up, and read over the gateway, "El Torre de Estrella."

He dismounted and entered the tent, and while Bertrand delayed him, Enrique entered in full armour. Someone called out: "Your enemy is here!"

"I am he! I am he!" shouted Pedro in a rage, and sprang forward, Enrique throwing a dagger in his face. They grappled together, and fell rolling on the floor, Pedro uppermost, and Enrique was on the point of perishing when a man named Roccaberti stabbed Pedro in the back, at the moment when Du Guesclin's nervous arms were dragging him back; and the half-strangled Enrique rose dizzy from the ground to find the blood of his mother and his three brethren avenged, and Pedro a corpse.

The unhappy king, whose savage passions had ruined fair abilities and high courage, was only thirty-five years of age when he thus perished, in the year 1362, caught like a wild beast in a trap.

CHAPTER XXIII.

THE LAST BRIGHT DAYS OF GRANADA.

MOHAMMED V. was a prosperous king. While affairs were still unsettled in Castille he seized Algesiras, and knowing he should not be able to keep it, destroyed its fortifications before he concluded with Enrique II. a truce which lasted for twenty years.

This period was the most prosperous of the Granaline kingdom, when, small as it was, it almost recalled the splendours of Cordova. Almeria was no longer a nest of pirates, but a great port of merchandise brought from Italy, Syria, Egypt, and Morocco. The Genoese themselves had a counting-house at Granada. Chivalry had always been congenial to the Arabs, and there was an interchange of friendly rivalries between them and the Christians, which led to romantic challenges and adventures, and polished the manners of the Spaniards; while both sides adopted a high code of mutual truth, honour, and courtesy. The Abencerrages and Zegris, and their kindred tribes, had warriors who were regarded as knights as much as if they had gone through all the ceremony of the vigil, the accolade, and the spurs, and who were the originals of the Rodomontes, and other gallant Saracen knights of Boiardo—nay, and of Othello himself. The Arab love of story-telling was fully developed in the numerous romances and poems which the Christians learnt from them; and many a ballad sung of the perilous love-stories of Christian and Moor, ending in the abduction of the lady by the side of her lover, or mayhap in his slaughter and her death.

When Aben Abd Allah Yousuf, the son of Mohammed V., married the daughter of the Emir of Fez, a succession of feasts and tournaments were given, to which knights came, not only from Christian Spain, but from France and Italy; and they were lodged by the Genoese in their factory.

Enrique of Trastamara was a thoroughly gallant and noble prince, and was commonly called by his people, El Caballero, or the knight. It was under him that the Spanish character began to assume that grave stately courtesy, and punctilious honour that ennobled it. He died of gout in his forty-seventh year, in 1379; and there were not wanting accusers who declared that he had been poisoned by a pair of embroidered buskins, sent to him by Mohammed, but no one credited the absurd story; and Juan I. lived in the same amity with this prince. The illegitimate birth of Enrique II. had caused his family to be so insecure on the throne, that they were continually on their guard against pretenders, and could not afford to quarrel with their Moorish vassals. The profound peace led to increased luxury at Granada, and a kind of mixture of the gallantry of the Arabian Nights and of the chivalrous romance of the Christians had even invaded the harem; and men, instead of in the Eastern fashion, holding woman as a being not to be mentioned, wore the devices of their lady-loves on the rich housings of their steeds—such as hearts pierced with arrows, a sail guiding a ship, an initial, and in colours, denoting their state of mind: yellow and black for grief, green for hope, blue for jealousy, violet and flame for ardent love. Large assemblies were held in the lovely houses and gardens, where hunting, poetry, music, and dancing were the occupations; but the grave learning and earnestness of Al Hakem's days had passed away, and the enjoyments had become far more sensual and voluptuous than in his time.

There prevailed all the vices of high civilisation and luxury closely packed. The high-born sons of the old Arab and Berber tribes did indeed preserve their personal courage, but the implicit obedience to the head of their Faith had been lost in revolutions. The treachery of the Berber had overcome the simplicity of the Arab, and the Moorish nobles were vain, unstable, and insubordinate; while the mass of the nation had the ordinary defects of manufacturing peoples, and were at once clamorous, vicious, and weak; their wealthy merchants indolent, the workpeople tumultuous and violent. The law devised by the rude Koreishite prophet had no elasticity to make it palatable to a state of advanced culture. It could not be a "living oracle," and there was no revivifying power within the body of Islam.

Mohammed would hardly have owned the graceful, luxurious pleasure-lovers of Granada, for the stern, hardy children of Islam; and Omar would have declared they were taking their paradise beforehand. The Koran was explained away into mysticism, and toleration was carried to the fullest extent of liberality. It is likely that the Spanish captive women in the harems had much leavened the character and feelings of these Moors, and made some Christian realities esteemed.

Juan I. was a good and brave man, but died in 1390 from a fall from his horse, when he was galloping over some ploughed fields with some horsemen newly returned from learning Berber fashions of fighting. His son, Enrique III., el Enfermo, or the sickly, came to the throne in the same year with Mohammed's son Aben Abd Allah Yousuf. Soon after the peace was interrupted in a curious manner. The Portuguese were at that time in a very fierce and eager state of religious zeal, and among them a hermit arose named João Sago, who went to the Grand Master of Alcantara, Don Martin Yanez de Barbuda, and assured him that he had had a revelation that, if he would attack the Moors merely in the name of the Gospel, not with any views to worldly advantage, he would drive them out of Spain without losing a man.

Don Martin believed him, and sent two squires to defy the King of Granada, and challenge him to a combat wherein one hundred Christian knights should maintain the cause of the Gospel against two hundred Moslems in defence of the Koran. The whole nation of the vanquished was then to embrace the religion of the victor.

The squires stood before Yousuf and gave this wonderful message. The age of ready faith was over with the luxurious Granadines; they treated the message with contempt, and Yousuf could hardly prevent them from offering violence to the squires. Don Martin, who was quite in earnest, set forth with his own knights and all he could collect in Castille, in spite of the opposition of King Enrique, who tried to prevent the truce from being broken. With about three hundred horse and a rabble of Almogarves and peasants, he entered the Granadine kingdom, and attacked the first fort he came to. He was beaten off with the loss of three men, and with a slight wound in his own hand. He called for the hermit and asked how this was, if the victory was to be a bloodless one.

The hermit said his promise did not relate to little castles, but to the great battle. Accordingly Barbuda and his troop hopefully awaited the army of five thousand Moors who attacked him. Not one of his knights survived to tell the tale, but, to the admiration of the Moors, everyone of them fell where he had stood; not a single wound was in the back.

Viewing the expedition as mere frenzy, Yousuf did not consider the peace to have been broken, and allowed the bodies to be carried honourably home. On the Grand-Master's tomb was the inscription:

"Hic situs est Martinus Yanius, in omni periculo experti, timoris animo."

It is said that the Emperor Charles V. on seeing the tomb and hearing the story said: "I wonder whether he would have snuffed out a lighted torch with his fingers!"

It was a time of great progress in literature in Spain, likewise partly caught from the Moors, partly from the Italian revival. The ballads of the Cid took their present form in this age, and hosts of songs were current, in a language whose sweet stately flow made the mere repetition of the words musical, as in the song called

> Fonte frida, fonte frida,
> Fonte frida, y con amor.

Magically sweet in sound, though most foolish, since it purports to be the love-song of a dove to a nightingale! Hundreds of romantic ballads were current, such as the famous cycle about the knight Don Gayferos carrying off his Moorish love, the fair Melisendra; or the savage one of Count Alarcos, who is required by the king to kill his wife, because he had deserted the Infanta to marry her.

Long romances in prose also began to be written, "Amadis de Gaul" being the chief and first, the book of all others which set the fashion in Europe of the long tales of adventures of knights-errant. And more serious writings also were made. Don Juan Ayala, who was present at the battle of Najara, and made prisoner by the English, wrote a spirited chronicle of the times, translated Livy into Spanish, and wrote a long rhymed satire on the corruptions of the Church and State. Treatises on government, science, and politics were produced or translated from the Arabic; and, while the Moors stood still, the Christians had entered on the march of improvement.

Yousuf died in 1396, as his people believed, of poison conveyed in a mantle sent him from the King of Fez, which ate into his flesh and separated it from his bones, so that he died in great torment.

His eldest son, Yousuf, was set aside by his brother Mohammed VI., and shut up in the castle of Schalobanyah, where he remained for the ten years of his brother's reign. In 1408, when Mohammed found himself fatally ill, he intended to secure the throne to his children, and sent the following letter to the Alcayde of Schalobanyah:

"My servant, so soon as thou receivest this letter,

thou shalt take the life of my brother, Syd Yousuf, and send me his head by the bearer."

The letter was given to the Alcayde while he was playing at chess with the prince.

"What ails thee?" said Yousuf. "Does the king want my head?"

The Alcayde handed him the letter. "Only let us finish our game," said Yousuf; "I am losing."

The Alcayde was bewildered and made false moves. The prince was coolly setting them right when two knights came galloping from Granada with tidings that Mohammed was dead and he was king; and a wise and prudent king he made.

Enrique the Sickly was likewise an able prince, and, among the remarkable events of his reign, was the interchange of civilities between him and Tamerlane, whom he admired as the conqueror of Bajazet. The Tartar made him the welcome present of two Hungarian maidens of noble birth, who had been found captives in the camp of Bajazet, and whom, no doubt, he supposed the Spanish king would welcome to his harem. Their Christian names were Maria and Angelina, but the Spaniards understood no more, nor did they attempt to send them to their remote home, but gave them in marriage to Castilian nobles. Enrique's own wife was Doña Catalina, or as we know her, Catherine of Lancaster, daughter to Pedro the Cruel's daughter Constanza, wife to John of Gaunt, and thus direct legitimate heiress. She was a good-natured, fat, foolish woman, not thought of highly by her husband, but a great favourite with the people.

Enrique III. died in 1406, leaving his young son Juan II., not quite two years old, under the care of his brother, the Infant Don Fernando. A dispute about the tribute led to a short war in which he took the city of Antequera. He was soon after called to the throne of Aragon, where King Martin died in 1414 without children, leaving his kingdom to the second son of his sister Leonor, since the jealousies between the rival kingdoms still ran too high for their union under the direct heir, the little Juan.

Queen Catalina became regent, and she continued in such close alliance with Yousuf that she constantly wrote for his advice in affairs of state, and the gentlemen, both of Castille and Aragon, continually came to adjust their quarrels on Moorish ground, either in the lists or by his wise arbitration. Catalina's sister, Philippa of Lancaster, was the noble wife of King João I. of Portugal, the first of the gallant house of Avis; and it was in 1415 that the Portuguese actually carried the war into Africa itself, and gained the city of Ceuta. But of their conquests and discoveries this history must not treat, and we return to the Spanish Moors, whose fall began to be prepared from the death of Yousuf III. in 1425, being in truth only delayed by the want of vigour in Castille, where Juan II. grew up a gentle, poetical, indolent prince, leaving his affairs to that splendid knight, Don Alvaro de Luna, to whom he gave the French title of Constable, or commander of the army.

Mohammed X., called Al Hayzari, or the Left-handed, made himself much disliked. He was meek and humble with the Christians and Africans, whom he dreaded, but rude and arrogant towards the Granadine Moors. He denied them audience for months, and angered them above all by refusing permission for those combats in the lists which they enjoyed above measure, and where his wiser forefathers had allowed the rivalry of the thirty-two tribes harmlessly to expend itself.

An uproar arose. Al Hayzari escaped in the disguise of a fisherman, and his cousin Mohammed XI., Al Zaquia, or the younger, became king; but he persecuted the Abencerrages as having been favourable to his predecessor, and they, taking refuge at the court of Castille, persuaded Juan II. to embrace the cause of Al Hayzari. He had likewise won the favour of the King of Tunis, and the Alhâmra was besieged by both Spaniards and Africans, till the usurper was delivered up by his own soldiers, and put to death by his rival in 1429.

The restored Al Hayzari profited by the weakness of the King of Castille to refuse his tribute, and a fresh war began, in the midst of which Yousuf, one of the Al Hamar, grandson to him whom Pedro the Cruel had assassinated at Seville, offered through a Mozarabic knight to restore Granada to its allegiance if he would espouse his cause. Juan consented; the Zegris, the chief tribe opposed to the Abencerrages, took his part, and defeated his enemies in a great battle, putting his rival to flight. He undertook to send Juan fifteen hundred horse to assist in all his wars, and to appear as a crown vassal at the Cortes of Castille whenever it sat south of Toledo.

Alvaro de Luna commanded the Castilian army, and defeated Mohammed the Left-handed at Caveca de los Guinetes, further making prisoner a large division of the army who were encamped on the top of a mountain. The army was in view of Granada, and a spirited ballad gives this dialogue between the king and a prisoner.

> Aben Amar, Aben Amar,
> Mero de Moreria—

which we can only render—

> Aben Amar, Aben Amar,
>   Of Moordom mighty Moor,
> They say upon thy natal day
>   Of omens there was store.
>
> The sea was lying in a calm,
>   And wax'd the moon on high,
> The Moor who with such signs was born
>   Must never tell a lie.
>
> Then made reply that gallant Moor
>   (His answer thou shalt know):
> "Nor would I tell thee one, my lord,
>   Though I my life forego.
>
> I am the son of Moorish sire
>   And captive Christian maid,
> And when I was an infant boy
>   'Twas thus my mother said:
>
> No falsehood ever should I speak
>   Great villainy 'twould be;
> Whate'er thou askest, señor king,
>   The truth I'll tell to thee."
>
> "Well likes me, Aben Amar,
>   This courtesy of thine:
> Tell me, I pray, what castles fair
>   On yonder mountains shine."
>
> "'Tis the Alhâmra, señor,
>   The Mosque you next behold;
> The third's the Alijovous,
>   Of wondrous work untold.

> They paid the Moor who built it
>   A hundred crowns a day;
> The day he did not labour,
>   The like he had to pay.
>
> There spreads the Generalife,
>   Garden unmatched on earth;
> There are the Crimson Towers,
>   Fortress of mighty worth."
>
> Then spoke out King Don Juan
>   Of Leon and Castille:
> "I'll wed thee, fair Granada,
>   Thy dower shall be Seville!"
>
> "I thank thee, King, I'm wedded,
>   I am no widow lone;
> The Moor who is my husband,
>   He loves my every stone."

It is rather disappointing that Aben Amar's truth was put to so very slight a test; but the secret of some of the nobleness of the Moorish knight is here betrayed by the mention of the Christian mother teaching her child that falsehood was "great villainy."

It was really deliberated in the council whether to lay siege to the city, but the nobles would not consent. They bitterly hated the Constable, as royal favourites were always hated in the Middle Ages, and did not choose that he should have the glory of driving the Moors out of Spain, so they would only consent to devastate the country; yet no sooner was the army on its way back to Cordova, than a report was spread that the Constable had been bought over by a bribe sent in a basket of figs. Yousuf, however, obtained the crown, but died at the end of the first half-year, in 1431, and Al Hayzari once more regained the throne.

There was a truce of two years between the two kings; but at the same time there was a continual border war, carried on by the Algarades on either side, and consisting in forays and the surprise of fortresses. The Christians gained Huesca, but the Grand Master of Alcantara was made prisoner by the vizier in an ambuscade in 1438. Granada and Castille were alike rent by discords: the one by the struggles of the Ben Zeregh, or Abencerrages, and the Zegris, who brought about a revolution and counter-revolution about once in two years; the other by the revolts of the nobles against Alvar de Luna, headed by Don Enrique, the king's eldest son, the first heir-apparent to bear the title of Prince of the Asturias. In 1453 they succeeded in the overthrow of that brave and able man, and the poor craven helpless king could not save him from being beheaded by his jealous and factious people; exactly as, at that very time, old Douglas Bell the Cat was hanging Cochrane for being too faithful a minister to the feeble James III. of Scotland. The unfortunate Juan II. did not survive his faithful friend a full year; and in 1454 was succeeded by Enrique IV., one of the weakest and most helpless of men.

In the meantime the unfortunate old left-handed Mohammed could not restrain the contentions of his nephews; and while one Aben Ismael retreated into Castille with a great number of Abencerrages knights, the other, Aben Osmin, overcame his uncle, who was dethroned for the fourth and last time. Osmin's rule, however, was distasteful, and Ismael was invited back in 1454. Osmin escaped to the mountains, and Ismael began his reign with higher hopes, because the tidings had arrived of the conquest of Constantinople by the Turks. Believing that this was an omen of success to Islam, Ismael refused to renew the truce with Enrique IV., and there was a renewal of the terrible warfare. The Spanish borderers were continually bursting on the Vega and carrying off the rich plunder from the beauteous country houses, burning the vines, driving off the flocks, and lighting fires, which the king could only behold from the terraces of the Alhâmra without bringing any aid. Enrique himself commanded one inroad, and put to the sword all the people of Mena, after which there was a truce, in the midst of which Aboul Hacem, a son of the king, with two thousand five hundred horse and ten thousand foot, made an inroad on the city of Estepa, and was returning with a great booty, when the eldest son of the Count of Arcos, Don Rodrigo Ponce de Leon, vowed to intercept him; and collecting one hundred retainers of his own family, rode towards the enemy, gathering up brave men as he went till his force amounted to two hundred and sixty horse and six hundred foot. With these he attacked the Moors near Peñarubia, and after a sharp fight put them to flight, as they evidently thought that this was but the vanguard of an army. Don Rodrigo had lost only one hundred and eighty men and they fourteen hundred; but the next morning the victors were alarmed by huge columns of dust, which they thought the heralds of their returning enemies. Happily before they had charged the foe, they found the dust was caused by the flocks of cattle and sheep making their way, as best they might, back to their pastures.

That same year the Duke of Medina-Sidonia besieged Gibraltar, and one of the commanders betrayed it to him, so much to Enrique's delight that he added King of Gibraltar to his titles, while Ismael, becoming convinced that the prosperity of Mahommedanism in the East did not affect Spain, sued for peace. The two kings met on the Vega, spent some days in feasts, and concluded a treaty which was signed in 1465, and was observed even after the death of Ismael. The Moorish and Castilian knights entered each other's cities freely; several Castilian gentlemen lived at Granada; and one, Diego de Cordova, became for some years the king's counsellor.

CHAPTER XXIV.

THE ABENCERRAGES AND ZEGRIS.

ENRIQUE IV. was one of those wretched princes whose misrule is only endured in hopes of its ending at their death. He was little better than an idiot, and his wife, Juana of Portugal, lived so as to be a public scandal; but as long as they were childless, public hope fixed itself on the king's younger brother, the Infant Don Alfonso, a promising high-spirited boy, born of the second wife of Juan II.

But when after eight years the queen gave birth to a daughter, Juana, whom the people were required to acknowledge as heiress, they could not endure the prospect of her reign, or of her mother's regency; they utterly denied her to be the king's child, called her La Beltaneja, after her supposed father, the unworthy favourite, Don Beltran de la Cueva, and at Avila, raised young Alfonso on their shoulders, proclaiming him king. He died, however, in 1464, in the midst of the war with his brother; and the insurgents then turned to his sister Isabel, a noble, wise, and devout maiden of sixteen, whom they would fain have proclaimed as their queen. She refused, however, to accept the crown while her brother lived; but she claimed to be acknowledged as heiress by the title of

Princess of the Asturias; and to this Enrique was forced by dire necessity to consent.

Many princes sought her hand, but she had made up her mind to bring together the two chief peninsular kingdoms by wedding no one save Fernando, the heir of Aragon. Fernando was the second son of Juan II. of Aragon, and had only become the heir through the crime of his mother, Juana Henriquez, and of the cruel step-mother who had most conduced to bring the term into disrepute.

Juan's first wife had been Blanca, queen in her own right of Navarre, who had died early, leaving three children, Carlos, Blanca, and Leonor. Carlos, though *de jure* king of Navarre, is always known as Prince of Viana, *i.e.* Béarn, as his father refused to give up the crown matrimonial to him. He was slandered, persecuted, and goaded into rebellion, overpowered, imprisoned, and though released, he died shortly after, with strong suspicions of foul play. His sister Blanca, after a no less miserable history, perished in the hands of her brother-in-law, the Count of Foix, to whose family the kingdom of Navarre passed; but Fernando was acknowledged heir of Aragon.

It had been at one time proposed that Carlos should marry the Infanta Isabel, and the plan held good for his young brother, and though Enrique did all in his power to prevent it, Isabel was resolute, and Fernando set forth from Aragon in disguise, and arrived in the middle of the night at Valladolid, where Isabel was residing under the guardianship of the Archbishop of Toledo. He was seventeen and she eighteen, when the prelate led him into the Infanta's presence, and Don Guherre de Cardeñas exclaimed "*Ese es*," ("This is he,") in memory of which the Cardeñas shield was enriched by the letters SS. The young pair were fair with the old Gothic complexion of Spanish royalty—Isabel small, slight, but queenly, and Fernando tall and manly. How much superior to him she was, was never known till her death. They were married in the presence of Isabel's little court at Valladolid, in 1467. Four years later, Enrique IV. died in 1471, and after a brief struggle the partisans of Juana were forced to consign her to a convent. Juan II. lived till 1479; but on his death Castille and Aragon became united under Fernando and Isabel—*los Reyes*, as their subjects called them, *los Reyes Catolicos* as subsequent history named them, for the sake of Isabel's deep devotion to the cause of religion. She was one of those high-minded women who have the power of inspiring men with their own lofty ardour and enthusiasm.

The days of the Moorish kingdom were already numbered when, in 1466, Aboul Hacem succeeded Ismael; but the disturbances in Castille emboldened him, and when, in 1476, the regular demand for tribute was made, he answered: "Those who coined gold for you are dead. Nothing is made at Granada for the Christians but sword-blades and lance-points."

Such was the last proclamation of war from the Moors. Even the Imaums disapproved and preached in the mosques of Granada, "Woe to the Moslems in Andalusia!" "The end is come," they said; "the ruins will fall on our heads!" Nevertheless, Aboul Hacem surprised the Aragonese city of Zahara with sixty thousand inhabitants, and put them all to the sword or sold them into slavery; but he was not welcomed, evil was predicted, and he became more and more hated when he put four of the Abencerrages to death.

The king and queen now began to prepare the whole strength of their kingdom for a final effort, not to be relaxed till Spain should be wholly a Christian land. Meantime the Adalides kept up an outpost war, full of wondrous adventures. Don Rodrigo Ponce de Leon, who had become Marquis of Cadiz, made a sudden night attack upon Alhâma, only eight leagues from Granada, and though the inhabitants fought from street to street he mastered it. He little knew that he had missed a troop of six hundred Moorish lances, who were besieging his wife in his own castle of Arcos, and would have taken her, if the Duke of Medina-Sidonia had not hurried to the rescue. There had long been a feud between the houses of Ponce de Leon and Guzman, which Queen Isabel had in vain attempted to end, until this gallant action made them friends for life.

Alhâma was a terrible loss to the Moors; and was bewailed in the ballad, "Ay de me Al Hâma," which so moved the hearts of the people that it was forbidden to be sung in the streets of Granada. It has been translated by Byron, who has in fact united two ballads, one with the refrain "Ay de me, Alhama," in the original.

> The Moorish King rides up and down
> Through Granada's royal town;
> From Elvira's gates to those
> Of Vivarambla on he goes.
>   Woe is me, Alhama!

Letters to the monarch tell
How Alhama's city fell:
In the fire the scroll he threw,
And the messenger he slew.
     Woe is me, Alhama!

He quits his mule and mounts his horse,
And through the street directs his course:
Through the street of Zacatin,
To the Alhambra spurring in.
     Woe is me, Alhama!

When the Alhambra walls he gained,
On the moment he ordain'd
That the trumpet straight should sound
With the silver clarion round.
     Woe is me, Alhama!

And when the hollow drums of war
Beat the loud alarm afar,
That the Moors of town and plain
Might answer to the martial strain.
     Woe is me, Alhama!

Then the Moors, by this aware,
That bloody Mars recall'd them there;
One by one, and two by two,
To a mighty squadron grew.
     Woe is me, Alhama!

Out then spake an aged Moor
In these words the king before:
"Wherefore call on us, O King?
What may mean this gathering?"
     Woe is me, Alhama!

"Friends, ye have alas to know
Of a most disastrous blow;
That the Christians, stern and bold,
Have obtained Alhama's hold."
     Woe is me, Alhama!

Out then spake old Alfaqui,
With his beard so white to see:
"Good King! thou art justly served,
Good King! this hast thou deserved.
     Woe is me, Alhama!

By thee were slain, in evil hour,
The Abenearrage, Granada's flower;
And strangers were received by thee
Of Cordova the Chivalry.
     Woe is me, Alhama!

And for this, O King! is sent
On thee a double chastisement:
Thee and thine, thy crown and realm,
One last wreck shall overwhelm.
     Woe is me, Alhama!

He who holds no laws in awe,
He must perish by the law;
And Granada must be won,
And thyself with her undone."
     Woe is me, Alhama!

Fire flashed from out the old Moor's eyes;
The Monarch's wrath began to rise
Because he answered, and because
He spake exceeding well of laws.
     Woe is me, Alhama!

"There is no law to say such things
As may disgust the ear of kings:"
Thus, snorting with his choler, said
The Moorish King, and doom'd him dead.
     Woe is me, Alhama!

Moor Alcayde, Moor Alcayde,[*]
Though thy beard so hoary be,

---

[*] On the authority of the ballad in Perez de Hyta, I have ventured to alter Alfaqui into Alcayde, as the person who was

> The King hath sent to have thee seized,
> For Alhama's loss displeased.
>> Woe is me, Alhama!
>
> And to fix thy head upon
> High Alhambra's loftiest stone,
> That this for thee should be the law,
> And others tremble when they saw.
>> Woe is me, Alhama!
>
> Cavalier and man of worth!
> Let these words of mine go forth!
> Let the Moorish monarch know,
> That to him I nothing owe.
>> Woe is me, Alhama!
>
> But on my soul Alhama weighs,
> And on my inmost spirit preys;
> And if the King his land hath lost,
> Yet others may have lost the most.
>> Woe is me, Alhama!
>
> Sires have lost their children, wives
> Their lords, and valiant men their lives;
> One, what best his love might claim,
> Hath lost, another wealth or fame.
>> Woe is me, Alhama!

put to death was the Alcayde, or governor, who lost the town, not the *Alfaqui*, or priest, who blamed the king, and at whom the king snorted, without doing anything worse:

> Eso dice el Rey Moro
> Relinchando de colera.

The Alcayde in Perez de Hyta's version pleads that the king had given him licence to go to his sister's wedding, and further tells how, when he sent to ransom his daughter, he was told that she was a Christian—Doña Maria de Alhama.

> I lost a damsel in that hour,
> Of all the land the loveliest flower;
> Doubloons a hundred I would pay
> And think her ransom cheap that day.
> > Woe is me, Alhama!
>
> And as these things the Alcayde said,
> They severed from the trunk his head,
> And to the Alhambra's wall with speed
> 'Twas carried, as the King decreed.
> > Woe is me, Alhama!
>
> And man and infants therein weep
> Their loss, so heavy and so deep;
> Granada's ladies, all she rears
> Within her walls burst into tears.
> > Woe is me, Alhama!
>
> And from the windows o'er the walls
> The sable web of mourning falls;
> The King weeps as a woman o'er
> His loss, for it is much and sore.
> > Woe is me, Alhama!

Alhâma had once before been taken by St. Fernando, but could not then be kept, and a council was held by the *Reyes Catolicos*, in which it was declared that it would take five thousand mules' burthen of provisions, sent several times a year, to support a garrison thus in the heart of the enemy's country. The high spirit of the queen, however, carried the day. She declared that the right thing to do was to take Loja to support Alhâma, and, after causing the three chief mosques to be purified as Christian churches, she strained every effort to equip an army with which Fernando was to besiege Loja. On the day before he set out Isabel gave birth to twins—one dead, the other a daughter; and this was viewed as an ill omen. The knights who carried the standards to be blessed looked dispirited, and all expected reverses. Most probably from the queen's illness, the expedition was not properly provided with good and tried warriors, and Ali Atar, one of the bravest of the Moors, defeated Fernando and forced him to retreat with the loss of his baggage.

Aboul Hacem was prevented from following up his success by the struggles of the women in his harem. His favourite wife was a Christian by birth, named Isabel de Solis, the daughter of the Alcayde of Bedmar; but she had become a renegade, and was commonly called Zoraya, or the Morning Star. Childless herself, she was vehemently set on the promotion of Abou-Abd-Allah, son of another wife, Ayescha, who is generally known by the Spanish contraction of his name, Boabdil; also in Arabic as *Al Zaquir*, the little, and in Spanish as *el Rey Chico*. Such disaffection was raised that Aboul Hacem was forced to return home, where he imprisoned Ayescha and her son; but they let themselves down from the window with a rope twisted of the veils of the Sultana's women, and, escaping to the palace or Albaycin, there held out against him, supported by the Abencerrages. The Zegris held by Aboul Hacem, and the streets of Granada ran red with the blood shed by the two factions till, in 1482, while the elder king was gone to relieve Loja, the younger one seized the Alhâmra; and Aboul Hacem, finding the gates closed against him, was obliged to betake himself to Malaga, where his brother Abd Allah, called Al Zagal, or the young, was the Alcayde.

Again Fernando and Isabel prepared an expedition to attack Malaga. It was led by the Grand Master of Santiago, Don Alfonso de Cardeñas, and victory was thought so certain that numerous merchants followed the army to seize or purchase the huge plunder that was expected in jewels, and the rich silks woven at Malaga. The way lay through the hills of Axarquia, thickly set with farms and villages, which the army harried as it marched, and on the third day arrived before the walls of Malaga.

But the light of the burning villages had served as beacons to warn the old king and his brother. They had sent forth a party, who, taking another road, occupied the passes, and El Zagal, together with a gallant warrior named Reduan, sallied out and gave battle to the Castilians before they had time to encamp. Their ranks were broken, and, when they tried to fly, they found their retreat cut off. The mountains they had ravaged bristled with avengers. Eight hundred perished in the field, sixteen hundred were made prisoners, and of the others many died an inglorious death by the hands of the enraged mountaineers, while only a few struggled home to tell the tale of disaster.

So high was the courage, so great the resources, of the Moors, that their fall was chiefly owing to their want of union. Boabdil, jealous of his father's success, resolved to eclipse it by a still greater victory; and with the able old captain, Ali Atar, whose daughter he had married, set forth for an attack on the city of Lucena, a rich but not well-fortified place.

No good auguries followed him. His title of "The Unlucky" was whispered as he mounted his horse, his lance-point was broken against the top of the gateway, and a fox was started by his troop, and made its escape untouched by darts.

The Governor of Lucena was Don Diego de Cordova de Aguilar, known by the curious title of Alcayde de los Donçeles, Master of the Pages. On the first alarm, he sent for help to his uncle, the Count of Cabra, and his two nephews Alfonso and Gonzalo, sons of a brother who had died early. The count arrived before the Moors were in sight, but the nephew came up while Boabdil was encamping. He thought himself surrounded by a huge force, and his infantry in terror began to fly. The horse fought gallantly, but Ali Atar, who was nearly ninety, fell mortally wounded from his horse. The Castilians closed in on the Moors, and Boabdil, finding that his snow-white war-horse, with its splendid caparisons, attracted attention to him, leapt off, and tried to hide himself in the willows that bordered the river Xenil. Here, however, he was attacked by three soldiers, and, after trying to defend himself with his dagger, he disclosed his name to save his life, and was taken to the Count of Cabra. Hosts of his best cavaliers were slain or perished in the river, and the survivors who reached home filled Granada with mourning and lamentation, for hardly a noble house but had lost a son.

Aboul Hacem was recalled and replaced in the Alhâmra, while Boabdil was carried to Cordova, where Fernando, knowing that his freedom would be much worse for the Moorish cause than his captivity, released him on condition of his freeing four hundred prisoners, paying twelve thousand doubloons a year, and attending Cortes as a vassal of Castille, as well as allowing free passage and supplying food to any troops sent against his father. On these terms *el Rey Chico* obtained his liberty and a truce for two years, giving his eldest son as a hostage. He and fifty Moors were then released, with magnificent gifts of horses, brocades, and silks; and the bribes of Zoraya prepared some of the citizens of Granada to admit him into the Albaycin palace.

Then began an unnatural war in the streets, and for a whole day there were skirmishes from house to house between the partisans of the father and the son. Night ended the conflict; and in the morning before it could begin again the wise old Imaum Macu stood forth, and thus addressed the chiefs: "Why do ye thus strike one another like deadly enemies? For whom do ye shed your brother's blood, which ought only to flow in defence of your wives, your children, your country, and your God? Ye, for a headstrong old man, unable to wield a sword or lead you forth against the enemy; ye, for a womanlike youth, without courage, virtue, or luck—a bad son, ruled by a woman, and the slave of the Christian. Give up both, and seek among the warriors of the royal race for one to whom we can safely entrust the safety of the kingdom."

The chiefs listened to his advice, and Al Zagal was at once chosen. Aboul Hacem gave way without contest to his brother, and soon after died; but Boabdil still tried to reign in the Albayein, so that there were two rival Abd Allahs, uncle and nephew, both kings in the one city. The uncle, wishing at any cost to prevent the civil war, proposed to his nephew to divide their power. Zoraya pretended to consent, but only to gain time, and the divisions were nearly as dreadful as ever. The nobles were chiefly for the uncle; but the poor, bought over by Zoraya's largesses, were for the nephew.

It is at this time that tradition and romance place a terrible incident, which probably has some foundation, though the most trustworthy Arabic histories do not mention it. In one of the great festivals, which the kings continued to give, one of the Zegris was killed by Zaide Aben Serady, an Abencerrage, both being lovers of the same lady—the fair Zayda—the subject of endless ballads. The feud becoming more deadly every day, the Zegris at last persuaded Boabdil that Hamet, the chief of the Aben Serady clan, had been lifting his eyes to one of Boabdil's own nieces. They had seen him, said two of the Zegris, meeting the queen at the fount of laurels; and they persuaded the king that his vengeance ought to fall on the entire tribe.

The Abencerrages were accordingly summoned to the Alhâmra, and admitted into the hall still called by their name. A well-armed band of Zegris and an executioner awaited them in the Court of Lions; a page was sent to summon them; and one by one they were beheaded over a huge vase of alabaster. Aben Hamet and thirty-five more had thus perished before one of the doomed men was followed by his page, who, seeing the horrible work that was going forward, dashed out at the door when the next was called in, and rushing down into the town met a band of warriors returning from a foray and brought them to the rescue. Others hurried up on the alarm, and there was a terrible fight, in which two hundred of the Zegris were killed. Aben Hamet's wife, the king's own sister, going to implore protection from Boabdil, was murdered by him with his own hand.

The places of these murders are still shown in the Alhâmra, and many a ballad sings of them; but their date is so uncertain that the best authorities disbelieve the facts, especially as Boabdil did not occupy the Alhâmra after his return from captivity. Romance further declares that the queen's innocence was to be proved by ordeal of battle; and that as no Moor was to be found to maintain her cause, four knights—namely, the Alcayde de los Donçeles, Don Juan Chacon, Don Alfonso de Aguilar, and Don Manuel Ponce de Leon —went in the disguise (or what was supposed to be such) of Turkish knights. Perez de Hyta even tells all their devices. Don Juan's was a wolf in a green field tearing a Moor, and above it a lily and the words, "For his crime he is devoured." Don Manuel had a lion also despatching a Moor, with the verse:

> A harder death would serve him right
> Who sins against the truth;
> For him it is scarce cruelty
> To die by lion's tooth.

Alfonso de Aguilar bore a golden eagle flying away with another unfortunate Moor bathed in blood, and the motto:

> I'll raise him to the skies
> That worse may be his fall,
> That the remorseless crime
> He did, be known to all.

And Diego de Cordova had a sword transfixing another Moor, with this legend:

> By my good sword's sharp edge
> Truth clearly shall be known;
> The good queen's freedom shall be won,

Of course the four knights gained a brilliant victory, and the king reinstated the queen in her honours. She sent a secret promise to her defenders to become a Christian, and assist them in the siege of Granada; and almost all the surviving Abencerrages went over to the Spaniards, three of them being baptised.

All this is pure invention. If civilisation, and, above all, printing, had not been so far advanced, these popular songs and tales would have formed the material of a magnificent epic, when the siege of Granada would have been as magnificent a centre for myth and legend as the sieges of Troy and of Paris; but though all the heroes and their stories are floating about in the world of fable, no one ever could believe in them enough to work them up into a poem of force sufficient to live and hold the imagination.

CHAPTER XXV.

THE SIEGE OF MALAGA.

Two years' truce from the Christians only enabled the uncle and nephew to struggle against each other more uninterruptedly. Indeed, as the truce only professed to be with the younger king Abou Abd Allah al Zaquir, or Boabdil, it hindered no one from making algarades on the country obeying Abou Abd Allah al Zaquir (also called Al Zagal), the uncle; and the unhappy Moors were robbed of their cattle, their harvests, and their vintage.

In 1484, the Cortes of Castille and of Aragon were convoked by their sovereigns, and each made a grant for the Moorish war to be pursued even to the end. Fernando de Talavera, the queen's confessor, when offered the Bishopric of Salamanca, answered that he would have no Bishopric but Granada. The war was preached as a crusade, and volunteers came from all parts—English Lancastrians banished by the House of York, French knights weary of the strict rule of Louis XI., Swiss and Italians, besides the great military orders, and the Hermandades or brotherhoods, a sort of voluntary mounted police which had lately arisen in Spain for the protection of the roads. There were ten thousand horse and forty thousand foot, artillery with all the latest improvements, and thirty thousand *gastadores* or *taladores*, whose systematic business was to destroy villages and mills, root up olives and vines, burn the crops, and make a wilderness of the fertile land so as to cut off all supplies from the cities, while the fleets of Biscay and Barcelona cruised round the coast.

Several places were taken; but when Loja was threatened, Boabdil sent to declare that it was his city, and the war was with his uncle, not himself, recommending him rather to attack Malaga; but Fernando replied that Loja was not included in the terms of the treaty. Whereupon Boabdil, knowing that he was suspected of cowardice, hastened to throw himself into the city. The siege was, however, carried on so steadily that he was soon in despair; and remembering that young Gonzalo de Cordova had been very courteous to him in his captivity, he sent for him and offered to make his submission. Fernando thereupon permitted the inhabitants to depart with what they could carry, giving them permission to settle in Aragon or Castille on the same terms as other "Mudejarres," or Moors among the Christians, who were at this time allowed toleration on condition of paying a tribute. Boabdil further engaged to deliver up Granada to the Spaniards whenever it should be possible, and to content himself with the title of Duke of Guadix; but this was kept secret, and he was escorted to Granada with the whole of the Lojans, none of them choosing to accept Fernando's terms. He found his uncle gone to relieve Velez, and thus was able to enter the Alhâmra, where he abstained from succouring Illora and Moclin, which were called the two eyes of Granada, and which were easily taken by the Christian army.

Al Zagal had gained a victory over the Count of Cabra, but had then been twice defeated. Reduan threw himself into Velez, and made so gallant a defence as to become the theme of many ballads and at last to obtain a favourable capitulation, and Al Zagal returned to Granada, but only to find that his nephew had closed the gates against him. On this he retired to Guadix, where he made a small kingdom of that city, together with Baeza and Almeria. So ended the campaign of 1486.

The next attack was upon Malaga. This was one of the richest and best-fortified of the Moorish cities. The walls were flanked by eighty strong towers and four huge citadels—the Gibalfaro and Alcazaba towards the land, and the Geneves and Atarazanas on the harbour protected it, all communicating with one another by underground passages. The two kings had each appointed a separate governor; but while Boabdil's was gone to treat with Fernando, Al Zagal's closed the gates, and manned the walls with a troop of Africans under Ibrahim the Zenete, a brave and merciful man. Fernando sent to try to buy him and the other defenders over by promises of lands and honours; but was answered by Achmet the Zegri: "My countrymen have shown by choosing me that they think me worthy. Thou wouldst make me base. If the insult be renewed, the messenger shall be treated as an enemy."

Fernando then tried to bribe the inhabitants, thinking the rich merchants and Jews would never endure the rigours of such a siege; but Achmet, finding out what was going on, threatened to turn his cannon on them if he saw any signs of treachery. It was a most gallant defence. Achmet and Ibrahim vied with one another in bravery; and the latter made several sallies on the Christians. In one of these, when he had driven in the outposts, he came into a field, where a number of the little *donçeles* or pages were at play; but he only patted them gently with his lance, and bade them run away to their mothers.

"Why not let them taste the point?" said a fierce warrior.

"Because I saw no beards," answered the generous chief.

Sickness broke out in the villages round, provisions became scarce, and a report became current that the queen had written to beg that the siege might be raised. Fernando knew that nothing but her presence would restore the spirit of the army. He wrote to her, and she soon arrived with her eldest daughter and a train of ladies; and as the Marquis of Cadiz and the Grand Master of Santiago escorted her into the camp, the troops were filled with joy and courage by her brave and gracious countenance. Fernando again offered favourable terms, adding that if these were not now accepted he would make everyone within a slave; but his proposals were again rejected, and the gallant Africans made sallies up to his very tents, in one of which the Marquis of Cadiz had nearly been made prisoner. The Granadines would fain have succoured them, but were prevented by Boabdil, who sent on his side servile messages of submission to the sovereigns, and presents of Arab steeds and rich raiment.

Isabel regarded the war as holy, and regulated her camp so as to prevent as much as possible all vice, licence, and profanity. She established hospitals for

T

the sick and wounded, and watched over them herself, kept up strict discipline, and arranged patrols to prevent disturbances, fires, or surprises.

The blockade thus established soon began to tell on the city. The armed men roamed the streets in search of food and pillaged the houses, and the populace began to die of hunger. Despair began to prompt strange deeds. A party of some hundreds of famished men dashed out upon the besiegers, to try to cut their way through, and perished to a man.

On the other hand, a fierce Dervish named Ibrahim Algerbi, of the tribe called Gomeres, became possessed with the idea that he was destined to save his country by slaying the king and queen. His fiery eloquence gathered together four hundred Moors, who set out from Guadix under an oath to cut their way through the enemy to the relief of the city. Half succeeded; the other half remained dead where they had fought; and in the midst knelt the Dervish, apparently unarmed and immovable, in the attitude of prayer. When questioned by the soldiers, he declared that he was Allah's messenger to the Christian king and queen, and must perform the bidding of Heaven.

Struck by his wild gestures and inspired mien, the men led him to the tent of the Marquis of Cadiz, who reported the occurrence to the queen. Fernando was then sleeping during the noontide heat, and Isabel said that the Dervish should be taken to the tent of Doña Beatriz de Bobadilla, Marchioness of Maya, where he might wait until the king awoke.

The tent was a very richly-adorned one, and in it were not only Doña Beatriz but Don Alvaro of Portugal, his wife, Doña Felipa, and several other persons of high rank. Ibrahim supposed himself in the royal presence, and in one instant his poniard flashed forth. He sprang like a panther upon Don Alvaro, stabbed him, and then flew upon Doña Beatriz; but in his wild haste, his weapon stuck fast in the heavy gold embroidery of her bodice, and, ere he could withdraw it, his arms were close pinioned by Don Lopez de Toledo, the queen's secretary. The guards dashed in, and, without any attempt at securing the man, absolutely cut him to pieces with their swords in a moment, and then in their fury hurled his mangled limbs into the town from their catapults. The besieged, who had learned his purpose from the two hundred who had come with him, gathered up the remains, did them all honour, and laid them in a splendid tomb, and then, by way of reprisals, killed a Galician prisoner and sent the body out of the gate on an ass.

After this no Moor was allowed to come near the royal tents, and a guard of the noblest young Castilian knights watched constantly round the tent of their beloved queen. Desperate fighting still went on; mines were met by countermines, and underground combats took place, while the famine became more terrible; children starved on pounded vine-leaves fried in oil; and boiled leather, and all the other wretched resources of the besieged eked out the subsistence of their elders; sickness and death thinned their numbers, and many citizens came forth and sold themselves for slaves to obtain a mouthful of food.

Yet the garrison fought with undiminished energy, till at last Achmet, moved by the sight of the deplorable misery of the inhabitants, withdrew into the Gebalfaro fortress, leaving the citizens to make the best terms they could for themselves. A merchant named Durdax was sent to offer terms of surrender, but the king sternly declared that the time of mercy was gone by; he would make no terms, but they must surrender at discretion. The reply filled the wretched people with despair, and they sent back again a message threatening that unless their lives and freedom were secured to them, they should hang from the battlements every one of their five hundred prisoners of war, shut up their women and children in the citadel, set fire to the town, and sally forth to kill every Christian they met, so as not to die unavenged.

Fernando sternly answered that if the hair of the head of one Christian should be touched he would not leave a Moor alive in Malaga.

There was agitation and tumult, but Durdax persuaded his fellows to trust to the king's pity, and a letter was written imploring him to act as his ancestors had done by the inhabitants of Cordova, Antequera, and the rest, and grant his supplicants at least life and freedom.

But the attempt at assassination had incensed Fernando, and the constancy of those who hold out a fortress without hope of relief is always viewed by a victor as an obstinate waste of his time and strength, exciting his wrath rather than his admiration. The petition was disregarded; Fernando could not forgive his five months' detention; and when Malaga surrendered on the 18th of August, 1489, and the Gebalfaro two days later, it was to slavery and destitution. The streets were so choked with dead that the king and queen could not at first make their public entry, to give thanks in the purified mosque. The brave leaders,

Achmet and Ibrahim, were thrown into a dungeon, and the whole of the inhabitants, about fifteen hundred in number, and all the soldiers, were collected to be portioned out for slavery. First, however, fifty maidens were chosen as a gift to the Queen of Portugal, another fifty for the Queen of Aragon, and a hundred of the finest men to serve in the Pope's guard, where, it is said, that in a year's time they had all become zealous Christians. The rest were then divided into three lots. The first were to be exchanged for Christians in captivity in Africa ; and with this view all persons who had relations captured or supposed to have been captured by the African pirates, were called upon to send in their names that they might be recovered. Another third was distributed to work as slaves among the nobles, as part of their spoil, each duke obtaining a hundred, each count fifty, and so on ; and the last third was sold to pay the expenses of the expedition. The severity was of course meant as a warning ; but Fernando was a man of sordid and avaricious nature, and his nobler-minded wife had only been able to keep his cruelty in check by appealing to his greed ; and when a wholesale butchery had been proposed, she had represented that to enslave the unfortunate men would be more profitable.

The Jews, four hundred in number, hoped to ransom themselves, but found their property was part of the spoil. However, their brethren ransomed them, and the other Malagans hoped likewise to buy themselves off by giving up all their treasure ; but in this they were cruelly disappointed. None of them were released, save those who were exchanged with the Africans ; and there was no mercy for renegade Christians who had become Mahometans, or Moors who had professed

Christianity for a time and then fallen away. They were delivered over to the Inquisition, and were either burnt or served for marks for the djerid.

The Inquisition, established to extirpate the Albigenses, had only recently been introduced into Spain. The Cortes both of Castille and of Aragon had been loath to accept it, and Queen Isabel had resisted it; but her confessor, Tomàs of Torquemada, had pressed it on her as a duty until she had yielded.

The world had yet to learn that matters of faith cannot be brought under secular jurisdiction; and the duty of a sovereign towards his country was thought to extend to the belief as well as the actions of men. To extirpate false doctrine was viewed as incumbent on every Christian prince; and Spain, which had begun with unusual toleration, was in each generation becoming more and more imbued with the spirit of persecution.

Malaga was to be a Christian city; the mosques were purified; the beautiful houses and lands of the unhappy Moors were freely given to settlers from Aragon and Castille; Don Garcia Fernandes was appointed alcayde, and attempted to restore the prosperity of the place; but it was long before its commerce returned. The mosques have been pulled down and modern churches erected; and the chief remains now left are the great citadel of Gebalfaro, and a beautiful marble horse-shoe arch, the entrance to the Moorish dockyard, but now left far inland by the retreating of the sea. On the 18th of August, the anniversary of the victory, the great bell of the Cathedral sounds three times.

"We must devour the pomegranate (*granata*) grain by grain," was the Spanish saying; and after a year's

CHAP. XXV.] THE SIEGE OF MALAGA.

delay, caused chiefly by a pestilence that was desolating Andalusia, the *Reyes Catolicos*, in 1488, prepared for a fresh attack on the small kingdom of El Zagal. The brave old Moor once more defeated Fernando's attempt on Almeria; but, in the spring of 1489, the queen herself repaired with the army to Jaen—the mountain city, lying like a dragon, with its tall castle and solid walls, to command the passes into the south. Baeza was her object; and to raise funds for the war she had pawned her jewels and mortgaged her lands to the merchants of Barcelona, who trusted her perfect good faith as they did not trust that of her husband.

It was while she lay there that, according to ballad-lore, the young Moorish hero Reduan felt himself obliged to fulfil a hasty boast once made that he could easily make himself master of Jaen. Lockhart thus gives the ballad:

'Thus said, before his lords, the king to Reduan.:
" 'Tis easy to get words, deeds get we as we can.;
Rememb'rest thou the feast at which I heard the saying,
' 'Twere easy in one night to make me lord of Jaen?' "

" Well in my mind I hold the valiant vow was said—
Fulfil it, boy, and gold shall shower on thy head;
But bid a long farewell, if now thou shrink from doing,
To bower and bonnibell, thy feasting and thy wooing."

" I have forgot the oath if such I e'er did plight;
But needs there plighted troth to make a soldier fight?
A thousand sabres bring; we'll see how we may thrive."
"One thousand!" quoth the king, "I trow thou shalt have five."

They passed the Elvira gate, with banners all displayed,
They passed in mickle state, a noble cavalcade;
What proud and prancing horses, what comely cavaliers,
What bravery of targets, what glittering of spears,

What caftans blue and scarlet, what turbans pleached of green,
What waving of their crescents and plumages between,
What buskins and what stirrups, what rowels chased in gold,
What handsome gentlemen, what buoyant hearts and bold.

In midst, above them all, rides he who rules the band:
Yon feather white and tall is the token of command;
He looks to the Alhamra, whence bends his mother down:
"Now Allah save my boy and merciful Mahoun."

But 'twas another sight, when Reduan drew near,
To look upon the height where Jaen's towers appear;
The fosse was wide and deep, the walls both tall and strong,
And keep was watched with keep the battlements along.

It was a heavy sight, but most for Reduan.
He sighed, as well he might, ere thus his speech began:
"Oh Jaen, had I known how high thy bulwarks stand,
My tongue had not outgone the prowess of my hand.

But since in hasty cheer I did my promise plight
(What well might cost a year) to win thee to a night,
The pledge demands the paying. I would my soldiers brave
Were half as sure of Jaen as I am of my grave.

My penitence comes late, my death lags not behind,
I yield me up to fate, since hope I may not find."
With that he turned him round: "Now blow your trumpets high!"
But every spearman frown'd, and dark was every eye.

But when he was aware that they would fain retreat,
He spurr'd his bright bay mare—I wot her pace was fleet;
He rides beneath the walls, and shakes aloft his lance,
And to the Christians call, if any will advance.

With that an arrow flew from o'er the battlement—
Young Reduan it slew, sheer through the breast it went;
He fell upon the green: "Farewell, my bonny bay!"
Right soon, when this was seen, broke all the Moor array.

THE SIEGE OF MALAGA.

Baeza was a very strongly-fortified place on the banks of a little river flowing from the Sierra Nevada, which was conducted through an elaborate system of canals to water the beautiful gardens that filled the valley. All these had to be laid waste, and the mere preliminaries of the siege occupied four months of constant labour, and perpetual fighting with the light squadrons of Moorish horse. The place was provisioned for fifteen months, and Fernando, finding that there was no hope of its yielding before the winter, would have given up the siege but for his wife, who not only kept up the ardour of the troops by her personal influence, but took care that they should be well supplied with all that could preserve their health in their winter quarters. Huts were built instead of tents to keep out the rain, in streets regularly laid out; pioneers were kept at work to render the mountain roads passable and to build bridges over the swollen torrents; fourteen thousand beasts of burthen were constantly going to and fro with supplies; and agents were everywhere employed to buy up corn for the army.

Even then sickness could not be averted, nor discontent. The gentlemen were especially disappointed that the king forbade them to accept those challenges to single combat with Moorish cavaliers which were their special pride and delight; and the infantry, who were suffering severely, began to murmur. On this, the queen herself, with her young son and daughter, came to the camp to share their perils and attend to their wants; and with her, as usual, the courage and perseverance of the army received a new impulse.

The Baezans began to despair, and Syd Yah-yah, El Zagal's nephew, began to treat with the sovereigns.

They were very gracious to him, and granted the most favourable terms they ever gave the conquered; permitting the inhabitants to retain their property and to settle in the suburbs as Mudajarras, while the troops were allowed to retire with arms, horses, and baggage. Syd Yah-yah himself seems to have been won over by the queen to become a Christian; and, indeed, there seems to have been a troop of Christian Abencerrages in her army, who had been alienated by Boabdil. On the surrender of Gaeza, many of the small cities in the Alpujarras offered to yield on the same terms, which were readily granted; and, indeed, most of them were bought from their governors for large gifts. Only the Alcayde of Purchena showed a nobler spirit, and when gifts were offered to him on his surrender he answered: "I am a Moor of Moorish lineage. I come not to sell what is not mine, but to yield what destiny has made yours. Had I not been weakened by those who should have strengthened me, you had gained the castle with my blood, not your gold. But as this may not be, I resign the place I cannot guard. All I ask is that the people may dwell in peace in their own religion, and all I will accept for myself is a safe conduct to Africa for me and my men!"

Syd Yah-yah then repaired to his uncle at Guadix, and showed him how irresistible was the Spanish force, and how the attempt to withstand it ended only in utter ruin and slavery, as at Malaga; while submission, while yet it was time, did save something for the unhappy race. The old man listened in silence, and did not move an eyelid while his nephew spoke. Then with a deep sigh he said: "Had not Allah decreed the fall of Granada, this arm would have saved her. The will of Allah be done."

It must have been very bitter to him to be shut out from the beloved city by the unworthy Boabdil, who had prevented him from making the resistance that might have saved the country for a time; but he resigned himself to yield up Almeria and Guadix, on retaining for his life the district of Andarax and the Alpujarras, with half the salt-pits of Malcha, and the title of King; just as, eight hundred years before, Theodemir had retained the title of King of Murcia. The brave old man was courteously treated by Fernando, who would not allow him to humble himself in homage.

CHAPTER XXVI.

THE LAST SIGH OF THE MOOR.

ONLY Granada remained of the kingdom of Al Hamar, and by treaty, Aboul Abd Allah al Zaquir, or Boabdil, was bound to surrender it to Fernando and Isabel when they should have overcome his uncle.

This, however, was impossible to him. The Moors, who refused to live under the Christians, had flowed in from all the places that had been taken, and were furious with him for not having stirred to assist them. Representatives of every Arab and Berber tribe were homeless fugitives in the streets of Granada, mourning for their lovely homes, raging against the king as a traitor and enemy to the Faith, and hardly withheld by the imaums from storming the Alhâmra. In the midst came the messengers from Fernando and Isabel to claim the performance of his promise. It was utterly impossible, and the ambassadors were forced to retire; but Boabdil—always a double traitor—sent a private message to invite the Count of Tendilla to appear with his troop in the Vega, assuring him that this would lead to its surrender. Then, when the count had arrived with the few forces at his disposal, Boabdil headed the best cavalry of the Zegris and drove him back with heavy loss. This was followed up by

CHAP. XXVI.] THE LAST SIGH OF THE MOOR. 285

the surprise of the little fortress of Alhendin; and in the general delight at this success, the mountaineers of the Alpujarras and the inhabitants of the towns on the coast rose upon the Spanish garrisons, and the Moors began to hope to recover their old boundaries.

It was only, however, bringing on the final struggle. The Marquis of Villena, warned by one of the Moors, put down the insurrection in the mountains, and the citizens were soon reduced, and found that they had forfeited the conditions on which they had surrendered. They were expelled from within the walls of their towns, though they were still allowed to live in the suburbs.

In the April of 1491 Fernando set forth from Cordova, with an army consisting of all the bravest warriors of Castille and Aragon together, with a troop of Moors under Syd Yah-yah—in all, numbering fifty thousand men. The city itself held altogether about two hundred thousand persons, of whom seventy thousand were fighting men. These were told off into two chief bodies, one to guard the gates and walls, the other to make sallies and fetch in convoys. The chief commander was Mousa Aben Abil Gazan, a Moorish knight of immense courage, skill, and agility, whom the romances of the siege make half-brother to the king.

Early in the month of May, Queen Isabel and her children arrived, to the extreme delight of the army, who believed that she always brought victory with her, and were enchanted to see her ride through their ranks in helmet and cuirass. Wishing to obtain a complete view of the Alhâmra, Isabel was escorted by the noblest cavaliers in the camp to the village of La Zerbia, where, mounting one of the flat roofs, she could have a fuller view of the palaces and mosques than her father, Don Juan, in the ballad. But the Moors on the walls saw her, and at once a large number hurried forth, hoping to secure such a prize, and fell on the guard of horsemen below, whom they at first scattered; and Isabel, kneeling on the house-top, saw her mailed warriors flying before the white-turbaned Moors. Before, however, the enemy could turn back to overpower the few who guarded the house, the Marquis of Cadiz, coming up with twelve hundred lances, broke them, and chased them back to the gates, then returned to escort the queen safely back.

About a month later, just as all had gone to rest, a lady chanced to hold her lamp too near the hangings of her tent; a fire broke out and quickly consumed all that quarter of the camp, with no loss of life, but of much of rich garments. All the queen's wardrobe was lost; but that same night Don Gonzalo de Cordova sent to Illora for a supply from the stores of his bride, Doña Maria Manrique, and so splendid and numerous were the robes and all the toilette necessaries which arrived, that Isabel jestingly told him that the fire had done the most damage in the coffers of Illora.

This accident led to the erection of a more solid town, by way of camp, than that which had been erected before Baeza. The buildings were of stone and mortar, and were so permanent that the army thought it deserved a name, and wanted to call it Isabel, but the queen begged that it might rather be known as Santa Fè. Between its trenches and the walls of the city endless encounters took place, and many a gallant deed was done. The following ballad, translated from Perez de Hyta, describes one of these encounters:

CHAP. XXVI.] THE LAST SIGH OF THE MOOR.

The camp of Santa Fè is girdled round with trench and palisade,
And, spread within, are tents of curtained silk, of gold, and of brocade;
There dukes, and counts, and captains bold, the nobles of the land,
And all the gallant men of war obey King Ferdinand.

It was at nine one morning that a horseman came in sight,
Mounted upon a charger, black, with a few spots of white;
Upon his haunches rose the steed, his master reined him in,
And showed the Christians all his teeth, displayed with mocking grin.

Scarlet and white and azure was the raiment of that Moor,
And over that gay livery a corslet strong he wore;
A double-pointed lance he bore, of steel most finely wrought,
An exiled Moor in Fez his buckler light had wrought.

And oh! the Pagan dog, behind his horse's tail he drew
The holy Ave Mary, full in the Christians' view;
And when he came before the tents he uttered thus his boast:
" Ha! is there any lord or knight, in all this warlike host

" Who'll come and prove his valour in this plain your camp before?
Come out, then, one or two, come out by three or four;
Alcayde of the pages come, thou art a man of fame,
Or Count of Cabra, come thou out, for mighty is thy name.

" Come out, thou Don Gonzalo, whom Cordova they call;
Or Martin of Galindo, brave soldier 'mong them all.
Portocarrero, come, of Palma the great lord;
Manuel de Ponce, come and try on me thy sword.

" Or if these will not come, then come, King Ferdinand,
And soon my might and valour I'll make thee understand."
The king's best knights stood listening the palisade before,
And each was begging licence to combat with the Moor.

There was young Garcilaso, a gallant stripling fair,
And hard he pleaded with the king that he the fight might dare.
" Nay, Garcilaso, for such work thou art yet over young,
There's many another in the camp to stop that Pagan's tongue."

Young Garcilaso took his leave in trouble and in pain,
That to attack the Moorish foe he could not licence gain ;
Then all in secret did he arm, and took a coal-black horse,
And rode forth from the camp unknown, disguised from all the force.

He went towards the champion, and thus defied the foe :
"Whether the king has valiant knights, oh Moor, thou now may'st know ;
Behold me here, the least of all, yet ready for the fight."
The Moorish champion turned him round, and rated low his might.

"Go back, my child, I never fight except with bearded men ;
Go, call thy bravest knight, my boy, and go thou back again."
Then Garcilaso in his wrath his steed with stirrup pressed,
And at the Moorish champion came with his good lance in rest.

Then swift as lightning wheeled the Moor, the combat is begun,
And, young as Garcilaso is, the victory he has won.
He gave a lance-thrust to the Moor that through his corslet sped,
And even as on the field he dropped, already was he dead.

While Garcilaso from his charger's back upon the ground hath sprung,
He hath cut off the grisly head, and to his saddle hung ;
Then from the horse's tail he took the Ave reverently,
And kissed the sacred words, and knelt on bended knee,

While to his lance he bound the scroll as banner of his pride,
Mounted again his steed, and led the Moorish horse beside.
Thus to the camp he came, and found the knights and warriors there,
All marvelling who had wrought that deed of prowess rare.

Great honour then both king and queen hath to that stripling shown,
And Garcilaso de la Vega is the name by which he now is known ;
Since where he slew the pagan was in the Vega's field,
And the king bade that "Ave Mary" should for ever grace his shield.

This David and Goliath battle really gave the name to the De la Vega family. It is also said that one of the Castilian knights in return rode up to the gates of Granada, in the face of the enemy, and nailed a cartel, bearing the words " Ave Mary," to the door with his dagger.

At first the city was too well supplied from the mountain district in its rear to be straitened for provisions; but as autumn came on, parties of Spanish soldiers were sent to ravage the country and prevent convoys from coming in. Then, in desperation, Mousa collected all his bravest men for an attempt on Santa Fè; but this sort of fighting necessarily depended chiefly upon infantry, and these were always the weakest point with the Moors. They fled on the first alarm, the cavalry could only charge ineffectually, and they were chased back even beyond their watch-towers, which were immediately occupied by the Christian archers.

The city was now entirely invested on all sides, famine began to be felt, and there was no hope of succour. The mob began to clamour for a surrender in time to save them from the rigours suffered by Malaga. Boabdil assembled his council, and all recommended a capitulation except the brave Mousa, who declared that defence was still possible, and that they had better still trust to their valour. The others all were resolved to capitulate, and a suspension of arms was agreed on; hostages were given on either side, and a spot between the two armies was appointed where the Vizier Aboul Hacem met Gonzalo de Cordova to agree on the conditions of peace.

If in two months' time the beleaguered city was not

succoured, Boabdil was to yield up Alhâmra and the Albayan, with all the other towers, gates, bastions; and all the sheiks of the tribes were to swear faith and homage to the King of Castille, who would become King of Granada; that all Christian captives should be released without ransom, that the Moorish prisoners of war should also be set free; that Granada should be a place of freedom for the Moorish slaves of the other provinces; that Boabdil should have an estate in the Alpujarras; that the inhabitants, even Christian renegades, should keep their wealth, houses, arms, and horses, and only deliver up their firearms; that they should retain their laws, customs, language, and dress, the exclusive use of their mosques and liberty of worship, and be tried by their own kadis, who should be assessors to the Spanish governors; that they should thenceforth pay the King of Castille such taxes as they had paid their native sovereign, but that for three years they should be wholly free from all imposts while they were recovering from the war. The convention was signed by the Vizier and by Gonzalo on the 25th of November, 1491.

The tidings filled Granada with misery. The streets were full of wailing, and the very people who had been crying out to be delivered from the pangs of hunger and the horrors of an assault, accused their chiefs of treason and apostasy, and insisted on burying themselves in the ruins of their city. Mousa, in the last divan: "Leave regrets to women and children," he said. "Let us show ourselves men, by shedding not tears, but blood to the last drop. I will lead you to find on the battle-field either an independence or an honourable death. Were it not better to be counted

THE LAST SIGH OF THE MOOR.

among those who died for their country than among those who looked on at its death? If you think that the Christians will keep their promises, and that you will find a generous conqueror in the king, you are mistaken. They thirst for our blood. Death is the least of the ills that threaten us. The pillage of our homes, the profanation of our mosques, cruelty to our wives and children, oppression, injustice, intolerance and its flames await the cowards who fear a glorious death, for I swear by Allah I will not endure them."

This speech met no response. The old spirit had died out of the wealthy and luxurious Granadines, and they had ceased to think—like their forefathers—that death in fight with the Giaour was an absolute boon, as a passport to paradise. Even Mousa's own speech was the speech of a patriot, but not the speech of one of the fiery fanatics whom his namesake had led against Don Rodrigo the Goth. Aggression is easier than defence, and the Moor was a very different being from the Arab. There was no assent from any member of the divan, and, after looking round upon them in vain, this last of the Moorish captains rose up, left the assembly, rode out at the Elvira gate in full armour, and was never seen again. The surrender then was agreed upon, and the king and his viziers decided against taking advantage of the two months' delay, since it was probable that a popular insurrection might take place and cut them off from all benefits of the treaty. So they offered to deliver up the city at the end of sixty days, and the capitulation was signed by the sovereigns and the chief nobles of the Cortes.

On the 2nd of July, 1492, Fernando and Isabel put off the mourning they had been wearing for their son-in-law, the Prince of Portugal. They advanced to within half a mile of the city, where the army was drawn up in full and glittering battle array, with every warrior in full armour and banners displayed, fresh pennoncels fluttering from the lances, and long files of clergy with crosses and pastoral staves. It was the final day of victory and compensation for the battle of Guadalete eight hundred years before, and well might the hearts of the son and daughter of Pelayo swell with thankful joy as they were thus borne in on the crest of the last triumphant wave of the tide which had advanced slowly, but steadily, from the Penamerella crags to the fair slopes of the Nevada.

In the meantime, from the deep horseshoe gateway of those strong walls came a dejected train—Boabdil first, then the ladies of his harem in their veils, and an escort of fifty horsemen. As they met, these riders dismounted, and Boabdil was about to do the same, but Fernando would not permit it, nor would the queen. On horseback, then, Boabdil kissed the king's right arm, saying: "High and mighty lord, we are thine; we yield thee this city and this kingdom, since such is Allah's will. Allah grant that thou may'st be merciful." With these words he yielded up the silver keys of the Alhâmra. Fernando handed them to the queen, and she gave them to their son, Don Juan, by whom they were transferred to Don Inigo de Mendoza, who was to be alcayde of the city.

The dispossessed Moorish royal family could not brook the sight of the Christians in their city, but rode on towards Purchena, the place he retained in the Alpujarras. When he came to the height of Padul, the last whence he could see the red towers of the Alhâmra, he drew his rein, sobbed out *"Allah akbar"* (God is merciful), and was for some minutes convulsed with weeping.

The spot has ever since been known as *El ultimo sospiro del Moro* (the last sigh of the Moor).

Zoraya turned on him in anger, exclaiming, " It befits thee to weep like a woman for what thou couldst not defend like a man."

" Hadst thou spoken thus at Granada," said the unhappy man, " I would have been buried under its ruins rather than surrender ! "

" Remember, O King," said his vizier, by way of consolation, " that great misfortunes make men as famous as great good fortune."

The reproach was so far true that had Boabdil been like his uncle, and able to take advantage of the courage and patriotism of the Moors, he might have postponed the fall of Granada for another generation or two ; but it had come to be only a matter of time that the Mohammedan power in Spain should perish. Not only did the union of the crowns array the whole Christian force against it, but the influence of the Koran as a ruling power was worn out. The whole elaborate Moorish civilisation was inconsistent with the patriarchal scheme of Mohammed; and when it becomes needful to explain away a religion, its constraining force is at an end.

While Boabdil paused weeping on the hill, the fourteen gates of Granada were thrown open, and the king and queen rode up the hill, their eyes fixed on the Alhâmra, whither the new governor had gone before them. Presently a huge silver cross, between the banners of Castille and of Santiago, was seen on the highest tower, and a shout was heard: "Granada, Granada, for King Fernando and Queen Isabel!" Then king, queen, and all the army dropped upon their knees, and a glorious "Te Deum" was sung, led by the singers of the royal chapel.

Tears of joy were shed by many a brave captain, who had inherited the struggle from his forefathers, as he came up to kiss the hand of Isabel as Queen of Granada.

Then they rode into the city. It was as a city of the dead. Not even a child looked from the balconies. The broken-hearted people were wailing in their houses while the tramp of the horse sounded through their streets, and Fernando and Isabel entered the Alhâmra as conquerors.

CHAPTER XXVII.

WOE TO THE VANQUISHED.

A FEW piteous pages must complete the history of the Moors in Spain. There are two ways of looking at everything, and to a devout queen it seemed her first duty to have a Christian realm, nor could the zeal of the fifteenth century understand that the wrath of man worketh not the righteousness of God.

The two races had hated one another too long to understand one another, and it was impossible not to give dire offence. When Syd Yah-yah, now Don Pedro de Granada, was made governor, it was no doubt thought that the people would be gratified; but they regarded him as an apostate and traitor, and were greatly incensed. One mosque was also consecrated as a cathedral, and this was regarded as a violation of the treaty. The Jews, who had not had terms made for them, were also expelled, and this produced much misery and impoverishment.

The elder Abd Allah sold his Spanish lands and retired to Oran, where he was pointed at as the unfortunate Moor, and where his descendants are said still to exist.

The unfortunate Boabdil could not bear to continue in Spain. He sold his lands and followed his uncle to

Africa, where, in less than a year, he died a soldier's death in a battle on behalf of the King of Fez.

Missionary priests preached diligently; but Christianity, as popularly understood in the Spain of the fifteenth century, was in the form most repellent to a Moslem, especially to a philosophical and scientific one. The essential points of Christianity are startling enough to a mind trained to the brief Moslem creed, and when to these were added the passionate adoration of the Blessed Virgin and the Saints, the teaching seemed to the Moors degrading in itself as well as hateful because coming from the conquerors. In old times the Mozarabic liturgy and the free use of the Scriptures, had made conversions far less difficult than since the strictest uniformity with Rome had been enforced, and with the more ardour in consequence of the distant echoes of the Reformation in Germany.

The preaching had little effect, and, in 1499, the greatest man in Spain—Francisco Ximenes de Cisneros, Archbishop of Toledo—came to assist. He advised claiming the families of all whose forefathers had fallen away from the faith and become Mohammedans. These he held to belong to the Church, and he thought that they might be constrained to conform; but the attempt raised a popular tumult. He was besieged in his house, and only extricated with great difficulty by the Count of Tendilla, who had to employ soldiers and cannon. This disturbance was held to forfeit all the immunities promised, and the Moors were threatened with the utmost penalties of rebellion, though those who became Christians were assured of pardon. Terror had its effect, and on the 18th of December, 1499, no less than four thousand Moors received baptism. It was reckoned that if the parents came hypocritically, the children might at least be saved. Much of the Arabic literature, which no doubt was of the immoral nature sure to be found among a sensual people like the later Granadines, was destroyed, the more valuable manuscripts being preserved; and the Scriptures, the Breviary, and the Liturgy were translated into Arabic.

The villages in the Vega followed the example of the capital; but in the Alpujarras there was a terrible revolt, in which Don Alfonso de Aguilar was killed. Fernando blockaded the mountaineers in their hills, and at last came to terms. All who chose to continue Moslems might go to Africa on paying a ransom of ten doubloons a head; the rest must embrace the Christian faith. This was carried out, but, unfortunately, the larger number were unable to raise the ransom, and remained either as absolute slaves or nominal Christians—Moriscos, as they were called, in opposition to those who proudly called themselves Old Christians. The Valencian Mudajarros were forced into the same appearance of Christianity in the early days of Charles V., and in 1526 the whole Peninsula had become so entirely Christian in appearance that the byword for seeking something impossible was: "It is looking for Mohammed in Spain."

But the Moriscos were thought to be still Mohammedans at heart; they still spoke and wrote Arabic, wore their own national dress, and secretly followed their own rites and customs. This lasted till the time of Philip II., when, on the complaint of the Inquisition they were commanded, within three years, to speak nothing but Spanish, leave off all Arabic customs, dress like the Christians, and send their women abroad unveiled. Even baths were destroyed and forbidden, lest ablutions should there be made religiously.

All this, as an old Moor named Francisco Nuñez Muley argued before the Council at Granada, was very hard, since what the Moriscos were required to give up might be quite consistent with Christianity ; but no mercy could be met with in Philip, and another dreadful insurrection took place in the Alpujarras. There was a desperate war lasting four years, ending in the deportation of all the Moriscos of the Alpujarras to Africa.

Those of Granada had been dispersed in the other provinces of Spain ; but though no external signs of difference were permitted, they were hated and avoided by the other inhabitants, and in 1611 were finally banished. The happiest took refuge in France ; those who were driven to Africa were despised and viewed as apostates by the Berbers, and made slaves. Some, escaped from their chains, returned to Spain, and entreated with tears to be allowed to live there as slaves ; but the hatred of a thousand years was too strong, and not even as genuine Christians were they tolerated. Spain had been growing more and more harsh, narrow, and unmerciful, and could not forgive the last descendants of those who had once trodden her down. The sense of the abilities of the Moors no doubt added to the vague fear and distrust of them. So much were they still esteemed the leaders of romantic fiction that Cervantes chose, as the supposed author of Don Quixote, the Moor, Cid Hamet Beneageli.

Thus perished the brightest blossom Mohammedanism had ever produced. The Christian perseverance had triumphed at last, but with the removal of the constant demand for watchful courage and resolution, the Spanish character began to lose all that was best in it, and deteriorated from the hour of the conquest of Granada.

THE END.

www.ingramcontent.com/pod-product-compliance
Lightning Source LLC
Chambersburg PA
CBHW022057230426
43672CB00008B/1198